ORDNANCE SURVEY
LEISURE GUIDE

CORNWALL

Produced jointly by the Publishing Division of the
Automobile Association and the Ordnance Survey

Cover: Boscastle – the harbour
Title page: Tin mine chimney, Wheal Coates, St Agnes
Opposite: Mending the nets at Looe
Introductory page: Mevagissey – fishing boats

Editor: Antonia Hebbert

Art Editor: Dave Austin

Design Assistants: Neil Roebuck and KAG Design

Editorial contributors: Rennie Bere (Wildlife); Dr V Challinor Davies (Gardens); David Clarke (Gazetteer; Directory; short features); Cornwall Archaeological Unit (The Ancient Landscape; The Industrial Landscape); Anne Duffin (Fighting Cornishmen); Des Hannigan (Long Distance Footpaths; Walks); Donald Rawe (Legends)

Picture researcher: Wyn Voysey

Original photography: Andrew Lawson

Typeset by Avonset, Midsomer Norton, Bath.
Printed and Bound in Great Britain by Butler and Tanner Ltd, Frome, Somerset.

Maps extracted or derived from the Ordnance Survey Holiday Map of the West Country (3¼ inches to 1 mile), 1:625 000 Routeplanner Series, 1:250 000 Routemaster Series and 1:25 000 Pathfinder Series with the permission of Her Majesty's Stationery Office. Crown Copyright reserved.

Additions to the maps by the Cartographic Dept of the Automobile Association and the Ordnance Survey.

Produced by the Publishing Division of the Automobile Association.

Distributed in the United Kingdom by the Ordnance Survey, Southampton, and the Publishing Division of the Automobile Association, Fanum House, Basingstoke, Hampshire RG21 2EA.

The contents of this publication are believed correct at the time of printing. Nevertheless, the Publishers cannot accept responsibility for errors or omissions, or for changes in details given.

Reprinted with amendments 1990
First edition 1987

AA ISBN 0 86145 512 6 (hardback)
AA ISBN 0 86145 511 8 (softback)
OS ISBN 0 319 00120 2 (hardback)
OS ISBN 0 319 00119 9 (softback)

Published by the Automobile Association and the Ordnance Survey.

CORNWALL

Contents

Using this Book

Each entry in the A to Z Gazetteer has the atlas page number on which the place can be found and its National Grid reference included under the heading. An explanation of how to use the National Grid is given on page 86.

Beneath many of the entries in the Gazetteer are listed AA-recommended hotels, restaurants, garages, guesthouses, camping sites and self-catering accommodation in the immediate vicinity of the place described. Hotels, restaurants and camping sites are also given an AA classification.

◇ **Please Note** The use of this symbol in this reprint indicates that the establishment is no longer in the AA scheme (it may even have closed) and the AA is therefore unable to verify the particulars.

HOTELS

1-star	Good hotels and inns, generally of small scale and with acceptable facilities and furnishing.
2-star	Hotels offering a higher standard of accommodation, with some private bathrooms/shower; lavatories on all floors; wider choice of food.
3-star	Well-appointed hotels; a good proportion of bedrooms with private bathrooms/showers.
4-star	Exceptionally well-appointed hotels offering a high standard of comfort and service, the majority of bedrooms should have private bathrooms/showers.
5-star	Luxury hotels offering the highest international standards.

Hotels often satisfy *some* of the requirements for higher classifications than that awarded.

Red-star	Red stars denote hotels which are considered to be of outstanding merit within their classification.
Country House Hotel	A hotel where a relaxed informal atmosphere prevails. Some of the facilities may differ from those at urban hotels of the same classification.

RESTAURANTS

1-fork	Modest but good restaurant.
2-fork	Restaurant offering a higher standard of comfort than above.
3-fork	Well-appointed restaurant.
4-fork	Exceptionally well-appointed restaurant.
5-fork	Luxury restaurant.
1-rosette	Hotel or restaurant where the cuisine is considered to be of a higher standard than is expected in an establishment within its classification.
2-rosette	Hotel or restaurant offering very much above average food irrespective of the classification.
3-rosette	Hotel or restaurant offering outstanding food, irrespective of classification.

GUESTHOUSES

These are different from, but not necessarily inferior to, AA-appointed hotels, and they offer an alternative for those who prefer inexpensive and not too elaborate accommodation. They all provide clean, comfortable accommodation in homely surroundings. Each establishment must usually offer at least six bedrooms and there should be a general bathroom and a general toilet for every six bedrooms without private facilities. Parking facilities should be reasonably close.

Other requirements include:
Well maintained exterior, clean and hygienic kitchens; good standard of furnishing; friendly and courteous service; access at reasonable times; the use of a telephone and full English breakfast.

SELF CATERING

These establishments, which are all inspected on a regular basis, have to meet minimum standards in accommodation, furniture, fixtures and fittings, services and linen.

CAMPING SITES

1-pennant	Site licence; 10% of pitches for touring units; site density not more than 30 per acre; 2 separate toilets for each sex per 30 pitches; good quality tapwater; efficient waste disposal; regular cleaning of ablutions block; fire precautions; well-drained ground.
2-pennant	All one-pennant facilities plus: 2 washbasins with hot and cold water for each sex per 30 pitches in separate washrooms; warden available at certain times of the day.
3-pennant	All two-pennant facilities plus: one shower or bath for each sex per 30 pitches, with hot and cold water; electric shaver points and mirrors; all-night lighting of toilet blocks; deep sinks for washing clothes; facilities for buying milk, bread and gas; warden in attendance by day, on call by night.
4-pennant	All three-pennant facilities plus: a higher degree of organisation than one–three-pennant sites; attention to landscaping; reception office; late-arrivals enclosure; first aid hut; shop; routes to essential facilities lit after dark; play area; bad weather shelter; hard standing for touring vans.
5-pennant	A comprehensive range of services and equipment; careful landscaping; automatic laundry; public telephone; indoor play facilities for children; extra facilities for recreation; warden in attendance 24 hours per day.

CORNWALL

Introduction

*With its spectacular coastline, idyllic villages, wild
moorland, great houses, exotic gardens and colourful
past, Cornwall is both beautiful and fascinating.
This guide introduces the rich Cornish legacy, its
legends and traditions, with detailed information on
where to go, maps, walks and motor tours.
Written entirely by people who live and work in
Cornwall, backed by the AA's research expertise and
the Ordnance Survey's mapping, this guide should
be equally useful to first-time visitors and those who
live here, as well as to those who are drawn back by
the magic of Cornwall year after year.*

The Ancient Landscape

We are all used to peeping over a hedge to glimpse a ploughed-up Bronze Age burial mound standing in a field of broccoli or oil seed rape; finding a fragment of mediaeval wall or arched window amongst the modern shops; or being drawn to the gaunt and dramatic engine-houses that stand on scrub ground. It takes a leap of imagination to think of the barrow in its original gladed sacred setting, or to picture the bustle of the mediaeval town. It is

equally hard to imagine the acres of wooden, tin-roofed processing buildings clustered about a smoking engine-house, the air thick with smoke and fumes of sulphur and arsenic.

The landscape, too, has changed. The remains of prehistoric stone round houses and mediaeval farmsteads on the now bleak hillslopes of Bodmin Moor and Penwith require us to recognise these as once productive and pleasant places to live. Since late prehistory, much of the county had been uncultivated moorland, surviving largely intact until the late 18th century. Once widespread in Cornwall, the traditional farm holding of field and moor now survives only in Penwith and around Bodmin Moor. It is within the former moorlands that the most dramatic landscape changes have occurred through mining, china-clay extraction, quarrying and enclosure for farming.

Hunters and gatherers, 8,000–4,000BC.

At the close of the Ice Age, 10,000 years ago, the coast of Cornwall lay up to four miles further out than today. The ice melted, raising the sea level, gradually drowning the coastal lowlands. The climate warmed rapidly and vegetation changed from tundra through coniferous and finally to mixed oak woodland. Bands of nomads hunted red deer, ox and pig in the forest and gathered berries, nuts, and plants. In summer they hunted on the open uplands, following the animals into the lowland woods in the winter. In the spring and autumn they moved to the coast, rich in fish, shellfish and grey seals. Little is now left of this, the Mesolithic period, but scatters of flint implements.

Settlers and monument-builders, 4,000–2,500BC

By 4,000BC the idea of agriculture had spread, and areas of woodland were systematically cleared. Excavations have shown that over the next few thousand years settled communities drastically changed the appearance of the landscape. In Cornwall, on the rocky summits of Carn Brea near

Left: Iron Age village street at Chysauster
Right: the Mên-an-Tol stone, near Lanyon
*Below left: the Hurlers, by the road just west of Minions.
Tradition says they are men petrified for playing hurling on the Sabbath*
Below right: aerial view of St Dennis, showing the Iron Age hill-fort in which the church stands

Camborne and Helman Tor, Lanlivery, massive stone ramparts were built around settlements of sub-rectangular houses. On the slopes below, plots were cleared for cultivation. At Carn Brea hundreds of flint arrowheads found in the excavations suggest that the settlement was sacked.

Little is known of where other people lived but Neolithic society was well-organised and capable of wide-ranging trade in Cornish stone axes, now found as far afield as Essex, and pottery made on the Lizard was distributed throughout the south-west. The great megalithic chamber tombs or quoits, a type common to the whole Atlantic seaboard, are well known. Built as expressions of religious belief and communal affiliation as much as repositories for the dead, they are mute evidence of the toil and skill required to erect them.

Farmers, ceremonial and burial monuments, 2,000–600BC

As the landscape filled up with the farms of round houses, sacred areas were set aside for many forms of ceremonial and burial monuments. Embanked ritual enclosures (with ditches on the inside) known as henges, as at Castilly, Bodmin, were succeeded by stone circles, standing stones (menhirs), and stone rows as important ritual monuments. Many are found in Cornwall, those on Bodmin Moor and Penwith being the best known. Around the Merry Maidens in Penwith is a fine example of a sacred area: several menhirs (the Pipers) and a cluster of burials surround the stone circle. One of these, Tregiffian, is an entrance grave: a Bronze Age development of Neolithic quoits, common in

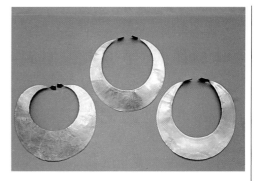

The gold collars, dating from about 1800BC, found at Harlyn Bay and (centre) St Juliot

Aerial view of Zennor, showing clearly the irregular pattern of the stone walls built on top of the original prehistoric field boundaries

Penwith and Scilly. Elsewhere, sacred areas contain cemeteries of burial mounds (barrows or stone cairns, marked tumuli on maps) erected over the cremated remains of prominent individuals. Several such cemeteries are visible, particularly those at Four Burrows and Carland Cross on the A30 north of Truro.

Surrounding them were farmland, pasture and settlements, now invisible in lowland Cornwall. It is on Bodmin Moor and in Penwith that Bronze Age landscapes can best be appreciated. Here on now bleak moorland stood hundreds of thatched stone round houses occupied at a time when the weather was some two degrees Centigrade warmer than today and soils were more fertile. On Bodmin Moor on the slopes of Roughtor and on the surrounding hills, over 500 ruined houses have been found with their associated stone-banked fields and nearby burial cairns and stone circles. Heaps of cleared stone and soil build-up (lynchets) against the lower edges of the fields are evidence of the cultivation that once took place. The farmers with their simple scratch ploughs would have been constantly reminded of their ancestors by the cairns that crown the hilltops and ridges all around. Below, in the more wooded valleys, lay deposits of tin gravel probably exploited at this early date to make, with copper, the bronze for tools, weapons and jewellery. Gold from further afield was beaten into armlets and neck pieces.

Hill-forts and the Celts, 600BC–AD43

The dominant monuments of the Iron Age are the hill-forts. Cornwall has an extraordinary number

and variety of defended sites. Even in decay their tumbled ramparts and silted ditches are impressive. Some have multiple defences with complicated entrances, others known as cliff-castles have huge ramparts thrown across narrow-necked coastal promontories (eg The Rumps, Pentire Head). These were the strongholds of the warrior aristocracy and the centres of tribal power from which they exacted tribute and directed trade.

Surrounding them were the smaller but nonetheless defended rounds: enclosed by a single bank and ditch they were probably the homes of freemen. Both these and other unenclosed farms sat amongst extensive fields that in Penwith have proved so durable that their form and layout still survives; in Zennor the stone walls defining small irregular fields lie on top of the original prehistoric field boundaries.

Also amongst the fields are courtyard houses: dwellings and farm buildings opening on to an unroofed courtyard. Chysauster is a village of over ten such houses arranged along a street. Carn Euny has, like many sites on the Atlantic seaboard, a fogou: an underground passage, presumably used for storage or ritual.

The Romans, AD43–410

Following the Claudian invasion of AD43, Vespasian with the second Augustan Legion marched west. By the mid-50s, the provincial capital Isca Dumnoniorum (Exeter) was founded to control the main territory of the Dumnonii, the Celtic tribe of Cornwall, Devon and West Somerset. The only known fort in Cornwall, at Nanstallon, Bodmin, housed a mixed 500-man auxiliary detachment of infantry and cavalry. The native strongholds were abandoned, and in the countryside life continued much as before in the rounds and courtyard houses. The enormous market of the Roman Empire widened trading opportunities, although tin was not at first in great demand as sources elsewhere were used. Fine tableware was imported to Cornwall from eastern Britain, the Continent and the Mediterranean, and coinage introduced.

The uplands, abandoned around 1,000BC because of deteriorating climate, were not reoccupied. The already developing farms in the lowlands helped to feed an expanding rural population. Towards the end of the period, early farms were abandoned and new hamlets established, and it is this pattern of settlements which survives to this day.

Cornwall appears to have been an isolated corner of the westernmost extremity of the Empire, still essentially Celtic in character and religion.

The Age of Saints and the kingdom of Cornwall, AD410–1066

The Celtic aristocracy was now free to rule and a network of independent kingdoms re-emerged over the British Isles. Cornwall was part of the kingdom of Dumnonia. The names of some rulers may be recorded on the inscribed memorial stones which dot the Cornish countryside. Their seats were re-fortified, defended sites, the most spectacular and renowned of which was Tintagel where excavations have revealed the trappings of a royal household.

Independence was short-lived, for by the 8th century the English had reached the Tamar, and by the 10th had nominal control of Cornwall. Dumgarth, drowned in 875, is the last Cornish king to be recorded; the Doniert Stone, St Cleer, may be his memorial. Although some rounds were inhabited until the 6th or 7th centuries, there was a gradual shift to unenclosed hamlets called trefs which by 1066 were the dominant settlement type: a move from stock-rearing to arable may be the reason. House styles were also changing: the earliest post-Roman buildings were round or oval, but at the 10th-century village of Mawgan Porth, rectangular houses were grouped around a courtyard.

Many farmers were also fishermen or tinners. The presence of Mediterranean pottery and continental influences on local styles suggests continuing trade with the Mediterranean, replaced by links with the Low Countries by the 9th century.

Christianity introduced from the Mediterranean and Wales brought fundamental changes. Nonetheless, ancient beliefs in the supernatural powers of springs lingered, and such sites were adopted as holy wells. Inscribed stones, commemorating important people, were set up beside tracks and fords, as well as in churchyards. Some have inscriptions in Ogham, the Irish stroke-alphabet, indicating the influence of Irish settlers in the spread of Christianity in Cornwall. True cross-carving began in the 9th century. The decorated crosses at St Neot, Cardinham, Sancreed and Lanherne are amongst the earliest and finest.

The 15th-century holy well at St Cleer was believed to be a healing well

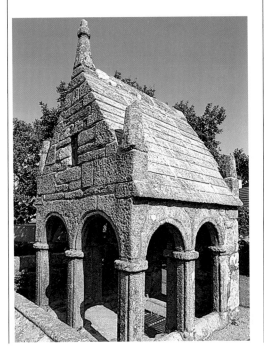

Restormel Castle, mostly late 13th-century, a prime example of military architecture

Castles and hamlets, church and trade, AD1066–1540

After the Norman Conquest the new aristocracy stamped its authority on the Cornish with a formidable series of castles: Launceston and Trematon being strongholds of Robert of Mortain, who held most of the Cornish manors. Other castles belonged to his chief sub-tenants, as at Restormel and Cardinham. By the 13th century the major castles all belonged to the Earls of Cornwall, and their subsequent history was of neglect, as the absentee earls and dukes resided in Wallingford, Berkhamsted and Kennington, supported by the income from their Cornish estates.

The predominant settlement pattern was of single farms and small hamlets, surrounded by their open fields, divided into strips by low banks. The Forrabury Stitches at Boscastle give some idea of how large areas of Cornwall must have appeared.

Most parishes and parish churches are mediaeval in origin, and many are on sites that had been in use for worship since the 5th or 6th centuries. Churches form Cornwall's largest reserve of mediaeval buildings. Most manors of any pretension had a domestic chapel, as at Cotehele. Other chapels stood at bridges and fords, or doubled as lighthouses and daymarks; some served Cornwall's many leper hospitals. Few of these sites survive. The most obvious and enduring monuments to mediaeval piety are the hundreds of granite crosses that marked the paths to churches.

By the 14th century no-one in the county would have been more than six miles from a market. Cornwall had many small towns, some of them little more than villages. Many were fishing ports. Seaports traded with Brittany, Wales, Ireland and Spain, often mixing trade with piracy and smuggling. Some of the coastal towns suffered at the hands of French and Spanish raiders: Fowey (1457), Marazion (1514), Mousehole, Newlyn and Penzance (1595). Block-houses and batteries were built in the 15th and 16th centuries to counter this and the threat of invasion; most notably Henry VIII's artillery forts at Pendennis, St Mawes and St Catherine's Castle, Fowey.

Compared to most counties, Cornwall had a particularly diverse economy which gave it a special character then as in later centuries. Most people worked the land but thousands more were involved in the tin industry or in quarrying slate or granite, while others fished, or worked in lively seaports where the Cornish language, still dominant in the west of the county, might be heard amid the cosmopolitan hubbub of Breton and French, Spanish and English.

The Industrial Landscape

Cornwall's landscape is scarred with the traces of both ancient and modern mineral extraction. The majority of the more obvious industrial remains belong to the last two centuries, but during the previous 4,000 years tin played an important part in the economy of the county. During prehistory, tin was dug from valley gravels and smelted in primitive bowl furnaces to produce metal ingots (some are in the County Museum, Truro). Tin at this time was mainly alloyed with copper to produce bronze, and from this implements, jewellery and weaponry were made. Evidence for prehistoric tinworks comes largely from finds recovered in abandoned streamworks reworked during the 19th century, which revealed numerous artefacts.

In the early years of the Roman period, the major source of tin for the Empire was the deposits in north-western Spain and Cornish tin was little exploited. However, in the 3rd century AD the gradual exhaustion of these sources led to the re-working of many Cornish streamworks. Unfortunately, no known Roman or earlier tinworks survive today, and the earliest visible remains probably date to the mediaeval period.

Documentary and archaeological work show the importance to the mediaeval economy of the tin industry and some of the earthworks in the valley bottoms (particularly on Bodmin Moor) date to this period. The tinners were tightly controlled by the Stannary Courts, which laid down laws, and upheld the privileges of those involved in the industry. Generally, tinners were exempt from manorial services and taxes, but in return, the tin which they produced was very heavily taxed at the nearest coinage town (Liskeard, Bodmin, Lostwithiel,

Main picture: mid-19th-century engraving of Botallack mine. Right: engine-house remains are a common feature of the Cornish landscape. Below left: the last rotative beam-winding engine in Cornwall at East Pool. Below right: tin-miner's helmet, an exhibit in Zennor's museum

Truro and Helston). Throughout this period, technology developed rapidly, with mining of the ore by opencast quarries and shallow shafts being introduced from the late 13th century. Before the tin ore could be smelted, it was necessary to separate the cassiterite (tin oxide) from unwanted minerals, and this was achieved by crushing and grinding the ore in water-powered stamping and crazing mills. It was then concentrated and smelted in blast-furnaces known as blowing-houses. The remains of these structures are still visible, although many hundreds have been destroyed by later mining. The tin was cast into large rectangular ingots, and then taken to be 'coigned' (taxed) and sold. Much of it was taken by sea to London where the majority was used in the production of pewter, but significant amounts were also used to make church bells, solder, artillery and bronze construction machinery.

The Cornish Industrial Revolution
The visitor to Cornwall cannot help but notice the remains of mine engine-houses in the landscape. They are found from the east of the county in the Tamar Valley and on the southern slopes of Bodmin Moor, through the area around Camborne–Redruth and on the cliffs of St Agnes to the clifftop stacks to the far west of Penwith. These are the relics of an industry which in the late 18th and for much of the 19th centuries made the

county one of the foremost tin and copper producers in the world, a major centre of invention and engineering during the Industrial Revolution. The development of transport networks was encouraged, and wealth was created that financed both the growth of the modern urban centres and the creation of many small mining villages in areas formerly moorland or heath. Ports often developed into important industrial centres in their own right, Hayle having at one time two of the largest iron foundries in the county, while Calstock grew beside the Tamar to serve the needs of the busy mining area to the west.

The surviving engine-houses and the acres of spoil and derelict buildings which now surround them represent only a small part of enterprises whose chief remains now lie abandoned deep underground, or which consisted of structures of an extensive but temporary nature – these have now been swept away but can be seen in abundance on photographs of the period.

The onset of the Industrial Revolution had demanded increasing supplies, not only of iron and coal, but also of tin and copper; two essential raw materials for engineering which Cornwall was able, almost uniquely in Britain, to supply. It was the local development of the steam engine which allowed extraction in the quantities demanded and from depths previously impossible to drain using earlier technologies.

The first beam engine was erected in Cornwall in about 1716 and despite the almost prohibitive cost of transporting coal from South Wales, in all nearly 1,000 engines were eventually installed to pump water, haul ore from workings up to 3,000ft deep, and drive machinery to crush and refine the ore. A large number of these engines was built in world-famous foundries like Harvey's of Hayle or Perran Foundry, which also supplied anything from a 50ft waterwheel to a miner's shovel. Gunpowder mills like the Kennal works at Ponsanooth, National Explosives at Hayle Towans and Bickfords Fuse Works at Tuckingmill and other manufacturers supplied all local demand from candles and clothing to gasholders and drain covers. The huge demand for steam coal and timber, and the massive tonnage of copper ore to be sent to Wales for smelting, spurred the development of industrial harbours linked to the mines by railways. Nationally famous inventors and engineers like Newcomen, Smeaton, Trevithick, Davey and Murdoch emerged as industrial expertise developed, gained at first hand in the mines, foundries and engineering works of the area.

The history of first copper and then tin mining in the period 1820-1890 was marked by both booms and slumps, and although always a dangerous undertaking for the miners themselves and a gamble for the adventurers who put up the capital and pocketed the profits, mining was the basis for the economic prosperity of the county.

Fortunes were made and lost virtually overnight: employment on copper mines in 1837 was around 30,000; from 1866 to 1874, Cornish copper mining collapsed after discoveries were made of vast deposits in Chile and Australia. Over 12,000 miners emigrated, and it was said that at the bottom of a mine anywhere in the world one could find a Cornishman working. In 1870 there were 300 tin mines at work in the county; by 1896 cheaper tin from Bolivia and Malaya had forced the abandonment of all but a handful. A brief world demand for arsenic staved off the end for a while, but by the turn of the century it was virtually all over, and areas that had been intensively worked for centuries were finally abandoned. In 1986 only three tin mines remained at work.

Top: spectacular landscape for drivers on the road which passes the china-clay mine at Stannon Downs
Above: the engineer Richard Trevithick holds a model of his locomotive

China-clay

China-clay extraction has the most obvious and spectacular impact on the landscape. First discovered by William Cookworthy in 1746, china-clay was originally used with china-stone for making fine porcelain, but nowadays is also used in paper-making, chemicals and other industries. The main centre of extraction lies within the Hensbarrow granite uplands north of St Austell, with smaller areas in Penwith, on Tregonning Hill near Helston and on Bodmin Moor. Two centuries of active working have changed the moorland landscape to one of sheer-sided quarries and water-filled pits, surrounded by the white dumps of waste mica and quartz sand. China-clay is formed by the decomposition of feldspar within the granite to a chalky powder: this is extracted by washing the working face with a powerful jet of water, and settling the clay from the stream in large pits or tanks. Originally the clay was dried naturally in large, open-sided sheds, but in the 1850s the pan kiln was introduced to speed the process. These long low buildings with a tall chimney at one end are still a distinctive feature of the area, although they have now been superseded by modern driers. Transport of the clay was mostly seaborne and ports which grew up to serve this need at Par, Fowey and Charlestown are still in active use, whilst that at Pentewan is disused. The Wheal Martyn Museum at St Austell displays the history and technology of the industry in a preserved works of the 1880s.

A landscape of stone: Quarrying

Stone-working has for centuries been part of the county's economy and in many areas quarry villages have grown up around the workings. The availability of a wide variety of stone and suitable materials for brickmaking ensured virtual self-sufficiency in building materials until recently, and the slate from the North Cornish quarries, many perched precariously on the cliff-faces, roofed most of the buildings of the county.

Not all stone was cut from quarries: most granite uplands are pockmarked with small surface workings where boulders and outcrops have been split into blocks for gateposts, millstones, crosses, quoins and mullions. Crushed stone used for road and railway building is traditionally the hard elvan stone, produced at Penlee and Dean Quarries. Dimension or shaped stone was used for building, for cobbles, kerbstones, gravestones and building ornament. Pentewan, Cataclews and Polyphant stone as well as granite were all used in Cornish churches from an early period. Serpentine and soapstone from the Lizard, although briefly tried as a source of pottery clay, were used for their varied colours. The larger granite quarries had cranes, tramways, dressing sheds and blacksmiths' shops for making and sharpening tools. Working methods have developed from wood wedges to tar and feathers, from gunpowder to high explosives and thermic lances.

Transport

Throughout the mediaeval period and into the 18th century most goods were moved by packhorse and donkey. Cornish roads were in many cases too rutted and narrow for carts, severely hampering the development of local industry, and the sea continued to be used for the despatch of goods and by long-distance travellers. But many of the navigable estuaries which had been important in the mediaeval and earlier periods became so choked with tinners' waste that important ports such as Helston, Tregony and Lostwithiel were left stranded far above navigable limits. Penryn, once the pre-eminent port on the Fal, was rapidly eclipsed once Sir John Killigrew, Governor of Pendennis Castle, had built the

Above: the slate quarry at Delabole has been in production for almost six hundred years
Inset: Brunel's Royal Albert Bridge takes the railway across the Tamar at Saltash

settlement of Pennycomequick, now Falmouth. Falmouth Haven, one of the world's great deep-water anchorages became a major naval station and packet port for the Americas. In the early 19th century Padstow became one of the largest embarkation ports for emigrant miners. Most of the ports and many of the tidal inlets once had flourishing shipyards building coastal traders, in part to serve the 300 or more lime-kilns used for agricultural fertiliser. Fishing boats, pilot gigs, river craft and larger ocean-going vessels continued to be built until after the First World War even in obscure places like Calstock, Portmellion, St Columb Porth and Gweek.

Turnpike trusts were set up in the late 18th century and improved major roads, but had little impact on the development of industry, although stagecoaches could now provide a reliable, although expensive, service to London. Several short canals were laid out to serve specific needs, but the hilly terrain was unsuited to major works of this kind; it was the advent of railways which allowed Cornwall's mining industry to expand to its 19th-century peak. From 1809 onwards, many tramroads and railways were built to serve industry and the local community. These were at first entirely independent and isolated within Cornwall, until the main line from London was finally opened to Truro in 1859, carried across the Tamar by Brunel's Royal Albert Bridge. However, the Cornwall Railway's adoption of the broad gauge effectively prolonged the county's isolation from through-communication with northern Britain until the gauge conversion in 1892. By this time, the heyday of Cornish mining and industry was over – the mineral tramways and harbours had carried the bulk of the traffic. The main line finally came into its own when tourists began arriving in large numbers, but this role was to be short-lived; the laying of the first tarmacadam on the A30 in 1919 heralded a new age of motorised road transport and a new era for Cornwall.

Above: the north front of Antony House, home of the Carew family. Left: portrait of the historian of Cornwall, Sir Richard Carew

Fighting Cornishmen

Richard Carew, the Cornish historian, wrote of his fellow Cornish gentlemen in 1602 that *'They keepe liberall, but not costly builded or furnished houses, give kind entertainment to strangers, make even at the yeeres end with the profits of their living, are reverenced and beloved of their neighbours, live void of factions amongst themselves (at leastwise such as breake out into anie daungerous excesse) and delight not in braverie of apparrell; yet the woman would be verie loth to come behind the fashion, in newfanglednes of the maner, if not in costlynes of the matter, which perhaps might over-empty their husbands purses. They converse familiarly together, and often visit one another. A Gentleman and his wife will ride to make merry with his next neighbour; and after a day or twayne, those two couples goe to a third; in which progresse they encrease like snowballs, till through their burdensome waight they breake againe.'*

Like other notable members of the Cornish gentry, Richard Carew's grandsons, Sir Alexander and John Carew, lived and died amidst great drama. Sir Alexander Carew was beheaded in London in December 1644 for plotting to deliver St Nicholas Island at Plymouth to the Royalist enemy; whilst in contrast, his brother John Carew was one of the judges who tried King Charles I, and was executed as a regicide at the Restoration in 1660. Their home, Antony House, in Carew hands from the 15th century, now belongs to the National Trust.

Also in eastern Cornwall are the houses of Mount Edgcumbe and Cotehele, both formerly properties of the Edgcumbe family; Mount Edgcumbe, still occupied by the family, is open to the public, and Cotehele belongs to the National Trust. Carew relates how in 1483, the Lancastrian Richard Edgcumbe was being pursued by the Yorkist Henry Bodrugan, and hid in the woods at Cotehele, overlooking the Tamar, *'which extremity taught him a sudden policy, to put a stone in his cap and tumble the same into the water, while these rangers were fast at his heels, who looking down after the noise and seeing his cap swiming thereon, supposed that he had desperately drowned himself, gave over their further hunting and left him liberty to shift away and ship over into Brittany'*, from which place he soon returned with Henry Tudor.

When Henry Tudor was crowned King Henry VII, after defeating Richard III, Richard Edgcumbe became powerful as one of the chief executors of crown policy. In February 1487 he was granted a commission to arrest Bodrugan and other Yorkist rebels 'who have withdrawn themselves into private places in the counties of Devon and Cornwall and stir up sedition'. The story goes that upon Edgcumbe's approach, Bodrugan slipped out of his house at Chapel Point near Mevagissey, leapt off the nearby cliffs and landed on a little grassy island 100ft below, where a boat was waiting to take him to a ship for France. The place is still known as Bodrugan's Leap.

In a later chapter in the history of the Edgcumbe family, after Sir Thomas Fairfax had led the Parliamentary forces across the Tamar in 1646, Colonel Pierce Edgcumbe conspired with some of his neighbours to surrender eastern Cornwall on advantageous terms, thus leaving the rest of the county open to the Parliamentarians and perhaps bringing about the ultimate collapse of the Royalist cause.

A sprightly gentleman

North of the Edgcumbe houses is Stow, one-time home of the Grenvile family, which has produced several Cornish heroes. Sir Richard Grenvile of the *Revenge* will always be remembered for his Elizabethan maritime successes, whilst his grandsons Sir Bevill and Sir Richard, were stalwart Royalists during the Civil War. Edward, Earl of Clarendon, historian of the Civil Wars, described Sir Bevill Grenvile as 'a gallant and sprightly gentleman, of the greatest reputation and interest in Cornwall' who was 'the generally most loved man of that county'. Sir Bevill has come to epitomise the Royalist cause in Cornwall, and inspired the poet Rev Robert Stephen Hawker to write:

. . . Call the hind from the plough, and the herd from the fold,
Bid the wassailer cease from his revel;
And ride for old Stow, where the banner's unrolled
For the cause of King Charles and Sir Bevill. . . .

At Braddock Down, near Boconnoc, a monument marks the site of the battle of January 1643 where, in a wild charge, Sir Bevill Grenvile led his servants and tenants down one hill and up another, so that they 'strook a terror' into the enemy. In May 1643, Sir Bevill and his fellow Cornish officers led their troops to another momentous victory at Stratton, near the Grenvile home at Stow. According to Clarendon, this 'seasonable victory' was celebrated by Sir Bevill Grenvile and Sir Ralph Hopton with 'public prayers upon the place and a solemn thanksgiving to Almighty God for their deliverance' and because of their success against the odds, Hopton is said to have declared that 'in the fight God blessed the King's party'.

Rebels across the Tamar

A plaque in Bodmin celebrates Thomas Flamank, a lawyer of the town. In 1497, a year of economic depression, Flamank and Michael Joseph, a blacksmith from the Lizard area, led 15,000

Mount Edgcumbe, near Torpoint, is still occupied by the Edgcumbe family

Plaque commemorating rebel-leaders Joseph and Flamank

Cornishmen to London to protest at being taxed to pay for a remote Scottish war. But the disillusioned and much-deserted Cornish force stood little chance of success against King Henry's 25,000 strong army at Blackheath on 16 June 1497. About 200 Cornishmen were killed in the ensuing battle, and both Flamank and Joseph were hanged, drawn, and quartered at Tyburn. This episode merely served to exacerbate anti-government feeling, so that the county proved to be an ideal springboard for Perkin Warbeck's claim, three months after the event, to be one of the Princes in the Tower who had not been murdered after all. Warbeck received a rapturous welcome in Cornwall, and in Bodmin was joined by some of the lesser gentry and proclaimed King Richard IV. He crossed the Tamar in September 1497 with 6,000 Cornish supporters, but they got no further than Taunton, where they were forced to surrender to the king.

In 1549, Bodmin again proved to be the natural centre of Cornish resistance to unpopular government measures. A full-scale rebellion broke out in reaction to the 1549 Act of Uniformity, with its enforcement of the Book of Common Prayer and its simplified service in English, in place of the old Latin mass. One of the complaints of the Cornishmen was that they could not understand

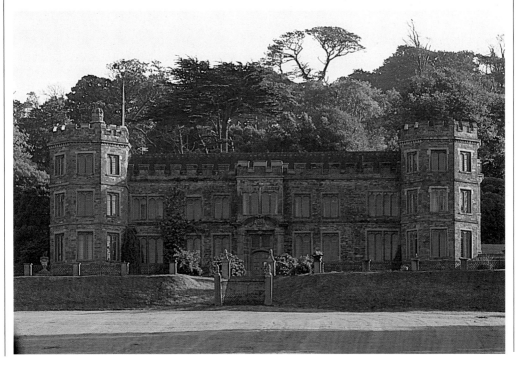

the new Prayer Book, 'and so we Cornishmen, whereof certain of us understand no English, utterly refuse thise new English'. Yet again an 'army' of Cornishmen marched from Bodmin across the Tamar, but with no more success than on previous occasions: they were routed by Henry VIII's troops in Devon, and their leaders executed. A century later, during the English Civil War, Bodmin maintained the same neutral stance as other Cornish towns, and entertained both Royalist and Parliamentarian officers in turn. However, in 1660-1661, the Mayors' Accounts record considerable expenditure on beer, buns, wine and bonfires in the streets, to celebrate the restoration and coronation of King Charles II. Not far from the town is Lanhydrock House, one-time home of the Robartes family, who through trade experienced a rapid rise in fortune and status in the early 17th century; by the mid-17th century Lord Robartes was one of the leaders of the Parliamentarian cause in Cornwall. Lanhydrock, more recently rebuilt after fire, is known as 'the grand old lady of Cornish houses', and is a National Trust property.

An honourable defeat

One of the ringleaders of the 1549 Prayer Book Rebellion was Humphry Arundel, a member of the oldest and most fanatically Catholic branch of the Arundel family. Humphry Arundel was executed for his actions, but the family maintained its faith, and partly because of this supported Charles I in 1642. Another branch of this family lived at Trerice Manor, eight miles south of Lanherne and three miles from Newquay. Sir John Arundell of Trerice, a staunch Royalist, was governor of Pendennis Castle, Falmouth, during the five-month siege of 1646. On 17 March 1646, Sir Thomas Fairfax occupied Arwenack Manor in Falmouth and ordered Arundell to surrender, only to receive this gallant reply: '. . . *having taken less than two minutes resolution, I resolve that I will here bury myself before I deliver up this Castle to such as fight against his Majesty*'. Eventually the garrison was starved into submission, but the Royalists maintained their dignity by making a surrender on honourable terms, and marched out of the castle

Above: memorial in Truro Cathedral to John Robartes, a leading Parliamentarian
Main picture: St Michael's Mount, centre of some turbulent episodes in history

with 'Drums beating, Colours flying, Trumpets sounding'. Pendennis Castle is open to the public; Trerice is a superb 16th-century manor house and belongs to the National Trust; Arwenack Manor is now private flats.

Falmouth harbour is overlooked on the other side by St Mawes Castle, which also supported the

Top: Pendennis Castle, the last Royalist stronghold in England to fall.
Bottom: St Mawes Castle also supported the Royalist cause

Royalist war effort in Cornwall, although it surrendered before Pendennis and without a fight. Sir Richard Vyvyan of Trelowarren suffered great financial loss by erecting another fort at Dennis Head in 1643-1644, at his own expense, to defend the Helford River for the king. Trelowarren has been the home of the Vyvyans since the 15th century. Sir Francis Godolphin of Godolphin House, near Helston, took up arms for King Charles I in 1642, and was governor of the Isles of Scilly; his younger brother, Sidney, the poet, was killed in the king's service at Chagford in 1643. His death was a major blow to his friends and contemporaries, Sir Bevill Grenvile writing to his wife that he '*was a gallant a gent as the world had*', whilst Sir Ralph Hopton said he was '*as perfect and as absolute a piece of vertue as ever our nation bredd.*' Godolphin House is in private (though not Godolphin) hands, and is sometimes open.

Rebellion's back-door
Some of the most turbulent episodes surround St Michael's Mount off Cornwall's southern coast. In 1473, after the Yorkist Edward IV had been established on the throne, the rebel Earl of Oxford seized St Michael's Mount by disguising his men as pilgrims. He was besieged by successive Sheriffs of Cornwall: Sir John Arundell of Trerice (who was killed in a skirmish on the sands dividing the Mount from the mainland, thus fulfilling a prophecy to that effect), Sir Henry Bodrugan, and Richard Fortescue. The siege lasted four months, far longer than the king considered necessary; indeed, according to tradition, Edward attributed this to the disloyalty of the Cornish, and he thereafter regarded Cornwall as 'the back door of rebellion'. Between 1642 and 1646 the garrison at the Mount was held for the king by its owners, the Bassett family of Tehidy. Sir Arthur Bassett surrendered the Mount to Parliament in April 1646. During the Commonwealth, St Michael's Mount passed into the hands of John St Aubyn, who had supported Parliament during the war; his descendant, Lord St Levan, is living there today.

Legends

As a land of legend Cornwall is difficult to surpass. Within its tiny area many hundreds of stories and myths have survived, some based on evident historical fact, others whose origins are lost in antiquity. Here is a fascinating field for the student of folklore.

The Cornish Giants and Fairy-Folk, or Piskies, are among the most notable of legends. The idea of the giants, it has been suggested, originated when the tall Celts arrived in Cornwall around 500BC. Being so much larger than the Neolithic and Bronze Age peoples before them, they were looked on as giants; conversely the Celts regarded their squat, dark predecessors as dwarfs or piskies.

Tales of the giants amused our ancestors down the ages, and were recorded mainly in West Cornwall. St Michael's Mount, that jewel of an island off Marazion, was said to have been built by the Giant Cormoran, or rather by his wife, Cormelian, whom he bullied into carrying huge granite blocks from the Penwith moors in her leather apron. One day as he dozed lazily on the hillside she decided to carry a great piece of greenstone which she found lying nearby, rather than trudge all the way back to the moor; but, waking up to what she was doing, Cormoran

administered her a kick which sent her sprawling
and broke her apron strings. The greenstone fell
some way short of the Mount, and hundreds of
years later, when the sea rushed in and engulfed
the area, the rock was left showing above the tide.

Another fearsome giant was Bolster, who in one
stride could step from St Agnes Beacon to Carn
Brea – about six miles. He fell in love with the
beautiful Saint Agnes herself, and to escape his
attentions she demanded that he should fill a great
hole in the cliff with his blood. The besotted giant
cut one of his veins and bled to death, not realising
that the bottom of the hole was connected to the
sea by a small tunnel.

But the most famous figure in Cornish folklore is
the ghost of Jan Tregeagle, who for his sins is
hunted across Bodmin Moor by the Devil and his
dogs. Tregeagle, the unjust Steward of the Lord of
Lanhydrock, is reputed to have robbed his master
of lands and extorted unfair rents from his tenants.

I WILL BROIL YOU FOR MY BREAKFAST.

*Left: the giant Bolster strides from St Agnes Beacon to
Carn Brea. This page, top: Jack 'the giant-killer' lures
Cormoran to his death in a pit on St Michael's Mount.
Right: Jan Tregeagle, sentenced to a series of grim tasks,
drops a sack of sand and creates Loe Bar. Finally, he
was condemned to bale out Dozmary Pool (above) with
a limpet shell with a hole in it*

After his death he was first sentenced to carry sacks
of sand from Porthleven to Marazion, and dropped
one across the mouth of the Cober River, creating
the Loe Bar. He was then set to spin sheaves of
sand at the mouth of the River Camel, but
annoyed the people of Padstow and St Minver,
and was shut into an oven at Trevorder; his
bellowings disturbed the peace of St Breock and
Wadebridge, so he was finally, with the aid of

monks and priests, established at Dozmary Pool near Jamaica Inn, and condemned to bale it out with a limpet shell with a hole in it. But on the wildest nights he is hunted across the Moor by a pack of satanic hounds.

The true story of Tregeagle emerges from no less than five successive generations of John Tregeagles who were active in the 16th to 18th centuries in mid-Cornwall. The first was indeed steward to Lord Robartes at Lanhydrock, and established a reputation as a severe magistrate. The second and third, his son and grandson, were Receivers-General to the Duchy of Cornwall and involved in a financial scandal. The combination of ill repute and apparent immortality has created the legend, embellished by the many 'droll-tellers' who travelled about, amusing cottagers with such stories at their firesides in winter.

Tales of the piskies are found in most parts of Cornwall. At St Allen near Truro a nine-year-old boy vanished for three weeks, and was then found asleep but unharmed in a bed of ferns; he told how he was taken away by the Little People into a palace of gold and silver and fed on fairy food. There are many accounts of people being 'pisky-led' – wandering around a field unable to find the gate, or led a dance over moorlands and becoming disorientated. In North Cornwall piskies were reputed to ride horses at night until they became exhausted; in West Cornwall cows would be milked dry at night.

Another story concerns an old furze-cutter who came across a tiny creature dressed in green cloth with diamond buckled shoes, asleep in the gorse. He took the little fellow home and kept him to entertain the family – he was a fine dancer – but the children let him out one day and he was claimed back by his own people. To have a pisky in the house always brought good fortune.

The spirits of the mines, known as Buccas or Knockers, were well-treated by the miners who always left underground a portion of their pasties or 'fuggans' (dough-cake) for them. Their

Tales of the Little People abound in Cornwall

There are many Cornish tales involving mermaids

knockings served as warnings of impending danger or rock-falls. The Buccas were said to be the spirits of Jews who had worked at smelting tin in Cornwall, and who were consigned after their deaths neither to Heaven nor Hell but a limbo in the tin mines.

Mermaids feature prominently in Cornish folklore. The Mermaid of Padstow, having lured a local fisherman into her embraces, was shot by him when he attempted to escape from her spell. In her dying moments she cursed the port – a terrible storm then raged, destroying many vessels, and threw up the great bank of sand known as the Doom Bar, on which hundreds of ships foundered during the centuries. The Mermaid of Zennor actually went to church and fell in love with the leading tenor in the choir, Mathy Trewhella; she successfully lured him down to the ocean bed, where he married her and had mer-children. At Cury near the Lizard an old man called Lutey found a stranded mermaid and helped her back into the sea, where she swam away to rejoin her merman husband and children, but not before she had granted Lutey three wishes. He would be immune to the spells of witchcraft, able to gain knowledge from the spirits, and his family would possess these powers for all posterity. But the sea-sprite told him she would come back to take him down to the sea-kingdoms with her, and nine years after the day she did re-appear, and the bewitched old man vanished with her into the waves.

Legends of lost cities around the coast of Cornwall undoubtedly represent folk-memories of inundations during the past. Between Land's End and the Scillies is claimed to lie the fabled land of Lyonesse, drowned in AD1099, and the bells of churches are said to have been heard ringing beneath the waters. Between Crantock and Perranporth once existed the great city of Langarroc. It was said to have been covered up by sand in a great storm about a thousand years ago, when most of its inhabitants perished, a punishment for their evil doings.

Encroaching sand has always been a great problem along the North Cornish coast, and St Piran's Oratory near Perranporth, a tiny chapel originally built by the saint himself about AD490, was for centuries covered up. Excavated in 1835, it was claimed to be the oldest extant building of Christian worship on mainland Britain – the second oldest after Iona Abbey. A long battle was fought to drain it and clear it of sand, but today, in order to protect it, the oratory has sadly been reburied and is now marked only by a rough stone saying simply 'St Piran'.

The saint was one of the hundreds of holy men and women who came to Cornwall from Ireland,

Above: St Piran's Oratory about 1900. Now it has been reburied. Left: St Neot was a pigmy. His life is told in the stained glass windows of St Neot's Church

Patron Saint of Cornish Miners, in celebration and commemoration of his discovery of how to smelt tin: one cold night he built up a bigger fire than usual in his cave on the foreshore at Perranzabuloe – 'St Piran in the Sands' – and a large black hearthstone cracked asunder in the heat, giving forth shining white tin metal. The Cornish Flag, a white cross on a black background, is thus named after him.

Among other notable saints was the virgin St Keyne, who blessed a well in the parish named after her in south-east Cornwall, and dedicated it to marriage. A poem by Robert Southey celebrates this: after the wedding husband and wife would rush to drink the well water, for 'he who first the water drinks, the mastery shall gain'. St Neot, whose church stands in a beautiful secluded valley near Liskeard, was a pigmy about 3ft high, whose life is remembered in the glorious mediaeval stained glass windows surviving in the church.

But the greatest Cornish saint was undoubtedly St Petroc, patron of Padstow and Bodmin, who established powerful monasteries at both places. He is said to have tamed the last great dragon ravaging the Cornish countryside, and binding his stole around its neck, mercifully led it to the sea near Padstow where it swam away. He also cast a spell over the warlike Prince Constantine who was hunting a little fawn and, converting him to Christianity, commanded him to spend the rest of his days in poverty and prayer at a cell near the bay named after him. The holy well of St Constantine and the remains of his mediaeval church can be seen among the dunes on Trevose Golf Course.

The relics of St Petroc were so venerated that in the 12th century a monk stole them and took them to St Méen across the Channel; Henry II of England, the Overlord of Brittany, commanded their return and gave a richly carved ivory casket in which to keep them.

Perhaps the most fascinating of all legends is that

Wales or Brittany, sister Celtic countries, between AD490 and AD650 – the 'Age of the Saints'. The saying goes that 'there are more saints in Cornwall than in Heaven', for every other village seems to be named after a saint, usually an obscure one about whom little is known. During the Dark and early Middle Ages the term 'saint' was used for a respected holy man or woman who had founded a cell and ministered to the local populace. Some of these were, however, great saints who have been recognised by the Catholic and Anglican churches, among them St Piran, who was widely venerated in mediaeval times.

He came, it is believed, from Ireland, and according to legend lived a roistering life, fond of his tipple, and died at the ripe old age of 206 by falling into a well when drunk one night. He is the of King Arthur, who was mortally wounded fighting his last battle against his treacherous nephew, Mordred. Many places in Britain claim Arthur, the great British hero who defeated the Saxons in 12 successive battles, but the tradition that he was actually a Cornishman has been strong in Cornwall since mediaeval times.

So tenacious were the Cornish in their belief that he would come again one day to rescue them from bondage that in AD1177 there was a riot in Bodmin church between visiting French monks and the local men; a Frenchman had scoffed at such an article of faith. The spirit of Arthur was believed to fly over the cliffs of Cornwall in the form of the Cornish chough – a bird now extinct in the county except for two or three pairs in captivity, at Padstow Bird Gardens and Newquay Zoo.

Tintagel Castle is the usual scene of Arthur's birth in romance and legend. Geoffrey of Monmouth, 12th-century author of the *History of the Kings of Britain*, was the first to record this belief. Evidence of a Celtic royal household has been found, but the remains of the castle there today, starkly situated on its island above towering cliffs, are Norman in origin. Another tradition associated Arthur with Castle-an-Dinas near St Columb, the

The myth of King Arthur has inspired writers and artists alike. The painting below portrays his death, the legendary site for which is at Camelford, near Slaughterbridge, where there is an engraved stone, the so-called 'Arthur's Tomb'

largest Celtic hill fort in Cornwall, which was also known as the seat of Cornish kings after Arthur's time. (Castle-an-Dinas has now been acquired from the Duchy of Cornwall by the Cornwall Heritage Trust, for opening to the public.)

Arthur's last battle was fought, according to Cornish legend, at Slaughterbridge near Camelford, where the river ran crimson with the blood of slain warriors. Sir Bedivere was sent to Dozmary Pool, six miles away on the moors, to return the sword Excalibur to the waters. And in the imagination of Alfred Lord Tennyson, the dying Arthur was carried down to the narrow loch-like harbour of Boscastle to be taken away in the funeral barge to Avalon.

Another legend, one of the greatest of love stories, has been given by Cornwall to the world: that of Tristan and Iseult, who shared the love potion mean for Iseult and her future husband, King Mark, and so were doomed to an illicit passion. Near Fowey is the stone inscribed with the earliest known form of the name Tristan, and not far from Helston in Meneage is a ford which was recorded as *Hryt Eselt* in the 10th century – the earliest known form of Iseult. King Mark, who sent Tristan to Ireland to bring Iseult back to be his queen, is traditionally associated with Castle Dore near Galant. And the earliest form of the romance, by the Norman-French poet, Béroul, sets the story firmly in south and mid-Cornwall, mentioning places such as Chapel Rock near Mevagissey (Tristan's Leap) and the Forest of Morrois (Moresk, near Truro), where the lovers fled to hide from Mark and his barons.

Cornish Wildlife

Algae and barnacles beside a rock pool on an exposed stretch of seashore.
Inset: a shore crab brandishes its pincers

Cornwall is almost an island, cut off from the rest of the country by the River Tamar. Its Atlantic situation as the most south-westerly part of England results in a relatively warm, wet climate with strong winds sweeping across the land. The county's natural history is influenced by these factors as well as by geology, and a number of exciting contrasts result, as can be seen easily enough when one travels about.

An obvious contrast is between the north coast and the south. The one is stark and wild with high, bare cliffs and few harbours. The other is gentler and more broken with numerous estuaries where wooded valleys run down to the sea – most of Cornwall's rivers flow southwards from the moors. Where breaks in the line of cliffs permit, as near Perranporth, there are more extensive sand-dunes on the north coast, with their own particular flora including burnet rose, sea rocket and sea holly. Salt-marshes, where sea spurrey and sea asters grow, are more frequent in the south. Beaches everywhere are regularly covered and uncovered by the tides to reveal the different

phases in the life of the seashore, with zoned banks of different seaweeds and the shelled creatures that live among them.

There are contrasts along the north coast itself where bare rock faces alternate with strips and cushions of brightly coloured flowers; and the stunted oak forest of the Dizzard, which stretches down landslip slopes almost to sea-level, has beside it some of the most uncompromising cliffs in Cornwall. Inland there are cultivated farmlands adjacent to industrial dereliction, the relics of china-clay workings and tin-mining in past centuries.

Above right: a fulmar in flight, its effortless gliding a familiar sight along the clifftops.
Above left: the burnet rose, a low-growing shrub 6–18in. high, forms large patches, especially in sand dunes

There are deep-cut ferny lanes with great splashes of colour provided by foxgloves, red campion and other colourful flowers; and mature old valley hardwoods contrasting with moorlands which look more barren than they really are, as the boggy ground supports numerous flowers. Cornwall's 'hedges' (stone walls) are almost bare on the windward side except for lichens, but full of colour on the other with stonecrops, rock spurrey and gorse. On walls, or wherever there are crevices, it is worth looking for ferns as the spleenworts in Cornwall include the rare bright green lanceolate spleenwort. Different again is the open water of Dozmary Pool and several reservoirs where great flocks of wildfowl pass the winter.

There are also many other wetland areas, among them Breney Common and Red Moor, near Bodmin, both owned and managed as reserves by the county Nature Conservation Trust. They are areas of heathland, ponds and willow carr where the trees grow in damp ground with reeds, rushes, mosses and the splendid royal fern; birds, including tits and such migrant warblers as the chiff-chaff, nest among the branches. A rich and varied animal life occupies the ponds, which have frogs, toads, palmate newts and countless invertebrates. Among the latter are diving and whirligig beetles, water boatmen, which swim on their boat-shaped backs, and Britain's only water-spider, which spins an air-filled 'diving bell' where it lives and breathes below the surface.

Soils are generally more acid than alkaline and relate to the underlying granite or to sedimentary rock formations; the latter are mainly Devonian

shales and sandstones, known as 'killas', or the carboniferous culm measures of north-east Cornwall. These are the remains of the heavily faulted Armorican mountain chain which stretched down south-west Britain some two hundred million years ago. Molten rock from the earth's interior welled up into the mountains, cooled and solidified until, exposed by erosion, it became the granite spine of the county (and of Devon): Bodmin and other moorland areas, West Penwith and the Isles of Scilly. There are a few exposures of volcanic rock, notably the pillow lava of Pentire Head, and the ancient pre-Cambrian rocks of the Lizard peninsula. There is very little limestone.

The rocks of the Lizard are mainly serpentine, gabbro and schists. They support a unique flora which makes this area one of Britain's classic botanical sites. Plants of special interest include Cornish heath (*Erica vagans*), pygmy rush, orchids and rare members of both clover and buttercup families; prostrate wild asparagus grows on a rocky islet off Kynance Cove. The level of the sea in relation to the land has varied greatly through the

Britain's only water-spider is found in ponds in some of Cornwall's wetland areas

during migration periods. Shelduck, among the most colourful of British wildfowl, also favour such places and sometimes nest in rabbit burrows along the verges.

Part of the charm of Cornwall's long coastline is that it offers many different kinds of beach – some rocky, others sandy or strewn with boulders, stones or pebbles – the degree of exposure to the waves and the weather varying greatly between beaches. Such factors determine the kind and abundance of seaweeds and of the marine animals likely to be found in rock-pools or attached to

Ornithologists are urgently trying to prevent the puffin (above left) becoming extinct in Cornwall
Above right: the dog whelk with its mass of egg capsules

ages, and this has produced a series of ancient marine platforms which is why a large part of Cornwall appears so flat.

In the spring and early summer the wild flowers of the coast are astonishing in their abundance and variety and can be seen at their best from the Coast Path. Cliff tops and exposed edges are outlined with thrift. Buttercups, violets, spring squill, sheep's sorrel and self-heal colour the maritime grassland. Gorse and hawthorn scrub are in full flower – thyme, western gorse and another range of plants appear later in the year to continue the panorama. Heathers are plentiful in some areas. Between bands of scurvy grass the cliff faces are bright yellow with flowers of bird's-foot trefoil and kidney vetch, variety being added by wild carrot, rock samphire and sea campion. At lower levels, where the influence of the sea is direct, there are sea lavender, orange lichens and green algae. In places bluebells and primroses, away from their normal woodland habitat, grow surprisingly close to the sea.

The birds are almost equally attractive. Gulls breed all along the coast, the main concentration of the beautifully sleek kittiwake being on St Agnes Head. Fulmars share some of their breeding cliffs, and there are a few pairs of that master falcon, the peregrine. Kestrels, buzzards and ravens are seen less often than they used to be but are still present. Auks do not breed north of Beeny, near Boscastle, but the commonest of them, razorbills and guillemots, are reasonably plentiful south and west of that point. There are very few puffins left thanks largely to the curse of oil pollution. Shags and oystercatchers occupy rocky beaches and sandy shores respectively. Choughs are now extinct in Cornwall but jackdaws are ubiquitous. Small songbirds are plentiful in the clifftop furze, while waders, such as sandpipers and godwits, are best seen on estuaries and salt-marshes in winter or

rocks. Mussels, barnacles, limpets, whelks, crabs and anemones are widely distributed. Ocean currents sometimes bring transatlantic species to Cornwall's shores, among them jellyfish-like animals and octopods. Whales and dolphins sometimes visit the coast or strand themselves on the beaches.

Of greater local interest, however, are the grey (or Atlantic) seals which breed on a few inaccessible stony beaches and in sea caves. They are a delight to watch as they hunt for fish or haul out on to their favourite rocky platforms, particularly when assembled during the autumn breeding season. The bulls arrive first to establish their territories and collect as many females as they can attract. Many of the females are already pregnant from last year's mating and drop their pups soon after joining the bull. They stay with their babies for about three weeks when these should be weaned and robust enough to fend for themselves in the sea. By this time the mother seal is ready to mate again, mating usually taking place in the water. The seals then disperse. At birth, baby seals have long silky white hair which they moult when fully weaned. Particularly when the weather is rough, these quite charming white babies can become separated from their mothers, and you sometimes find them apparently abandoned on various Cornish beaches. It is best to leave them where they are as the mother usually follows her baby out to sea and is likely to be somewhere nearby waiting for darkness and the high tide.

The greatest concentration of seals is on the Isles of Scilly where also there are very large numbers of breeding sea birds, mainly on outlying islands and sea-stacks – for instance, both storm petrels and Manx shearwaters breed on Annet Island. Several common land birds are absent but rare visitors from North America, blown off course across the Atlantic, appear so often that searching for and watching rare birds on the islands has become a well-established branch of the tourist industry. Another interest – this time for botanically-minded visitors – lies in deciding which of the many plants they find are genuine natives and not unusual garden escapes; there are several local varieties of wild plants on the islands. There is also a Scilly shrew, not found on the mainland, which is hunted by rats on stony beaches and, for the lepidopterist, there is a local sub-species of the familiar meadow brown butterfly.

There is more to Cornwall than the coast, though no place is more than 15 miles from the sea, and the hinterland is dominated by the granite moors which reach their highest point on Brown Willy (1371ft). There are rocky tors and clitter slopes but most of the open land has been so improved for grazing that little heather is left and only scattered bilberry bushes remain. Many bogs have been drained; those that survive support an interesting flora with sphagnum moss, cotton grass, bog asphodel, orchids, insect-devouring sundews and much else besides. Pools and streams, often bordered by ferns, provide yet another colourful scene; yellow flags contrast with purple marsh orchids and blue forget-me-nots, while several species of dragonfly hawk for insects. Too many of the woods which used to occupy the margins of the moors have been cleared away.

There are numerous heathlands, both dry and wet, away from the main moorland areas, and they are very characteristic inland Cornish habitats. Dry heath has often developed on land laid waste by former tin-mining and streaming activities and is typified by the common ling heather, with minute leaves and pink flowers, as well as the purple-flowered bell heather. The now rare Dorset heath grows in a few such places. Wet heathland, which occurs in relatively small patches throughout the county, is dominated by purple moor grass; if any heather occurs it is most likely to be the cross-leaved heath. Heath spotted orchids are fairly common.

The green hairstreak butterfly at rest, showing its green underwings streaked with a fine white line. It appears in May and June, mainly in woodland

The yellow flag iris thrives beside Cornwall's pools and streams

Numerous insects thrive in such surroundings with marsh fritillary butterflies, bush crickets, grasshoppers, blue agrion damselflies and four-spotted hawker dragonflies among the most attractive. Spiders are numerous.

The bird life of the higher moors tends to be dominated in the winter by large flocks of lapwings, golden plovers and curlews, solitary pairs of which breed in many moorland valleys. Meadow pipits, which are often parasitized by cuckoos, are the commonest small bird of the open moor; linnets, stonechats and skylarks are also widespread. Foxes are widespread; badgers make their setts among the boulders. Several butterflies occur, among them the uncommon green hairstreak, whose caterpillars feed on gorse and bilberries, and the dark green fritillary which is associated with violets.

Most of the ancient woods in Cornwall are dominated by sessile oak (which has stalkless acorns) with ash, holly and other trees. A few of those that survive were mentioned in the Domesday Survey; other woods unfortunately have been cleared away to make room for conifer plantations, farming, mining and even building development. Among those that remain, Drayne's near Liskeard, Pelyn near Lostwithiel, Lanhydrock near Bodmin and the valley woods of the south coast are the most important; and conservation of the remaining deciduous woods is now a vital task. They support a rich and varied ground flora with mosses, ferns, fungi and, among lichens, the large plate-shaped tree lungwort which shows the relative absence of pollution in the atmosphere. Among flowering plants are wood anemones, bluebells and snowdrops.

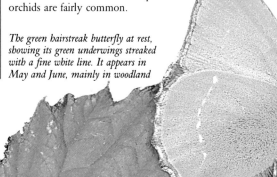

The bird and animal life of Cornish woods is generally similar to that found in damp valley woods elsewhere, with badgers, foxes, stoats and weasels. The insect life includes many woodland butterflies. Otters, which are becoming increasingly rare in Britain, still inhabit a few Cornish rivers, mainly where the banks are well wooded, and they may eventually be re-introduced elsewhere now

Above: Cornwall is one of the few areas of Britain where the otter is still found.
Left: the southern marsh orchid

that a branch of The Otter Trust has been established near Launceston. It is to be hoped that competition from the alien mink, now widely distributed, will not prove too strong. Red deer occur in certain woodland areas in east Cornwall.

The delightful badger is normally looked upon as a beneficial species, but was believed to be responsible for the spread of bovine tuberculosis in West Penwith and in the east of the county during the 1970s. Badger setts were gassed and hundreds of animals killed in an attempt to wipe out the disease. This is a highly complex issue about which much could be written, but naturalists did not believe that badgers were the guilty parties and at the time of writing the killing of badgers has almost ceased – without any apparent increase in the

The grey seal, Britain's largest wild mammal, comes ashore only to breed and to bask

spread of tuberculosis among cattle. The argument continues. Badgers in Cornwall are found not only in woods and on the moors; they are quite plentiful in coastal scrub.

What is being done to preserve all this wildlife?

Firstly, the Nature Conservancy Council, the Government's official watchdog, has listed more than 60 Sites of Special Scientific Interest and has established the Lizard National Nature Reserve, covering 1,000 acres of valuable heathland. The National Trust owns over a hundred miles of coast, including some of the best areas, like Pentire Head and Dodman Point, and some fine old deciduous woods inland. The Cornwall Bird Watching and Preservation Society owns two sanctuaries and leases the rights over parts of certain reservoirs where wildfowl and waders feed. The Cornwall Trust for Nature Conservation, the one body concerned with all forms of nature conservation throughout the county, owns or leases or manages 28 nature reserves covering some 3,000 acres, most of Cornwall's major habitats being represented. Many other areas are carefully monitored. Cornwall, moreover, is fortunate in the co-operative attitude of County and District Councils, but pressures remain formidable.

Gardens

Those travellers with a keen eye for the landscape who make the journey from London or the north towards the south-west will appreciate the rich pastures of Somerset and the lush beauty of lowland Devon. Continuing westwards across the Tamar and on down the long peninsula of Cornwall might well raise expectations of a land even more exotic in garden and hedgerow.

At first sight the very reverse would appear to be true. For Devon's rolling hills, its rich red earth, its high hedges and narrow lanes soon give way to a bleak granite upland, effectively separating north coast from south. So it is that many of the Duchy's summer visitors return home with memories of a coastline that is incomparable (especially if the weather has been clement), but of an interior that is nothing but an uninviting windswept moorland.

If this is so they have not travelled wisely, for this superficially forbidding land is one of only two areas in the islands of Great Britain (the other is a narrow maritime belt of western Scotland) that are genuinely able to grow plants from warm temperate climates out of doors.

To the south of the central spine of granite and moors there is some shelter from the worst of the great westerly gales. The land descends gradually in rolling 'downs' to a coastline that is generally far less rugged than the north. The short-lived streams that cut their way through the downs, such as the Lynher, the Fowey and the Fal soon become deep-water estuaries enclosing a system of inlets and drowned valleys penetrating well inland. The Fal is the finest example of these drowned valleys, where a complex of beautiful, wooded creeks meets to form the great estuary of the Carrick Roads. It is along this coast from the Tamar to the Helford and again in the south-facing part of Mount's Bay that the effect of the Gulf Stream is most pronounced. The climate is relatively mild with a high humidity; frost and snow are rare and fleeting. Almost as important for the gardener, the

Main picture: the dovecote and pool at Cotehele
Inset: as the rhododendrons at Tregothnan near the end of the flowering period, the paths are strewn with petals

Falmouth - St. Mawes
MARITIME HERITAGE
TRAIL

Explore the rich maritime history of
Falmouth & St. Mawes by land and sea

Enjoy the Maritime Heritage of Falmouth, St. Mawes and St. Anthony Head

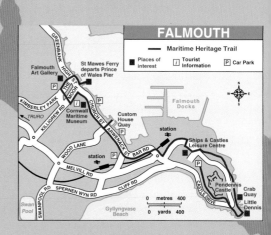

Pendennis Headland

Coastal defences survive at Pendennis Headland from every period of foreign threat during the last 450 years. The original castle was built by Henry VIII in 1545, and Queen Elizabeth incorporated this into a massive fortress, with high ramparts and a dry moat.

The trail starts from the reconstructed Hornworks, the forward defences of Pendennis during the Civil War siege of 1646. After visiting the Castle, continue to Pendennis Point at first following the moat, and then passing Half Moon Battery and the Maritime Rescue Centre. At the Point descend to Little Dennis Fort, built by Henry VIII to provide auxiliary fire-power at sea-level.

Return to the car park and descend to the 18th century Crab Quay Battery. The route can now be easily followed using the map.

Falmouth Waterfront

Along Castle Drive a layby provides an unsurpassed viewpoint of Falmouth's waterfront and dockside activities, including ship repair.

Arwenack House is the former manor house of the Killigrew family, who planned Falmouth. After the Killigrews built Custom House Quay in 1670 Falmouth rapidly developed into a major port. The grand classical building in Arwenack Street is the present Custom House, opened in 1814. Close by is the King's Pipe, a brick chimney built to burn contraband tobacco.

Cornwall Maritime Museum has displays, model boats and artefacts which tell of Falmouth's fascinating maritime past. There is also a strong maritime theme at Falmouth Art Gallery, from where it is a short walk to the Prince of Wales Pier.

Falmouth Quay Punt, Cornwall Maritime Museum

Cornwall Maritime Museum exhibits

A Half Day Extension

During summer, the St. Mawes to Place Ferryboat provides access to the fine coastal walks and maritime heritage of St. Anthony in Roseland. The ferry lands near Place House, the private residence of the Spry-Grant-Dalton family. The suggested 3 $\frac{1}{2}$ mile circular walk follows the coast path from Place, visiting the 13th century Church of St. Anthony, and St. Anthony Lighthouse, built in 1834 to mark the entrance to Carrick Roads. St. Anthony Battery was armed with two 6" guns from 1887 until 1956, when coastal defence was abandoned.

Just above Porthbeor Beach turn left and join the road. Turn right and almost immediately left into Bohortha, where a footpath descends to Place.

St. Mawes seafront

Ill cannon, St. Mawes Castle

Guarded by the twin castles of Pendennis and St. Mawes, the Fal Estuary is one of the finest natural harbours in the world. Situated at the gateway to the English Channel, Falmouth flourished for 200 years as the second busiest port of the British Empire. Inbound sailing ships replenished supplies and outward-bound vessels sheltered awaiting favourable winds. Forty sleek, swift brigantines of the Post Office's Packet Service were based here until the Napoleonic Wars.

Today the Fal Estuary is better known for its unspoilt natural beauty, but the area's great maritime heritage can easily be discovered on this trail. Use your mind's eye to recreate the bustle of Falmouth's wharves, and get afloat to see the wonderful views on the foot ferry between Falmouth and St. Mawes.

View over cannon, Pendennis

Henry Scott Tuke (b1858), Falmouth Art Gallery

Main photo: Pendennis Headland

Falmouth-St. Mawes Ferry

DAILY SUMMER SERVICE

From Falmouth (Prince of Wales Pier)

Mondays to Saturdays
0830, 0945, 1015, 1045, 1115, 1145, 1215, 1315(NS),
1345, 1415, 1445, 1515, 1545, 1615, 1645, 1715
Sundays
1000, 1100, 1200, 1400, 1500, 1600, 1700

From St Mawes (The Harbour)

Mondays to Saturdays
0900, 0945, 1015, 1045, 1115, 1145, 1215, 1245(NS),
1345, 1415, 1445, 1515, 1545, 1615, 1645, 1715
Sundays
1030, 1130, 1230, 1430, 1530, 1630, 1730

NOTES

NS Not Saturdays
Summer Service operates Easter, May Day Bank Holiday
period and Whitsun to 30 September. During the
remainder of April and October check with the ferry
company.

WINTER SERVICE

Mondays to Saturdays

From Falmouth (Prince of Wales Pier)
0830, 1015, 1115, 1315, 1415, 1615

From St Mawes (The Harbour)
0900, 1045, 1145, 1345, 1445, 1645

**There are no
winter Sunday services**

Operated by St. Mawes Ferry Company
(01326) 313201

St. Mawes to Place Ferryboat

DAILY SUMMER SERVICE   5 May - 30 Sept

From St Mawes (The Harbour)
1000, 1030, 1100, 1130, 1200, 1230,
1330, 1400, 1430, 1500, 1530, 1600, 1630

From Place
1015, 1045, 1115, 1145, 1215, 1245,
1345, 1415, 1445, 1515, 1545, 1615, 1645

There are no winter services

Operated by Balcomb Boats (01209) 214901

Opening Times

Cornwall Maritime Museum
Not on phone
Easter - 31 October:
Daily 10am - 4pm
1 November - Maundy Thursday:
Mon - Sat 10am - 3pm

Falmouth Art Gallery (01326) 313863
Until 31 October 1995:
Mon - Fri 10am - 4.30pm
Sat 10am - 1pm during exhibitions
Not open on bank holidays
Re-opens Spring 1996 after Gallery renovations

Pendennis Castle (01326) 316594
1 April - 30 September: Daily 10am - 6pm
1 October - 31 March: Daily 10am - 4pm

St Mawes Castle (01326) 270526
1 April - 30 September: Daily 10am - 6pm
1 - 31 October: Daily 10am - 4pm
1 November - 31 March: Wed - Sun 10am - 4pm

Getting There

Truro - Falmouth Line Regional Railways (01872) 76244
Bus links to Falmouth and St. Mawes
Western National (01209) 719988
Ordnance Survey Maps   For detailed map information
O.S. Landranger 1:50,000 Sheet No. 204,
O.S. Pathfinder 1:25,000 Sheet No. 1366 Falmouth & St. Mawes

FURTHER INFORMATION
Falmouth Tourist Information Centre,
28 Killigrew Street, Falmouth,
Cornwall TR11 3PN (01326) 313457

Produced by the Dodman - Fal Estuary Countryside Service with funding
from Carrick District Council, Cornwall County Council, Cornwall Tourist
Board, Countryside Commission, English Heritage, European Regional
Development Fund, Falmouth Town Council, Roseland Chamber of
Commerce, Rural Development Commission, St. Just in Roseland Parish
Council, St. Mawes to Place Ferryboat (Balcomb Boats), The National Trust.
Photographs courtesy of David Brenchley (Really Wide Picture Company),
George Hogg, Dawn Runnals, St. Mawes Ferry Company and sponsors.
Guide designed in Cornwall by Creative Copy (01736) 60284 and
printed by Rowe The Printers, 1995.

moderating effect of the sea temperature ensures a relatively cool summer. The final part of the pattern is set by the way in which the various forms of mainly Devonian rock weather into a strongly acid soil so essential for the cultivation of many exotic plants.

It was mainly in these secluded southern valleys that the great gardens of Cornwall were developed. The perceptive will notice the bewildering pockets of 'micro-climate' often magnified by cunningly sited planting of shelter belts. Some who garden in the small area between Truro and the Helford describe it as 'the banana belt' (a title that can most kindly be described as unproven).

Up-country enthusiasts intent on discovering as much of the best of the botanical treasures as he or she or both may have time for will ask: 'When is the best time to come?' A good question indeed! March for the camellias, April for the magnolias, May for the rhododendrons – unless the spring is very mild or very cold. A good compromise is the last week in April and the first in May.

Start your tour from the Cornish side of the Tamar Bridge. Lining the western side of that broad river, on strategic sites overlooking the Sound or commanding some of the many miles of creek are a number of great houses with gardens which, if not entirely in the Cornish tradition, should not be missed: Cotehele, Ince Castle, Port

Eliot, Antony House and Mount Edgcumbe. There is not space here to do justice to all these and if only a few miles apart as the crow flies they involve long detours by road. *Mount Edgcumbe* with its wonderful views across the Sound to Plymouth is now a country park covering nearly

900 acres and open every day of the year. Unique in Cornwall are the magnificent formal gardens containing many rare plants in landscaped settings. Here, too, the National Camellia Collection is being established. It is only too easy to believe that Mount Edgcumbe was coveted by Medina Sidonia, Commander of the Spanish Armada who swore he would live there if the English were defeated. On the River Lynher is *Ince Castle*, perhaps the only major brick building in Cornwall. The gardens of about five acres are of relatively recent creation but already have great charm and are well worth a visit.

Follow the main road to Liskeard and then turn off towards the coast and *Caerhays Castle*. Caerhays is the mecca of all those who enjoy the three Cornish staples: the camellia, magnolia and rhododendron. Here, on a great sloping hillside 100 acres in extent and leading down to the very edge of the sea is one of the world's great collections of these, and much else besides. Three generations of the Williams family, beginning with the renowned John Charles Williams (chief sponsor of such supreme plant collectors as Forrest and Wilson), created this garden. Not only were hundreds of seedlings planted but 'J.C.' alone made some 250 rhododendron crosses of which barely 3 per cent have been named. Nor is this prodigious raiser remembered for his rhododendrons alone, for his interest in this field began with daffodils and included camellias in great number. There are few gardeners who do not know of the *Williamsii camellias* or the *Williamsianum rhododendron*. Caerhays is the plantsman's paradise.

Back now along the winding lanes between the Cornish hedges covered in spring with sheets of wild flowers to the A390 and *Trewithen*. It is sometimes referred to as Cornwall's most beautiful garden – an impossible assessment to make, but there is no doubt that here the visitor will discover a veritable treasure trove of rare and tender plants

A spring carpet of many colours in one of Cornwall's most delightful gardens, Trewithen

growing to perfection and superbly maintained. Unusually for Cornwall, the garden is mainly level, its most striking feature being the lawn which stretches away from the fine, early Georgian house for 200 yards, its gently curving edges framed by great banks of rhododendron overhung by magnolia after magnolia, the perfection of which is a reflection of the garden's creator, George Johnstone, for whom they were his special interest. Do not miss the *Rhododendron macabeanum* reputably and deservedly Britain's finest form of this deep-yellow flowered species.

Continuing on your way south and west, much of the woodland to the left of the road belongs to the *Tregothnan* estate, the gardens of which are open to the public only twice a year in spring. They are ever-increasingly worth a visit, the great lawns backed by proportionately sized scarlet rhododendrons up to a century old. This great garden/park of some 80 acres enjoys a continuing planting process which ensures something new and something more every year.

A few miles farther on, past the triple-spired cathedral at Truro, and a brief detour brings us to *Trelissick*, one of the leading gardens of the National Trust in Cornwall. High above the deep, salt-water inlet formed by the Fal there are splendid panoramic views across the Carrick Roads to Pendennis Castle. Trelissick is also a summer garden renowned for its collection of species hydrangea.

To the south of Falmouth we enter the 'Fox country'. To that town in 1759 came George Croker Fox, a Quaker merchant and banker who prospered mightily so that by the turn of the century the family was spreading out around the town and very shortly owned eight fine estates all within a radius of some five miles. Three of these estates developed outstanding gardens with some characteristics in common – one being that they stood at the head of deep valleys running down to the sea or the Helford River. The parent garden was *Penjerrick*, the story of which is as romantic as any in our gardening history. Here, the soil is

Top: the maze at Glendurgan, planted by Alfred Fox in 1883 with laurel, an unusual choice
Above: early morning mist in the valley at Trebah

deep, never drying out and never flooding. The eye is led down a lawn flanked by purple beeches and contrasting conifers framing the sea a mile away. The rate of growth is prolific and the dense planting provides a near-tropical effect. It was at Penjerrick that Samuel Smith, head gardener for half a century, produced the glorious Penjerrick hybrid rhododendrons. It is said that though distributed among many gardens in England and Scotland nowhere do the Penjerrick hybrids flower as they do on their native soil. Still to be seen (and in increasing need of careful maintenance), are the original shrubs which were the product of these crossings.

Glendurgan shared in many of the botanical treasures from Penjerrick whilst developing its own atmosphere. Of particular interest are enormous specimens of liriodendron (the tulip tree) and a huge range of camellias and magnolias. At the foot of the garden is the tiny village of Durgan, a jewel of a place and not to be missed at any time of year. A few hundred yards from Glendurgan is the third of the great Fox gardens, *Trebah*. A major planting exercise is in hand to restore the depleted shelter belt so vital to all Cornish gardens. Everywhere the views are breathtaking. A small stream provides a water garden as far as the neck of the ravine which is packed with rhododendrons and camellias, many of enormous size and perhaps a hundred years old. From the terrace in spring one looks down on a vast carpet of many colours, for once seeing these flowering trees from above. Graded paths wind down each side of the ravine, which provides almost entirely frost-free shelter for tender Asiatic

and Australasian plants with the tree fern *Dicksonia antarctica* growing in abundance.

Just outside the historic town of Helston, in a secluded valley is *Trevarno*. Here is another truly superb woodland garden not to be missed. Trevarno opens on several days in April and May and comprises several acres of gently terraced gardens crammed with rare plants and especially interesting for the remarkably comprehensive and excitingly planted conifers, many very rare in cultivation. A large ornamental lake at the foot of the garden makes a perfect foil for rich and continuing planting.

Along the coast of Mount's Bay, *St Michael's Mount* can be mentioned in the gardening context for, very occasionally, Lord and Lady St Levan open their private gardens to the public. If your visit coincides with such an opening do not miss it! Situated on a series of narrow terraces suspended between the rocky shore below and the fairy-tale silver granite walls of the castle 250ft above, a new, rapidly expanding and improving garden is taking shape where many tender plants too numerous to mention successfully defy the salt spray of winter storms.

Through Penzance and just off the road to Land's End is *Trengwainton*. It was founded on the wealth from the slave trade; Wilberforce's Act (which ended the slave trade) ruined the original owner and Trengwainton passed to the Bolitho family. It is now run by the National Trust. Perhaps the most frost-free garden on the mainland of Britain, Trengwainton can lay claim to its most comprehensive collection of rare, sub-tropical plants able to be grown outdoors. Near the entrance to the drive is a complex of five walled gardens providing almost total shelter for these rarities. The long drive itself is flanked by a tumbling stream lavishly planted with massed primulas, meconopsis and many other water and bog species, backed by massed rhododendrons both species and hybrids. Around the house are some of the finest magnolias in Cornwall. A mainly 20th-century garden, Trengwainton owed much to the gift of plants and good advice from the other owners of estate gardens in the county.

A great many splendid gardens, large and small, must perforce be left undescribed. *Bosahan*, for instance, on the opposite side of the Helford to Trebah and offering equally superb views and dramatic sub-tropical effect. *Chyverton*, near the north coast and sheltered by fine woodlands, begun in the 1790s and planted up continually ever since, has a collection of typical Cornish plants to complement that of Caerhays itself. It is open by appointment. Much farther to the north in seemingly inhospitable country is the smaller garden of *Tremeer*, where six acres of vivid colour and pervading scent are set between the Atlantic and Bodmin Moor.

There are many, many others, especially the newer, smaller gardens made between or after the wars.

Information on National Trust gardens is given in the Directory, page 82. Except where specified, most of the other gardens described are open only during the peak flowering period, in April, May and June.

The Cornwall Garden Society produces a 'Gardens Open Calendar' annually in February (price 50p) which gives most of the information visitors will need. It can be obtained from The Secretary, 'Chysbryn', Bareppa, Mawnan Smith, Falmouth, Cornwall. Please send 50p and a large, stamped, addressed envelope.

Long Distance Footpaths

Cornwall's coastline, its wild flowers, its scenery make exploration on foot a must. Around the coast runs the 268-mile Cornwall Coast Path; inland are the 30-mile Saints' Way and the less well-defined 13-mile Tinners' Way, based on routes used by people for over a thousand years. All lend themselves to short explorations along sections of their lengths.

Cornwall Coast Path

The Cornwall Coast Path is 268 miles long and runs from Marsland Mouth on the north coast round Land's End and on to the shores of Plymouth Sound. It is the central part of the 520-mile South West Way, the longest continuous footpath in England.

Like the whole of the South West Way, the Cornwall Coast Path is usually walked from north to south, a psychologically 'downhill' journey that leads the walker from the great 600ft cliffs at Marsland to the granite knuckle of the Land's End Peninsula then back to the east, along the gentler south coast.

Physically, the CCP is one of the most challenging expeditions in the country. It lacks the great heights of the mountain footpaths, but in total demands such a series of ups and downs that it could match Everest foot by uphill foot!

Main picture: view from the Cornwall Coast Path over Kynance Cove.
Inset, this page: on the clifftop path near Zennor.
Inset, opposite page: the sun sets beyond Cape Cornwall

How the path began

Much of the Cornwall Coast Path is based on the tracks that marked out the regular 'beats' walked by coastguards. In 1947, a new National Parks Committee suggested that a continuous pathway round the British coast was a possibility. Cornwall offered the ideal conditions for a continuous county path but it was not until May 1973 that the Cornwall Coast Path was officially opened.

Since then there have been steady improvements so that today a continuous route is open to the experienced walker as a challenging journey of unsurpassed beauty and variety.

On the way

The Cornwall Coast Path can be divided into three convenient sections for both planning and description's sake.

The first is from Marsland Mouth on the Devon border to St Ives in Penwith, a distance of 112 miles. The second is from St Ives, via Land's End and Penzance, to the Lizard, a distance of 64 miles. The third is from the Lizard to Plymouth, a 92-mile final section.

All three sections are quite different in character, their underlying geology dictating the type of landscape and coastal formations, and in many cases the local natural environment.

Marsland Mouth to St Ives (112 miles)

Imperceptibly the main South West Way leaves Devon at Marsland Mouth and enters Cornwall to follow the western edge of that enchanting northern extension of the county, bounded by the infant River Tamar on the east and the Atlantic on the west.

This is not yet Celtic Cornwall, more a unique little island in its own right, remote and particularly lovely. The great cliffs of the culm-measures buttress the coast at Marsland and Sharpnose, where black fins of rock thrust seawards from the main cliff. The path leads across occasional valley bottoms by Morwenstow and Coombe and so on to Bude, the first of the great breaks in the coast, where vast sands stretch into the distance at low tide and the huge Atlantic breakers thunder on to the shoreline.

Beyond Bude the route is marred in places by land-slip and diversion. It is easily navigable, however, and graced with superb views as it leads the walker to the more isolated sections at Buckator and Beeny Cliff before Boscastle is reached in the lovely Valency Valley. The coast is less dramatic than the previous section but equally fascinating.

Beyond Boscastle with its strange chasm-like

harbour lies the 'romantic' Tintagel, awash with Arthurian myth and unashamed commercialism. Crowds and cream teas are soon left behind for the magnificent stretch of coast that leads on to the Camel Estuary, another major inlet on the Cornish coast.

For the walker, the estuary is approached via the splendid Rumps Point and Pentire Point where there are breathtaking views across the infamous Doom Bar to Stepper Point and Trevose Head. In summer a passenger ferry will transport the walker from Rock to the busy and charming port of Padstow, whence the Saints' Way leads across Cornwall to Fowey on the south coast.

From Padstow, the CCP leads to Trevose Head and on towards Newquay, past superb beaches where sprawling holiday developments are balanced by the wild magnificence of such places as Park Head and Bedruthan Steps.

At Newquay, the walker can pause for a while to savour once more the necessary contrast between the various tourist needs. Beyond here the coast is again particularly lovely as the path follows the edge of great beaches and traverses green-backed headlands towards the strange industrial landscape of the St Agnes mining coast, then goes onwards to Godrevy Point, the northern outlier of St Ives Bay and the gateway to the Land's End Peninsula.

St Ives to the Lizard (64 miles)

The lovely town of St Ives is forever linked to the Cornish fishing industry, a trade that has shaped the character of the modern town as both tourist resort and artists' haven. Beyond here the walker enters the Land's End Peninsula along the wildest and most remote part of the coast path as it winds its way towards the west, by greenstone and granite cliff above seas of aquamarine and beautiful beaches of white shell-sand.

Here the ancient moorland of Penwith rises steeply from the coastal shelf by Zennor and Morvah, where farming is still carried on within the same fields that Iron Age settlers used. It is an area particularly rich in ancient memorials, where stone circles, burial 'quoits' and Iron Age villages have survived, partly because of their granite resilience, although much more has been lost by plunder and carelessness. The National Trust plays a vital part in conserving the important landscape features which remain and in 1986 launched a £200,000 appeal.

This remarkable stretch of the coast path includes the desolate industrial landscape round Pendeen and St Just, an area that was once a mining heartland but is now sadly redundant since the closure (1986) of Geevor Mine, Cornwall's last coastal working. There the landscape has a desolation that is not without its own rather strange attractiveness.

Several miles beyond here lies Land's End, the attractions of which may be diminished for the walker after the miles of beautiful coastline already covered.

Here the walker turns away from the Atlantic coast along the finest granite cliffs of all, by Gwennap Head and Porthcurno, and on to the busy town of Penzance and Mount's Bay, dominated by the offshore island of St Michael's Mount with its splendid castle. (The 34-mile stretch of coast path from St Ives to Penzance is often tackled as a separate expedition, if the walker has only a few days to spare.)

From Penzance the long-distance route hugs the eastern shore of Mount's Bay by beach and shattered headland, by the dramatic Mullion Harbour and the lovely Kynance Cove, and so runs on to the serpentine country of the Lizard and the most southerly point of the mainland of Great Britain.

Rich and colourful vegetation by the coast path above Lizard Point

The Lizard to Plymouth Sound (92 miles)

From Lizard Point to St Anthony Head on the Falmouth Estuary, the Cornwall Coast Path changes character in a remarkable way. The vegetation becomes more lush, the headlands and the charming fishing coves, like Cadgwith and Coverack, are less rugged and more subtly complex in their forms. Two great waterways divide the land at Helford and Carrick Roads, creating enchanting networks of creeks and wooded river banks that cause the walker some problems of navigation.

There are various ferry crossings but these can be seasonal, so the coast path walker should make a careful check beforehand of local details.

Falmouth is a substantial Cornish town only a few miles from the county town of Truro, the very heartland of cultural and commercial Cornwall, seemingly far removed from those great raw-boned cliffs of the north and west. Beyond Falmouth lies the lovely Roseland Peninsula where our route leads on by Gerrans Bay and Nare Head to the great headland of the Dodman, with its magnificent Iron Age ramparts. To the north lie Gorran Haven and Mevagissey, immensely popular with visitors but nevertheless retaining much of their charm in the surviving architecture of the traditional fishing village.

The scene changes to St Austell Bay with its industrial hinterland amidst the white clay 'alps' of Hensbarrow, the bay itself enclosed by Gribben Head, with Fowey to the east at the southern termination of the Saints' Way.

From here the coast path leads on through Polperro and Looe to where the great sweep of Whitsand Bay brings the walker to Rame Head and the delightful Mount Edgcumbe which stands on the shores of Plymouth South – the effective culmination of one of the great coastal walks of the British Isles.

The Tinners' Way (13 miles)

One of several standing stones on the Tinners' Way, on Mên Scryfa Down near Madron

The Tinners' Way is a 13-mile walking route from St Just to St Ives on the Land's End Peninsula.

It is a relatively new concept and is still being defined. Right of access may not exist throughout its length, although the lanes and tracks involved have existed for many years as part of a network of ancient ways across the peninsula.

The Tinners' Way follows a line of a high granite ridgeway that was probably one of the original lines of communication in pre-history, when the bare summit of the ridge stood clear of the densely covered lowland.

There is evidence that the route was used for transporting minerals from the Bronze Age up until the 19th century, a period of almost 4,000 years. It would have been part of a network of tracks connecting seashore ports with the country inland and with their counterparts on the opposite coast.

The modern concept of the Tinners' Way, or 'Forth an Stenoryon' as it is known in Cornish, is an imaginative creation based on what remains of this ancient network of communications. It should be said that archaeologists are sceptical about the route, but it nevertheless makes for a full day's expedition through some of the most magnificent country in Cornwall.

The Tinners' Way starts at Cape Cornwall near St Just. From the car park the route follows the coastal path northwards before turning inland to cross the main north coast road at Truthwall. It leads up on to the high moors, the most ancient of Cornish landscapes, punctuated frequently by the granite monuments of early people, including standing stones, burial chambers, Iron Age castles, ancient villages and stone circles.

For eight miles the Tinners' Way traverses the lonely moors before reaching the delightful little church of Towednack in a valley leading up from the sea. From here, alternative routes can be taken by road, or along the old field paths that lead down to the coast at St Ives.

The Saints' Way

(30 miles approx.)

Cornwall's Saints' Way, or 'Forth an Syns' as it is known in the ancient language, is an imaginative reconstruction sponsored by the CRS Community Programme. It follows one of the cross-country routes travelled by Welsh and Irish 'saints' of the Dark Ages, between AD400 and 700.

It traverses the 'waist' of the county from Padstow on the north coast to Fowey on the south, and throughout its length is waymarked by distinctive Saints' Way signposts.

The Saints' Way is about 30 miles long and runs through a dozen parishes, across landscapes which are vivid and varied and as Cornish as the county's more famous coastline.

The route is linked by significant relics of Cornish history, from the ancient shrines and burial chambers of Neolithic times to the handsome mediaeval churches founded by the Normans and the sterner Wesleyan meeting houses of the 18th century.

The 20th century intrudes but the Saints' Way goes across the grain of the land and modern roads are quickly crossed. The side roads, which in places have supplanted the old byways, are themselves relatively peaceful.

Its religious connections apart, the Saints' Way would have been a traditional trade route linking the north and south coasts of Cornwall. For many centuries Welsh and Irish merchants disembarked at Padstow before crossing overland to Fowey and the shores of St Austell Bay, where they re-embarked for Brittany. It was a journey taken in preference to the sea-passage round Land's End,

Relics of St Petroc in Bodmin Church

whose savage and storm-battered coast must have had as bad a reputation in ancient times as Cape Horn has today.

The symbolic starting point for the Saints' Way is the south door of Padstow parish church, where, in AD520, the Welsh St Petroc established a small monastic settlement. From here the route goes southwards through Padstow Parish by footpath, lane and field, to the combined parishes of the charmingly named Little Petherick and St Issey.

The influence of St Petroc along this northern part of the Saints' Way is evident, in place names and in religious foundations. The name Petherick is a mediaeval form of Petroc, while the Saint's spirit and influence travel on towards St Breock and Bodmin. From St Breock Downs, superb views can be had to the Camel estuary in the north and to the white clay 'mountains' near St Austell in the south.

From here the Saints' Way continues to the Parish of Withiel, with the great rocks of Helman Tor leading the walker on through Lanivet Parish to the south of Bodmin, until reaching the Helman Tor gate on the bounds of the parish of Lanlivery.

Here the modern Saints' Way divides, one route going via Lanlivery, with its fine church tower, and St Samson's Parish, its church small but full of interest, and on to Fowey; while the other goes via Luxulyan, especially lovely at bluebell time, St Blazey, and Tywardreath, site of a priory founded soon after the Norman Conquest of which nothing remains.

Helman Tor is literally the high point of the Saints' Way. It is truly characteristic of the 'Granite Kingdom' with its great wind-eroded rocks surmounting the hill-top above acres of willow and gorse, the whole area retaining some of the flavour of that ancient country traversed by saint and trader alike.

The eastern route to Fowey via Lanlivery goes through the wooded estuary of the Fowey river, traditional meeting place of Tristan and Iseult. The western route, which is slightly longer, takes in part of an ancient track with handsome granite stiles and cobbled causeway, whose rediscovery in 1984 was the inspiration for the present Saints' Way.

The accepted end to this remarkable journey across Cornwall is the Church of St Finbar at Fowey. Finbar was a 7th-century Irish saint, who travelled via Cornwall to Brittany and Rome and founded a Christian cell at Fowey. Thus for the modern pilgrim the Saints' Way is linked from Padstow to the southern shore.

Holy well at Luxulyan, one of several wells whose waters were believed to have healing powers

> *For more information about these paths, contact Cornwall Tourist Board, Old County Hall, Station Road, Truro TR1 1BR.*
> *Tel: (0872) 74282, ext 3101.*

CORNWALL

*Each entry in this Gazetteer has the atlas
page number on which the place can be
found and its National Grid reference
included under the heading.
An explanation of how to use the National
Grid is given on page 86.*

Above: The Hurlers, near Minions

Altarnun

Map Ref: 95SX2281

Sheltering beneath the eastern heights of Bodmin Moor, this attractive village is bisected by a peat-brown stream rushing under a 15th-century packhorse bridge to join the Tamar. Well-tended gardens stand before granite, slate-hung and colourwashed cottages, and dominating all is the impressive pinnacled tower of the church, dedicated to St Nonna (the mother of St David, patron saint of Wales). It is known as 'The Cathedral of the Moor'. Its spacious, light interior, barrel-roof, carved rood screen and decorated Norman font make it one of the finest West Country churches. Over 70 delightfully carved 16th-century bench-ends are the work of Robert Daye. Another great craftsman, the sculptor Nevil Northey Burnard, was born in the village in 1818. This wayward genius became a fashionable sculptor in London, but died penniless in Redruth workhouse. John Wesley frequently visited Altarnun while staying at nearby Trewint, and a carving of his head by Burnard surmounts the door of the Georgian Wesleyan Meeting House with its external staircase and ground floor stables.

Across the A30 road to the south lies the Forestry Commission's Halvanna Nature Trail.

A fine church, with pinnacled tower and (right) many carved bench-ends, overlooks the stream and narrow bridge at Altarnun

Blisland

Map Ref: 94SX1073

Reached by twisting lanes on the western slopes of Bodmin Moor, this pretty, well-kept village overlooks the valley of the River Camel. Around the rim of a large, tree-lined village green – one of the few in Cornwall – stand Georgian and Victorian houses and cottages, a manor house, forge, schoolhouse, rectory and old inn, the Royal Oak. The Norman and mediaeval church, dedicated jointly to St Protus and St Hyacinth and known locally as St Pratts, has a white-walled interior deservedly described as 'dazzling and amazing' by Sir John Betjeman. Columns rise unevenly from the slate floor to an irregular barrel-roof, and a brightly-painted rood screen, the work of F C Eden in 1894, stretches the full width of the building.

Bodmin

Map Ref: 92SX0767

The bustling, narrow streets of this hillside town owe their origins to a Welsh missionary, St Petroc, who settled here in the 6th century. The town grew up around a monastery and priory, and by the time of Domesday Book it was the only town in Cornwall to boast a market. The mighty 15th-century church is the largest in the county and once contained the relics of St Petroc.

Bodmin became a centre for Cornish rebellion, and one of its sons, Thomas Flamank, led an ill-fated march on London in 1497, to protest against taxation. In 1549 the mayor was hanged for refusing to use Cranmer's English prayer book. Winning the Right of Assize in 1835, Bodmin became the county town and its growth was further aided by the arrival of one of the earliest railways in Britain, linking it with the port of Wadebridge. Only with the growth of Truro has Bodmin's role declined, but it remains a town of great character, its Assize Court and Tudor Guildhall being particularly worthy of note. The once-feared Bodmin Jail, scene of many public executions, is now an hotel, and the former headquarters of the Duke of Cornwall's Light Infantry now houses a Regimental Museum. Overlooking the town is an obelisk memorial to Sir Walter Raleigh Gilbert, a major in the British Army in India.

To the east of the town, at Fletchersbridge, is Bodmin Farm Park with tame animals and a nature trail, and to the north-west, near Washaway, stands the spacious Georgian mansion, Pencarrow House. Sir Arthur Sullivan composed the music for *Iolanthe* here and the 500 acres of gardens contain fine camellias and rhododendrons – a blaze of colour in spring.

AA recommends:
Hotels: ◇ Tredethy Country, 3-star Country House Hotel, *tel.* (020884) 262 (off B3266)
Hotel Allegro, 50 Higher Bore St, 2-star, *tel.* (0208) 73480
Westberry, Rhind St, 2-star, *tel.* (0208) 72772
Self Catering: ◇ Barn Cottage, The Coach House, Orchard Cottage, The Tallet & Court Flat, *tel.* (0208) 4951
◇ Penbugle Cottage, *tel.* (0208) 2844
Campsite: Camping & Caravanning Club Site, Old Callywith Rd, 2-pennant, *tel.* (0208) 73834
Garages: Kinsmans, Russell Garage, Dunmere Rd, *tel.* (0208) 72669
Wadham Stringer, Liskeard Rd, *tel.* (0208) 3145

Writers

The names of many writers are inextricably linked with Cornwall, none more so than that of Bodmin-born author and literary critic, Sir Arthur Quiller-Couch. Under the pseudonym of 'Q' he wrote lovingly about Cornwall and Fowey, his home for 50 years, which appears as 'Troy Town' in his novels. The writer Kenneth Grahame, a friend of 'Q', paid many visits to Fowey and was partly inspired by the woody creeks and the sight of so many people 'messing about in boats' to write *The Wind in the Willows*.

Cornwall's china-clay country has produced two distinguished writers: the poet and novelist Jack Clemo, deaf and blind for most of his writing career, and the historian, poet and leading authority on the Elizabethan Age, Dr A L Rowse. Another celebrated poet, Charles Causley, still lives in Launceston, while at Carnkie in the shadow of Carn Brea, the poet and author of *The White Hotel*, D M Thomas, was born.

Many writers born east of the Tamar have also sought inspiration in Cornwall. The Valency Valley will forever be linked with Thomas Hardy and his first wife Emma, whom he met while restoring St Juliot church. The high north coast cliffs and lush inland valleys are strikingly invoked in his novel *A Pair of Blue Eyes*.

D H Lawrence wrote much of *Women in Love* while living in a cottage surrounded by Iron Age fields in Zennor in the early years of World War I. The flickering lamp in his window was thought by the villagers

Self-portrait of D H Lawrence

to be a signal to enemy submarines, and both Lawrence and his German-born wife Frieda were suspected of being spies and asked to leave. Dylan Thomas and his wife Caitlin had a more pleasant sojourn in Cornwall after their marriage in Penzance. They lived for a while at Mousehole, which Thomas described as 'really the loveliest village in England', and it is possible that the fishing village of Llaregyb in *Under Milk Wood* owes

as much to Mousehole as to his home village of Laugharne in Wales.

Virginia Woolf's childhood holidays in St Ives and picnics near Godrevy provided the background setting for her novel *To the Lighthouse*. Cornwall also provided the background for all of the most famous novels by Daphne du Maurier. *House on the Strand* is based in Tywardreath, near St Austell, while the famous 'Manderley' in *Rebecca* is based on Menabilly, west of Fowey, where she lived for a while. When Daphne du Maurier stayed at Jamaica Inn on Bodmin Moor between the wars and wrote her tale of Mary Yellan, Joss Merlin and his smuggling activities, it was in fact a Temperance Hotel. Another smuggling base, a quiet inlet off the Helford River, was immortalised by her novel *Frenchman's Creek*.

The area around Polzeath is renowned as John Betjeman Country, for it was here that he spent happy childhood holidays. He later wove its villages, lanes, churches, coastline and golf-courses into his evocative poems. Further west, around Perranporth and St Agnes, we are in Poldark country, the setting for Winston Graham's ten *Poldark* novels depicting life in a late 18th-century mining community. More recently, the novelist E V Thompson chose the heights of Bodmin Moor and several south coast ports as the locations for his books *Chase the Wind* and *Ben Retallick*.

Bodmin Moor

Map Ref: 95SX2075

Less fearsome than neighbouring Dartmoor, the granite uplands of Bodmin Moor are wild and desolate, topped by brooding tors. Bronze Age settlements encircle the jagged outcrop of Rough Tor, and an exhilarating walk from Camelford leads to Cornwall's highest point, the summit of Brown

Willy (1,377ft) which commands a view over the length of Cornwall. At the moor's centre, on the main A30 road, stands Jamaica Inn. This slate-hung 18th-century building, which inspired Daphne du Maurier's novel, has long been a welcome stop, for smugglers carrying illicit cargoes from coast to coast and for coaches crossing the bleak moor. On the lonely moorland to the south is Dozmary Pool where, according to legend, King Arthur's

sword Excalibur was received by a hand rising from the water. The pool is said to be bottomless, but wild moorland cattle can often be seen wading at its centre. Another local legend relates how Jan Tregeagle, an unjust local steward, was condemned to perform several impossible tasks, one being to drain Dozmary Pool with a limpet shell.

Rough Tor, one of the jagged outcrops that tops Bodmin Moor

Steep slate cliffs run down to the little harbour at Boscastle

Boscastle

Map Ref: 94SX0990

The narrow fjord-like entrance to
Boscastle harbour – little more than
a cleft in the slate cliffs – leads to a
long heather-clad valley and a tiny
16th-century pier from which slate
and corn were exported. Higher up
the coombe, limewashed cottages
cluster round the water-mill at the
foot of the pretty hillside village.
During the Napoleonic Wars soldiers
were recruited in two old coaching
inns, the Wellington and the
Napoleon. On the opposite hillside
a few stones are all that remain of
the castle, once held by the Breton
Bottreaux family, which gave the
village its name. An unusual
Museum of Witchcraft contains
many sinister artefacts. The novelist
Thomas Hardy often visited
Boscastle when he was a young
architect, restoring the hillside
Church of St Juliot. He courted and
married the rector's sister-in-law,
Emma, and many of his poems and
the novel *A Pair of Blue Eyes*
describe the area. A riverside walk
leads up the valley of the River
Valency to St Juliot Church at
Hennett and back along the south
side of the valley, passing the
churches of Lesnewth and Minster.

AA recommends:
Hotels: Bottreaux House, 2-star, *tel.*
(08405) 231
◇ Riverside, The Harbour, 2-star, *tel.*
(08405) 216
Self Catering: ◇ Cargurra, St Juliot, *tel.*
(08406) 206
◇ Cobblers Cottage, High St, *tel.* (0208)
850277 or 850617
◇ The Cottage, *tel.* (08405) 313
Guesthouse: St Christophers Country
House Hotel, High St, *tel.* (08405) 412

Breage

Map Ref: 90SW6128

The old church of St Breaca at the
centre of this small farming
community contains a series of bold
wall-paintings, discovered last
century under a layer of limewash.
Painted in the 15th century by
peripatetic monastic artists, they
depict St Christopher and Christ
blessing the Trades.
   Nearby Godolphin House, home
of the royalist Earls of Godolphin,
with its supporting row of Tuscan
columns and elaborate plaster
ceilings, was built in the 17th and
18th centuries.
   To the west, beyond the wide
beach of Praa Sands, is Prussia
Cove, a narrow cleft in the rocky
coast where the notorious smuggler,
John Carter, waged a private war
with the Preventive Men.

*Breage Church has several 15th-century
wall-paintings*

St Juliot Church, Boscastle

Bude

Map Ref: 95SS2106

Once a busy port, from which
cargoes of sand and seaweed
were carried to Launceston for
fertiliser along an ingenious
canal, Bude was developed as a
family resort in Victorian and
Edwardian times. The treacherous
cliffs of Cornwall's north coast
here give way to wide sandy
beaches, backed by grassy downland
and sandhills. The small castle on a
mound by the canal entrance was
built in 1850 by Sir Goldworthy
Gurney.
   About a mile inland, the small
market town of Stratton was the
birthplace of Anthony Payne, the

Bude harbour and canal entrance

'Cornish Giant'. Born in the Tree Inn he stood over 7ft tall and fought beside his master, Sir Bevill Grenvile, at the nearby Battle of Stamford Hill in 1643.

Widemouth Bay to the south is one of Cornwall's most spectacular surfing beaches.

AA recommends:
Hotels: Hartland, Hartland Ter, 3-star, *tel.* (0288) 55661
◇ Strand, The Strand, 3-star, *tel.* (0288) 3222
Camelot, Downs View Rd, 2-star, *tel.* (0288) 2361
Penarvor, Crooklets Beach, 2-star, *tel.* (0288) 2036 due to change to 352036
Self Catering: ◇ Downland Holiday Flats, Maer Lane, *tel.* (0288) 4994
Guesthouses: Atlantic Beach, 25 Downs View, *tel.* (0288) 3431
Cliff Hotel, Maer Down, Crooklets, *tel.* (0288) 3110
Dorset House Hotel, 47 Killerton Rd, *tel.* (0288) 2665
◇ Surf Haven, 31 Downs View, *tel.* (0288) 2998
Campsites: Budemeadows Touring Holiday Park, 4-pennants, *tel.* (028885) 646
◇ Bude Holiday Park, Maer Lane, 3-pennants, *tel.* (0288) 2472
Wooda Farm Camping & Caravanning Park, Poughill, 3-pennants, *tel.* (0288) 2069
Garages: Cann, Medland & Co, Bencoolan Rd, *tel.* (0288) 2146
◇ Flexbury, Ocean View Rd, *tel.* (0288) 2008 (day) & 2114 (night)

Cadgwith

Map Ref: 91SW7214

Sheltering east of the Lizard, Cadgwith is a small, picturesque fishing community of pink and whitewashed cottages, their thatch held down against winter gales by heavy chains. A rocky promontory, the Todden, divides two steep shingle beaches up which fishing boats are hauled over wooden rollers by a winch. Today the chief catches are crab and lobster, but in the 19th century Cadgwith held the record for catching pilchards –

1,300,000 in a single day. The old pilchard cellar, where the fish were packed in barrels, stands next to the old inn where fishermens' voices are raised in salty song on Sunday evenings.

Along the springy clifftop to the south is a collapsed sea-cave known as the Devil's Frying Pan, while a short walk to the north is the delightful Poltesco Valley. Green serpentine stone was quarried and cut here, but the old water wheel which powered the machinery now stands idle. A nature trail winds along the peaceful valley beside a bamboo-fringed lagoon. Twisting lanes of sweet-smelling flowers lead up to Ruan Minor where the flat Lizard landscape is broken by a squat church tower of serpentine stone which acts as a daymark to shipping.

AA recommends:
Self Catering: ◇ CC Ref 307 EL (Character Cottages), *tel.* (03955) 77001
◇ CC Ref 316 EL (1, 2 & 3 flats) (Character Cottages), *tel.* (03955) 77001
Guesthouse: ◇ Cadgwith Cove (Inn), *tel.* (0326) 290513

Callington

Map Ref: 93SX3669

This small market town of slate-hung houses stands on high land between the valleys of the rivers Lynher and Tamar, surrounded by lush fruit-growing country. The water from the Dupath Well, bubbling to the surface inside a 15th-century chapel, is said to cure whooping-cough. Meandering lanes lead past orchards and market gardens to the secluded village of St Dominick with its 13th-century church, but dominating all is Kit Hill to the north. Surmounted by the chimney of a derelict copper mine, this hill was given to the people of Cornwall by Prince

Charles, Duke of Cornwall, and its summit affords a spectacular view across Bodmin Moor and Dartmoor.

AA recommends:
Campsite: Honicombe Holiday Village, 3-pennants, *tel.* (0822) 832583
Garages: Newport Mtr Bodyworks, Church St, *tel.* (0579) 83432
Palmers, Liskeard Rd, *tel.* (0579) 83372

Calstock

Map Ref: 93SX4368

The 12 graceful arches of the railway viaduct tower over the town of Calstock, sprawling along the steep northern bank of the River Tamar. It was the coming of the railway that caused the town's former glory as a river port to decline. Stone and copper ore from nearby quarries and mines, and fruit and produce from the surrounding orchards and farms, had formerly been shipped from local wharves. A walk is recommended up the steep streets to the Parish Church of St Anthony for a fine view of the snaking, thickly-wooded Tamar Valley and the ivy-covered chimneys of long-disused copper and tin mines. Inside the church are memorials to the Edgcumbe family whose home, Cotehele, lies round a bend in the river. A scenic railway journey or a boat trip up the river from Plymouth provides an ideal way of reaching Calstock.

AA recommends:
Restaurant: ◇ Boot Inn, 1-fork, *tel.* (0822) 832331
Self Catering: ◇ The Danescombe Mine, *tel.* (062882) 5925
Guesthouse: ◇ Boot Inn, Fore St, *tel.* (0822) 832331

Today lobster and crab have replaced pilchards as the main catch of Cadgwith's fishermen

Camborne

Map Ref: 90SW6440

The area surrounding Camborne and Redruth was once the most intensely mined in the world. In the 1850s two-thirds of the world's copper was produced by nearly 350 mines employing 50,000 underground workers. The deepest mine was Dolcoath (3,000ft deep), but like most of the others it closed early this century when cheaper deposits of tin and copper were discovered overseas. Miners and their families were forced to emigrate and thousands of 'Cousin Jacks and Jennys' sailed for America, Australia and South Africa.

Jackdaws now nest in the derelict, ivy-clad engine-houses, arsenic calciners and 'count houses' (for book-keeping) that surround the town and provide a rich source of interest to industrial archaeologists. The engineer Richard Trevithick, born at Penponds in 1771, designed the high pressure steam engine which revolutionised mining, and also the first steam locomotive to carry passengers. His statue stands in front of the town's library and he is joyfully remembered each April when a colourful Trevithick Day procession is held in the town.

Modern Camborne is a busy shopping centre with light industry flourishing at its outskirts. Several fine Wesleyan chapels bear witness to the success of Methodism among mining communities, and at the town's centre stands the 15th-century parish church.

At Pool, to the north, are the East Pool Cornish Beam Engines, working, pumping and winding engines owned by the National Trust. A colourful display of rock and mineral specimens can be seen at the School of Mines Museum, and close by is Carn Brea Leisure Centre with its swimming pool and squash courts.

AA recommends:
Campsite: Magor Farm Caravan Site, Tehidy, 1-pennant, *tel.* (0209) 713367
Garage: ◇ J K Motors, Gurneys Lane, *tel.* (0209) 715021

Pool, near Camborne, is rich in mining remains.
Main picture: whim beam engine.
Inset: upper chamber, Taylor's Shaft

Camelford

Map Ref: 94SX1083

The humped camel decorating the weathervane on the town hall is misleading, for the town's name probably stems from the Cornish words 'cam pol' or 'winding river', an apt description of the watercourse that meanders through neighbouring meadows after descending the northern heights of Bodmin Moor. Slate predominates in this old wool town and former pocket borough. A coach-house has been converted into the excellent North Cornwall Museum and Gallery where folk items and a fully furnished cottage interior are displayed. A road leads east to Crowdy Reservoir, where anglers can try their luck fishing for brown and rainbow trout, and continues to a car park from where a walk can be taken to the rocky outcrop of Rough Tor.

AA recommends:
Guesthouses: Countryman Hotel, Victoria Rd, *tel.* (0840) 212250
◇ Warmington House, 32 Market Pl, *tel.* (0840) 213380
Pencarrow (farmhouse), *tel.* (0840) 213282
Campsite: Juliot's Well Holiday Park, 4-pennants, *tel.* (0840) 213302

Charlestown

Map Ref: 92SX0351

Unlike most Cornish ports, whose development and growth can be traced back to mediaeval times, Charlestown sprang from the drawing-board to reality in a mere ten years. Almost entirely due to the enterprise of one man, Charles Rashleigh, a local industrialist, it was completed in 1801 for the import of coal and the export of china-clay from the St Austell area. Local workers fell into one of two categories: those with clay-white faces and clothes and those covered with coal-dust. The harbour, wharves and lock-gates were designed by the engineer John Smeaton, responsible for the Eddystone Lighthouse, and the entire 'town' was carefully planned at one stroke, with a broad, tree-lined, main street running down to the harbour.

Right: Charlestown harbour, built in 1801 and still a working port of great charm

Charlestown is still a working port, and Georgian houses, dock offices and a chandler's stores provide an evocative picture, while the unspoilt charm of the place have led to it becoming popular as a film location, *Poldark, The Onedin Line, The Voyage of Charles Darwin* and *The Eagle has Landed* all being partly filmed here. A portrayal of 19th-century life in the port together with items concerning shipwrecks and diving can be seen in Charlestown Visitors Centre. Along the coast to the east is the broad sandy beach of Carlyon Bay, the Cornish Leisure World and the Cornwall Coliseum, where internationally famous artists appear throughout the year.

Inventors

Towards the end of April each year, the flag-hung streets of Camborne are crowded with people and steam-powered traction engines in honour of the local engineering genius and 'Father of the Locomotive', Richard Trevithick. Born in 1771, Trevithick unquestionably did more for the development of the steam engine than anyone else, including the better-known James Watt and George Stephenson, and ran his first steam road-carriage in 1802. Half-way up a hill it ran out of steam and rolled back to the bottom, an occasion recalled in a favourite local song, *Going up Camborne Hill, Coming Down*. Trevithick built a second more powerful locomotive and took it to London. Called the 'Catch-me-who-can', it carried passengers on a circular track at 15mph. In 1804 he took another engine to Wales where it hauled ten wagons of coal, each weighing ten tons. This was 20 years before Stephenson's first successful running of 'Locomotive One'.

The high-pressure steam pumping engines developed by Trevithick, Newcomen and West allowed mines to be kept relatively water-free and miners to drill to much deeper levels. The lack of national fame accorded Richard Trevithick is probably due to his tendency to spread his genius thinly over a wide range of projects, often leaving others to develop and consolidate his ideas. As well as devising a Thames tunnel and a tower taller than Eiffel's, he also invented a

Trevithick's statue, Camborne

steam-powered lift, dredger and threshing machine. Following an 11-year spell working in the Peruvian silver mines, Trevithick returned to Cornwall and died in poverty in 1835. A statue to the great man, holding a model of his steam-carriage, stands in front of Camborne public library.

Another great pioneer of steam-power, Goldsworthy Gurney, was inspired as a youngster by Trevithick's machines. Born at Padstow in 1793, Gurney began his career in the medical profession, also studying chemistry and mechanical science. In 1823 he experimented using steam boilers to power road vehicles that 'resembled common stage coaches, but without horses'. A year later he succeeded in carrying 18 passengers, six inside and 12 on top of the carriage, from Bath to London at 15mph. A regular service of Gurney coaches linked Gloucester with Cheltenham in 1831. Like Trevithick, Gurney's interests were wide-ranging, his other achievements including an oxy-hydrogen blow pipe for quenching fires in mines, the 'Gurney Stove', used to heat the House of Commons, and a mock castle built on sand at Bude. Goldsworthy Gurney was knighted in 1863 and died 12 years later.

At the head of Market Jew Street in Penzance, only yards from his birthplace in 1778, stands a statue honouring the scientist and inventor, Sir Humphry Davy. When only in his early twenties he lectured at the Royal Institution and later became president of the Royal Society and a founder of the London Zoo. Best known as the inventor of the miner's safety lamp, responsible for saving so many lives, Davy also conducted pioneering research into gases. One of these, nitrous oxide or 'laughing gas', was later to be used as an anaesthetic. However, Davy's greatest achievement was probably his work on electrolysis. He isolated and named sodium and potassium, the gases chlorine and fluorine and the metals barium, strontium and calcium.

Cotehele

Map Ref: 93SX4268

The grey granite home of the Edgcumbe family, built mainly in the last decade of the 15th century and overlooking the Tamar valley, is now in the care of the National Trust. In 1553 the family moved to Mount Edgcumbe, 10 miles to the south, and Cotehele was subsequently only occasionally occupied. The Tudor home has remained virtually unaltered since the addition of a tower in 1627, and most of the original furnishings are intact. As well as beautiful furniture, needlework and armour, almost every room contains a glowing tapestry. Well-tended gardens and banks of rhododendrons surround a restored mediaeval dovecote, and a path winds down through dense woodland to the riverside, passing a small chapel by a gorge. This was the spot where Richard Edgcumbe hid from Richard III's men after throwing his cap down the hillside to put his pursuers off the scent.

Alongside the River Tamar at Cotehele Quay, is a small museum, a splendidly-restored boathouse and *Shamrock*, one of the last sailing-barges to carry stone down the river. A short woodland walk leads to a watermill restored to working condition, a cider press, forge and wheelwright's shop.

Coverack

Map Ref: 91SW7818

Sheltered by the Lizard from fierce south-westerly gales, this charming fishing village with its tiny pier and pretty thatched and slate-hung cottages has remained relatively unspoilt. Over the years its lifeboat crew performed many heroic deeds, rescuing mariners and vessels wrecked on the dreaded Manacle Rocks further along the coast. Like many such isolated fishing communities, Coverack was formerly known for its smuggling activities and several of the cottages have secret hiding-places under their stone floors. Bracing clifftop walks lead around the rim of the Lizard plateau, north to Porthoustock and south to Cadgwith.

AA recommends:
Campsite: Little Trevothan Caravan Park, 3-pennants, *tel.* (0326) 280260

Crackington Haven

Map Ref: 95SX1496

A long, peaceful, gorse-clad valley owned by the National Trust opens out on to a sandy beach washed by high, and sometimes dangerous, surf. Sheltered by towering cliffs, the beach was formerly used as a

Above: Crackington Haven, its beach sheltered by tall cliffs.
Left: Mordern Mill, Cotehele

small port for unloading Welsh coal and limestone and exporting locally quarried slate. Sand and seaweed for the land were carried up the valley by donkeys. An energetic walk south leads to High Cliff, 730ft above The Strangles beach.

The hamlet of St Gennys (pronounced with a hard 'g') to the north commands wide coastal views as far as Hartland Point. Alongside a green common stands the Norman-towered Church of St Genesius, and its churchyard looks out over Castle Point, sometimes identified as an Iron Age fort surrounded by banks and ditches but probably a natural formation.

AA recommends:
Hotels: ◇ Coombe Barton, 2-star, *tel.* (08403) 345 ◇ Crackington Manor, 2-star, *tel.* (08403) 397
Self Catering: ◇ CC Ref 331 P (Character Cottages), *tel.* (03955) 77001 ◇ Gunnedah (flats), *tel.* (08403) 265 ◇ East & West Emetts, *tel.* (08403) 338
Guesthouse: Manor Farmhouse, *tel.* (08403) 304
Campsite: Hentervene Farm Caravan & Camping Park, 3-pennants, *tel.* (08403) 365

Crantock

Map Ref: 91SW7960

This ancient village of colour-washed cottages and pretty gardens is separated from the bustle of Newquay by a long narrow estuary, The Gannel. The village stocks stand outside the church and the thatched Old Albion Inn contains a secret chamber, used by smugglers, under its stone floor. Legend tells of the large city of Langarroc and its seven churches which existed hereabouts before the lawlessness of the inhabitants invoked the wrath of God, who drowned it in sand. Substance was given to the legend when local farmers ploughed up numerous teeth and bones from the sandy soil.

Over the dunes is Crantock Beach with its cliff caves, and along tamarisk-edged lanes to the south are the surfing beaches of Porth Joke, known locally as Polly Joke, and Holywell Bay.

AA recommends:
Hotels: Crantock Bay, West Pentire, 2-star, *tel.* (0637) 830229 ◇ Fairbank, West Pentire Rd, 2-star, *tel.* (0637) 830424
Self Catering: ◇ Halwyn Farm Cottage, ◇ Scantlebury & Trevalsa Cottages, West Pentire, *tel.* (0637) 830277 ◇ Treago Malthouse & Treago Cottage, *tel.* (0637) 830277
Campsites: Trevella Tourist Park, 5-pennants, *tel.* (0637) 830308 Treago Farm Caravan Site, 3-pennants, *tel.* (0637) 830277

Delabole

Map Ref: 94SX0784

Slate quarrying has been carried out in this area for almost 600 years, and Delabole Slate Quarry (1½ miles in circumference and 500ft deep) is the largest man-made hole in Britain. 500 men were once employed here, blasting, cutting and splitting the blue-grey slate into standard sizes known as Ladies, Countesses, Duchesses, Queens and Imperials. Cheaper substitutes have caused a decline in the industry, but about 50 men are still employed, practising the old skills. The public is not allowed into the quarry, but a viewing area alongside a museum affords a dizzying view of the workers far below.

AA recommends:
Hotel: ◇ Poldark Inn, Treligga Downs, 2-star, *tel.* (0840) 212565
Campsite: Planet Park, 3-pennants, *tel.* (0840) 213361

Below: Pendennis Castle, Falmouth

Falmouth

Map Ref: 91SW8032

Its position at the entrance to a large stretch of deep, sheltered water – the estuary of seven rivers – made Falmouth ideal for development as a defendable port. Before Tudor times it was a small fishing village known as Penny-come-quick, but the enthusiasm of Sir Walter Raleigh and the foresight of the local piratical Killigrew family, caused quick growth in the late 16th century. Pendennis Castle and its smaller neighbour across the water, St Mawes, were built on either side of the entrance to Carrick Roads to defend the port against invaders, and were designed on a 'clover leaf' plan.

Falmouth became known as 'the Front Porch of Britain', being an ideal place to replenish supplies for inbound ships and suitably sheltered for outward-bound vessels awaiting favourable winds. For 200 years it was a base for the Packet Services (letters and packets being dispatched by fast sailing-ships to America, Spain and Portugal), and became the second busiest port in Britain after London, a position maintained until the end of the last century when sail gave way to steam-power. The arrival of the railway in 1863 brought renewed affluence, and the south-facing side of the town was developed as a holiday resort, visitors also enjoying the nearby beaches of Gyllyngvase, Swanpool and Maenporth.

Falmouth today is a popular yachting centre, earning prosperity from tourism, shipping and ship-repairing. Its busy main street, decked with flowers in summer, snakes along the foot of a steep hillside, with numerous alleyways leading down between the shops to the waterside and views of bobbing boats and dazzling water. At the town's centre is the Prince of Wales Pier from where pleasure trips can be taken or the ferry caught to Flushing or St Mawes. Close by is a tree-lined open space known as The Moor, flanked by steep hillsides of houses. The town hall houses the art gallery, and on the opposite side is a precipitous flight of 111 steps known as 'Jacob's Ladder'. Alongside the Custom House is a chimney where contraband tobacco was burnt, and a tiny harbour which has witnessed the arrival and departure of many record-breaking voyages. It is also the permanent home of the tug *St Denys* which houses Falmouth Maritime Museum. At the southern end of the main street is Arwenack, the 17th-century manor house of the Killigrew family who developed the port.

AA recommends:
Hotels: Penmere Manor, Mongleath Rd, 3-star Country House Hotel, *tel.* (0326) 211411
Royal Duchy, Cliff Rd, 3-star, *tel.* (0326) 313042
Hotel St Michaels, Stracey Rd, 3-star, *tel.* (0326) 312707
Crill House, Golden Bank, 2-star, *tel.* (0326) 312994 (2½m w on unclass rd)
Restaurant: ◇ Continental, 29 High St, 1-fork, *tel.* (0326) 313003
Self Catering: ◇ 22 Greenbank (cottage & flats), *tel.* (0326) 314853
◇ 2 Stratton Place, *tel.* (0326) 314853
Guesthouses: ◇ Bedruthan, 49 Castle Drive, Sea Front, *tel.* (0326) 311028
◇ Gyllyngvase House Hotel, Gyllyngvase Rd, *tel.* (0326) 312956
◇ Maskee House, Spernen Wyn Rd, *tel.* (0326) 311783
Penty Bryn Hotel, 10 Melvill Rd, *tel.* (0326) 314988
Campsites: ◇ Maen Valley Caravan Park, 4-pennants, *tel.* (0326) 312190
◇ Golden Bank Caravans, Swanpool Rd, 3-pennants, *tel.* (0326) 312103
Tremorvah, Swanpool, 3-pennants, *tel.* (0326) 312103
Garages: Boslowic, Boslowic Rd, Swanvale, *tel.* (0326) 312765 (day) & 312097 (night)
Dales, Ponsharden, *tel.* (0326) 72011 (day) & 72013 (night)

Falmouth's harbour opens out into the deep protected waters of Falmouth estuary

Celtic cross of the old type, with circular head, Feock churchyard

Feock

Map Ref: 91SW8238

This creekside village near the mouth of the River Fal consists of a cluster of whitewashed and thatched cottages and a number of modern, affluent properties. Its small church nestling in a green bowl of yew trees has a separate tower and an interesting lych-gate with a slate-hung upper storey. A lane descends steeply to shingly Loe Beach where vessels of all sizes and shapes take to the safe waters of Carrick Roads. To the south the long arm of Restronguet Point reaches out across the mouth of a creek. At its tip travellers may signal for a ferry to the opposite, darkly wooded bank by hoisting a flag. A peaceful creekside walk from Feock follows the old tram-road from Penpol to Devoran.

The mackerel catch is unloaded on the long harbour front at Flushing (below and inset)

Flushing

Map Ref: 91SW8033

Said to have the mildest climate in Britain, the trim little village and quay of Flushing faces Falmouth across a narrow strip of water filled with white sails and fluttering flags. It owes its name to 17th-century Dutch builders from Holland who came to construct piers and sea-walls and settled here. The village retains a distinctly Dutch atmosphere and its narrow streets contain several Queen Anne houses, the former homes of packet-ship captains. A lane winding up between delightful gardens leads to a small park and vantage point over the village rooftops.

AA recommends:
Guesthouse: ◇ Nankersey Hotel, St Peters Rd, *tel.* (0326) 74471

Fowey

Map Ref: 92SX1251

An historic town overlooking a deep-water anchorage, Fowey (pronounced 'Foy') is one of Cornwall's most picturesque and romantic places. The pace of life in its narrow streets is easy and there are few concessions to modern 'development'. Colourful old houses, ranging in architectural style from Elizabethan to Edwardian, radiate from a market hall and 14th-century church. The shipping of tin ore from here to France was halted by the Hundred Years War when over 700 local seamen were recruited to sail against the French. Known as the 'Fowey Gallants', many were later to become much-feared pirates, raiding any ship that strayed within Cornish waters. After the French ransacked the town in 1457, blockhouses were built on either side of the entrance to Fowey harbour and a chain stretched between them to de-mast any invading ships. To further strengthen the defences, Henry VIII built one of his many castles along this coast at Readymoney Cove. Many Edwardian visitors were attracted to the town by the writings of Sir Arthur Quiller-Couch in which Fowey was thinly disguised as 'Troy Town'. His home stands below the Esplanade overlooking the boat-filled river. The rail link with Lostwithiel in 1864 and the great depth of the river have enabled Fowey to become one of Cornwall's leading china-clay exporters, freighters of 10,000 tons nosing their way through pleasure craft to the harbour north of the town.

Right: view over Fowey to Polruan

Walk along the high narrow lane of Bull Hill for a panoramic rooftop view of the town and river, or follow the winding length of Fore Street to visit the Noah's Ark Museum where charming domestic items are displayed in period settings. An exhibition describing the town's history can be found in the Town Hall Museum; and the Ship Inn, once the home of the Rashleigh family, boasts some fine Elizabethan panelling and plaster ceilings. The romantic neo-Gothic building towering over the town is Place House, the seat of the Treffry family. Dating from the 15th century but largely rebuilt in the 1840s, it is only occasionally open to the public. The Bodinnick car ferry crosses the river at Caffamill Pill and a passenger ferry goes through a flotilla of yachts to the small port and hillside village of Polruan on the opposite bank.

A few miles up-river from Fowey is Golant, a cluster of riverside cottages with a church containing a pulpit made from old carved bench-ends. This area has strong links with the tragic lovers Tristan and Iseult, and Tristan's father, King Mark of

Cornwall, is said to have lived at Castle Dore, a circular earthwork to the west of the village.

AA recommends:

Hotels: Fowey, The Esplanade, 3-star, *tel.* (072683) 2551
Marina, The Esplanade, 2-star, *tel.* (072683) 3315
◊ Old Quay, Fore St, 2-star, *tel.* (072683) 3302
◊ Penlee, The Esplanade, 2-star, *tel.* (072683) 3220

◊ Riverside, 2-star, *tel.* (072683) 2275
Restaurant: Food for Thought, The Quay, 2-fork, *tel.* (072683) 2221
Guesthouses: Ashley House Hotel, 14 Esplanade, *tel.* (072683) 2310
Carnethic House, Lambs Barn, *tel.* (072683) 3336
Wheelhouse, 60 Esplanade, *tel.* (0726) 832452
◊ Trezare (farmhouse), *tel.* (072683) 3485
Garage: Cotswold, Lambs Barn, Polvillion Rd, *tel.* (0726) 833468 (day) & (0726) 832653 (night)

Food

'Tes plain and nothin' fancy, but it do stick to your ribs,' was how one St Just housewife described Cornish food. She might have added 'full of variety', for everything is grist to the Cornish cook's mill. The pie was for many years the medium through which her art was revealed: pilchard pie, mackerel pie, bream pie, conger pie, curlew pie, giblet pie and ram pie all being popular dishes. Squab pie contained young pigeons; Nattlin pie, pig's entrails; Likky pie, leeks; and Muggety pie was made with sheep's entrails. Starry-gazy pie contained pilchards with their heads poking out through the crust. It is hardly surprising that the devil never came to Cornwall for fear of being put in a pie.

The ubiquitous Cornish pasty bought from a shop or supermarket bears little resemblance to the crimped foot-long home-made concoction enjoyed by farm-workers in the fields or miners deep underground for their 'croust'. Often marked with the consumer's initial in pastry, the pasty was an early convenience food, being held in one hand and eaten from the end. The genuine article, made from short-crust pastry, contains chunks of the best steak (*not* minced meat), potatoes, onion, turnip, salt and plenty of pepper, but the contents vary from one family to another and remain the subject of endless debate.

Cakes and puddings also form an integral part of 'croust' as well as 'high-tea'. Heavy cake (not as indigestible as it sounds) is composed of flour, butter, cream, sugar and currants, rolled out flat and scored with a fish-net pattern. Tatie cake is made from mashed potatoes, fat, flour, currants and sugar while Figgy pudding is made from raisins ('figs') baked with suet, flour, eggs and sugar.

Traditional tea-treats, still held in most villages, culminate in communal hymn-singing and the eating of Saffron buns – yeast buns coloured yellow with saffron from the crocus flower and dotted with currants. Always fond of a 'dish of tay' (cup of tea) many Cornish people stave off the winter cold with something a little stronger. Shenagrum is a warming mixture of rum, brown sugar and a slice of lemon in hot beer, and Mahogany is gin beaten with treacle. Metheglin or mead, made from fermented honey, is also enjoyed in some parts of west Cornwall.

Clotted cream is a basic ingredient of any true Cornish tea and no slice of blackberry or apple tart would be quite the same without its dollop of cream. At one time almost every cottage or farm-kitchen had a bowl of golden-encrusted clotted cream cooking slowly on the range. This is one dish that has not suffered from being produced on a large-scale, the tubs of locally-made cream retaining the home-made quality while having a much longer 'larder-life'. With a butterfat content of 60 per cent, it is slightly thinner than Devon cream and is easier to spread. Eaten with Cornish splits (yeast buns), the jam is spread before the cream, but for Thunder and Lightning the cream is spread first, then coated with a trickle of syrup.

Cornish pasties – the real thing

Grampound

Map Ref: 91SW9348

Rushing through this modest village on the main A390 road, it is difficult to believe that it was once an ancient borough of great importance. Originally the lowest bridging point on the River Fal, it was a busy market town in the centre of a rich agricultural parish, sending two MPs to Parliament. Bribery and corruption were rife and the town was denied representation in 1820. Its steep main street still contains several interesting buildings, notably a toll-house by the bridge, a guildhall and clock-tower and a tannery where traditional bark-tanning methods are still used.

AA recommends:
Self Catering: ◇ Golden Keep Cottage, *tel.* (087253) 500
◇ Golden Manor Flat, *tel.* (087253) 500
Guesthouse: ◇ Tregidgeo (farmhouse), *tel.* (0726) 882450
Campsite: ◇ Lynwood Camping & Caravan Park, Mill Lane, 3-pennants, *tel.* (0726) 882458

Gulval

Map Ref: 90SW4831

A showpiece village of Victorian houses and cottages, compactly grouped round the church, Gulval lies on a south-facing slope bright with flowers. A few miles inland (take the St Ives road and branch left at Badger's Cross) is the Late Iron Age settlement of Chysauster, one of the oldest villages in Britain. Nine courtyard houses, one of which is a semi-detached unit, are grouped on either side of a village street. Dating from the first century BC and abandoned four centuries later, each building consists of a courtyard surrounded by a series of small rooms (stables, living quarters, stores, etc), each of which would originally have been roofed with thatch. Each house has a small terraced garden-plot, presumably for the growing of herbs. Nearby is a fogou, a long, walled ditch which was originally roofed and was used for religious or storage purposes.

Gunwalloe Church, on the dunes

Gunnislake

Map Ref: 95SX4371

The graceful seven-arched New Bridge, built in 1520, made Gunnislake the lowest crossing point on the River Tamar until modern times. It was also the upper tidal reach of the river and locally-mined copper, tin, wolfram and arsenic were shipped downstream from here and Calstock until the early 1900s. Narrow streets of miners' cottages rise steeply up the hillside, and from the top of the main street you can see numerous ruined mine-chimneys and look over the Tamar Valley to the dramatic Morwell Rocks, backed by dark woodland on the opposite bank.

AA recommends:
Hotel: ◇ Cornish Inn, The Square, 2-star, *tel.* (0822) 832475
Guesthouse: Hingston House, St Anns Chapel, *tel.* (0822) 832468 (1m w A390)
Garage: Central Motors, New Bridge Hill, *tel.* (0822) 832432 (day) & (0836) 274855 (night)

Gunwalloe Fishing Cove

Map Ref: 90SW6522

Little more than a scattering of fishermen's cottages, Gunwalloe Fishing Cove lies at the eastern tip of Mount's Bay, where a long shingle beach gives way to the rising cliffs of the Lizard plateau. A short walk south takes you to Gunwalloe Church Cove where the small Church of St Winwalloe sits in the dunes beside the beach, surrounded by a hedge of tamarisk. Together with its separate bell-tower, the church appears to be in constant danger of being swept away by waves during storms. It was from the high grassy headland of Poldhu Point to the south that Marconi transmitted the first trans-Atlantic radio signals in 1901.

Gweek

Map Ref: 91SW7026

At the head of the beautiful Helford River, this peaceful little village with its two bridges was once a busy port, taking over Helston's trade when that town became cut off from the sea by the formation of Loe Bar. As Penryn, Truro and Falmouth grew, so Gweek's trade declined and the river slowly became choked with silt. The last cargo was carried from its wharves in 1880, and today its waterfront is a popular place for family boating. Set in pleasant woodland and sloping fields on the north bank is the Cornish Seal Sanctuary, where injured seals are cared for after being washed in on the north coast beaches.

The Seal Sanctuary at Gweek

Gwithian

Map Ref: 90SW5841

Backed by high 'towans' or sand-dunes, the three-mile stretch of sand on the eastern side of St Ives Bay offers plenty of space for holidaymakers, even in high summer. The pocket-sized village of Gwithian at the northern end contains some charmingly thatched cottages, a tiny Methodist chapel, an inn and farmhouses. The church is dedicated to St Gothian, an Irish missionary whose monastic cell was unearthed nearby during the last century, but which has now once again been engulfed by sand. Offshore from a high turfy headland owned by the National Trust stands Godrevy lighthouse which formed the haunting image in Virginia Woolf's *To The Lighthouse*, her novel recalling childhood holidays in St Ives.

AA recommends:
Hotel: ◇ Glencoe House, 23 Churchtown Rd, 2-star, *tel.* (0736) 752216
Self Catering: ◇ Sandbank Holiday Flats, *tel.* (0326) 311063

Hayle

Map Ref: 90SW5637

A landing place in early times, Hayle sprang to prominence last century when its foundries manufactured the boilers, machinery and engines for use in Cornish mines. Richard Trevithick, the great Cornish engineer, built his first steam-powered 'road-carriage' here in the early 1800s, and one of the first railways in the world ran from Hayle to Redruth. Tin and copper were smelted at Copperhouse to the north-east, where a large pool is formed by lock-gates across a stream. The River Hayle is now heavily silted but a few vessels still use the old wharves. The Victorian buildings of the town are overshadowed by the lofty granite railway viaduct carrying the London to Penzance line. At Paradise Park, south of the town, rare birds and endangered animals can be seen in luxuriant surroundings. Brightly-coloured parrots fly free and also here is the red-billed Cornish chough, once a familiar sight around the coast but now locally extinct.

AA recommends:
Hotels: Hillside, I Grist Lane, Angarrack, 2-star, *tel.* (0736) 752180 (1½m e off A30) ◇ Penellen, Riviere Towans, Phillack, I-star, *tel.* (0736) 753777
Self Catering: ◇ Tolroy Holiday Village, *tel.* (0872) 40400
Campsite: St Ives Bay Holiday Park, 73 Loggans Rd, Upton Towans, I-pennant, *tel.* (0736) 752274

Ponsance Cove, by the waters of the Helford River

Helford

Map Ref: 91SW7526

The peaceful, wood-fringed waters of the Helford River, with its deep, sheltered creeks and winding inlets, is one of the most attractive areas of Cornwall – a world away from the windswept cliffs of the north coast – and a yachtsman's paradise. The snug village of Helford, on the south bank, straggles beside a tidal creek and contains a thatched inn and an award-winning restaurant, The Riverside. A ferry from the point beyond the inn goes across the river, past yacht-masts as dense as reed-beds, to Helford Passage and another hostelry of character, the Ferry Boat Inn. West of Helford, and best seen by boat, is Frenchman's Creek, a smuggler's hideaway made famous by Daphne du Maurier's novel.

Steep lanes of sweet-scented flowers lead south to Manaccan where colour-washed cottages and a thatched inn lie on a valleyside at the head of a tidal creek. An ancient fig-tree sprouts from alongside the Norman doorway of the granite church. To the east a lane meanders alongside a creek to St Anthony-in-Meneage and its well cared for waterside church.

The village of Helford, on a creek of the Helford estuary

While exploring the waters of Helford River, keep an eye open for Morgawr (Cornish for 'sea giant'), Cornwall's answer to Nessie. First seen in 1926, it has been spotted on numerous occasions in this area and was described by one witness as being a 'hideous hump-backed creature with stumpy horns'.

AA recommends:
Restaurant: Riverside, 2-forks, *tel.* (032623) 443

Helston

Map Ref: 90SW6527

The 'quaint old Cornish town' of the well-known song is decked with flags and flowers on 8 May for Flora Day, a celebration to welcome spring. No song is sung, and the rather formal, jigging dance is known not as the Floral but the Furry, from the Cornish word 'Fer' or Feast Day. This 17th-century celebration is preceded on the same day by a much older mumming play, the Hal-an-Tow.

Helston was once a thriving port and ships sailed the Loe River to load locally streamed tin, but during the 13th century a bar of shingle formed at the mouth of the river, cutting off access to the sea. The freshwater lake, Loe Pool, that built up behind the barrier is one of the two sites in Cornwall reputed to be where King Arthur's sword, Excalibur, was received by a hand rising from the water. (See also 'Bodmin Moor'.) A delightful walk leads around the borders of the lake. Edward I selected Helston as one of Cornwall's stannary towns, where the quality of locally-produced tin was tested ('assayed'), and the wide, sloping main thoroughfare, which has water from the surrounding mines running down 'kennals' on either side, is called Coinagehall Street. The town contains many modest Regency and Georgian buildings and its dipping, winding streets have a genteel quality all their own. The 16th-century Angel Hotel stands below a classic Victorian Guildhall, beside which steps lead down to the Butter Market Folk Museum, crammed with interesting items. Across the valley rises the tower of the parish church, destroyed by lightning in 1727 and rebuilt in 1830. In the churchyard is a memorial to Henry Trengrouse, inventor of the life-saving rocket apparatus used to save

so many lives around the coast. A thatched cottage in Wendron Street is where 'Battling' Bob Fitzsimmons, the only Englishman to become world heavyweight boxing champion, was born. The Blue Anchor Inn, a resting place for monks in the 1400s and one of a growing number of inns in Britain selling their own beer, stands at the lower end of the main street. On market day (Monday) Coinagehall Street is lined with colourful stalls.

South of Helston is the Royal Naval Air Station of Culdrose where Sea-King helicopter pilots are trained. There is a public viewing area by the car park.

One of Cornwall's leading tourist attractions, Cornwall Aero Park and Flambards Village, can be found close by. This large all-weather attraction features displays of aircraft and helicopters, wartime exhibitions and a Concorde flight-deck. 'Flambards Village' is a splendidly evocative recreation of streets, shops and domestic interiors dating from the turn-of-the-century, while 'Britain in the Blitz' features a wartime street complete with shops, pub and living room with its Morrison shelter. Surrounding all are landscaped gardens, lakes and children's rides and games.

North of Helston, near the former mining village of Wendron, is another important tourist attraction, Poldark Mine. Here you can explore the workings underground and experience conditions first-hand. Above ground is a working beam-engine and a fine collection of mining artefacts as well as a childrens' play-park with rides and games.

AA recommends:
Hotels: Gwealdues, Falmouth Rd, 2-star, *tel.* (0326) 572808
◇ Angel, Coinagehall St, 1-star, *tel.* (03265) 2701
Nansloe Manor Country Hotel, Meneage

Flora Day dancers weave through the streets of Helston

Rd, 2-star Country House Hotel, *tel.* (0326) 574691
Self Catering: ◇ Greenacres Holiday Bungalows, Clodgey Lane, *tel.* (03265) 2620
Guesthouses: ◇ Hillside, Godolphin Rd, *tel.* (0326) 574788
Strathallan, Monument Rd, *tel.* (0326) 573683
◇ Wheal Tor Hotel, 29 Godolphin Rd, *tel.* (03265) 61211
Campsites: Glenhaven Camping & Touring Park, Clodgey Lane, 3-pennants, *tel.* (03265) 2734
Trelowarren Chateau Camping, Trelowarran, Mawgan, 3-pennants, *tel.* (032622) 637 (3m s off B3293 to St Keverne)
Garages: Helston, Meneage St, *tel.* (0326) 573415
Helston Auto Centre, Clodgey Lane, *tel.* (0326) 563671 (day) & (0209) 831896 (night)

Lamorna

Map Ref: 90SW4424

Set between towering pinnacles of weathered granite is Lamorna Cove, as peaceful and beautiful as its name suggests with a small crescent of sand, a stout stone pier and a sprinkling of cottages. To one side is a granite quarry from where stone was cut to build the Thames Embankment and several lighthouses. A flower-bordered lane leads up a deep sheltered coombe to the tiny village and an old flour-mill. The famous inn, The Wink, was originally only licensed to sell beer, but a wink to the landlord would produce something a little stronger. Follow the road up the valley and turn left to reach The Merry Maidens, a Bronze Age circle of 19 stones said to be a group of young girls turned to granite for dancing on the Sabbath. Two large standing stones in nearby fields, The Pipers, are reputed to be the musicians who accompanied the dancers and met the same fate.

AA recommends:
Hotel: ◇ Lamorna Cove, 3-star Country House Hotel, *tel.* (0736) 731411
Campsites: Boleigh Farm Campsite, 1-pennant, *tel.* (0736) 810305

Land's End

Map Ref: 90SW3425

Known as Belerion, 'Seat of Storms', to the Romans, this most westerly point in mainland England draws countless visitors. Walk south from the hotel along the coastal footpath to witness some of the most magnificent cliff scenery in Britain, the granite worn, battered and shaped by Atlantic gales into jagged spires, gaping chasms, fractured pillars and holed headlands. Beyond the jutting reefs of Enys Dodnan and the Armed Knight are the Longships lighthouse and the Seven Stones reef where the *Torrey Canyon* came to grief in 1967. On the horizon are the Wolf Rock lighthouse and the Isles of Scilly, 28 miles distant. Close to the hotel, now known as the State

House, are exhibitions tracing the maritime history, wildlife and geology of the area, while the First and Last House contains a craft workshop. South-east, in Nanjizal Bay, archways of orange lichen-encrusted granite rise from the dazzling ultramarine sea. Continue to the southernmost tip of the peninsula to find Porthgwarra, two small smugglers' coves divided by a headland through which local miners carved a tunnel, formerly used for smoking fish.

Lanhydrock House

Map Ref: 92SX0863

Lanhydrock belonged to the Augustinian Priory of St Petroc at nearby Bodmin before being surrendered to Henry VIII in 1539. Bought by the Robartes family in 1620, it remained their home until it was given to the National Trust, together with 400 acres of surrounding land, in 1953. Built amidst wooded parkland on the edge of the River Fowey valley, the house is approached along an avenue of beech trees. It appears to be Tudor, but the majority of the 17th-century house was destroyed by fire in 1881. The charming two-

storeyed gatehouse, entrance porch and north wing remain intact, but the remainder of the house is a Victorian copy in the Tudor style. The interior provides a vivid picture of life in Victorian times,

The fine plaster ceiling of the Long Gallery, Lanhydrock House

particularly 'below stairs'. The mighty kitchen with its roasting spit, the larders, dairy, bakehouse, cellars and servants' quarters contain many interesting domestic details. Her Ladyship's room, the dining room, steward's room, drawing room and the Long Gallery are all worthy of inspection. Its windows look out on to the formal gardens of clipped yew. On the hillside behind the house is the 15th-century Church of St Hydrock, and the surrounding gardens are a mass of colour in early summer.

AA recommends:
Guesthouse: ◇ Treffry (farmhouse), *tel.* (0208) 4405

Lanlivery

Map Ref: 92SX0859

The 15th-century tower of Lanlivery church stands almost 100ft high and is one of the finest in Cornwall, being visible from many miles around. Inside the church are slate memorials, a charming ringer's rhyme and a large carved font. Next to the old village inn is Churchtown Field Studies Centre where mentally and physically handicapped youngsters come to enjoy activity holidays. A road and then a footpath running north-west leads to the summit of Helman Tor with its rocking logan stone and dramatic views over mid-Cornwall.

AA recommends:
Guesthouse: ◇ Treganoon (farmhouse), *tel.* (0208) 872205
Campsite: Powderham Castle Caravan & Tourist Park, 3-pennants, *tel.* (0208) 872277

Land's End

Launceston

Map Ref: 95SX3384

Known as 'Lanson' by the local people, this old market town close to the Devon border is proudly Cornish and has retained much of its character. Built on a hill topped by a Norman castle, the town's origins lie across the valley of the River Kensey to the north where a community grew up around an Augustinian priory and the Church of St Stephen. It is here that you will find the 15th-century mother church of Launceston and the Byzantine-style Roman Catholic church, built early this century, where lie the relics of the priest Cuthbert Mayne who was martyred in the town in 1577. On the south side of a mediaeval footbridge spanning the Kensey is the tiny Church of St Thomas, built in 1182, which contains the largest font in Cornwall. The castle which dominates the town was built following the Norman Conquest, but the outer and inner baileys are 12th- and 13th-century. Despite its strategic position, the castle was stormed four times during the Civil War. Originally called Dunheved, the walled town of narrow streets which grew up around the castle took the name of the neighbouring community and eventually became the capital of Cornwall, only relinquishing that title in 1838 when the Right of Assize passed to Bodmin.

The finest stonemasons in Cornwall were assembled by Sir Henry Trecarrel to decorate St Mary Magdalene Church in memory of his wife. The delicate carving on this magnificent 16th-century building is also a splendid monument to their own skills. As well as several well-preserved red-brick Georgian houses, this busy shopping centre also boasts a small art gallery over the South Gate and a local history museum in Lawrence House. To the west of the town, Launceston Steam Railway runs for 1½ miles along the beautiful Kensey valley. The secret world of the wild otter can be experienced at the Tamar Otter Park at North Petherwin, north of Launceston.

AA recommends:
Hotel: ◇ White Hart, Broad St, 2-star, *tel.* (0566) 2013
Self Catering: ◇ Higher Bamham Farm, *tel.* (0566) 2141
◇ Primrose Cottage, Langore, *tel.* (0566) 3216
◇ Tredidon, St Thomas, *tel.* (056686) 288
Guesthouse: ◇ Eagle House Hotel, Castle St, *tel.* (0566) 2036
Campsites: ◇ Travadlock Hall Holiday Park, 1-pennant, *tel.* (056682) 392
Garages: Greenaways, *tel.* (0566) 2222 (day) & 3265 (night)
◇ St Stephens (R L Curran), *tel.* (0566) 2546

Lelant

Map Ref: 90SW5437

Lelant grew as a flourishing port on the western bank of the Hayle estuary in the Middle Ages, but as the river became clogged with silt, so its importance declined. The estuary marshland, known as the Saltings, is now a sanctuary for wading birds, and cars can be left at the nearby station before a journey along the scenic rail line to St Ives. The village's golf course, renowned in the golf world, offers fine views across to Hayle Towans and Godrevy lighthouse, and nestling in the dunes at its edge is the 15th-century church dedicated to St Uny, a 6th-century Irish saint, the brother of St Ia who founded St Ives.

Close to the village is Cornucopia, a tourist attraction depicting various aspects of Cornish life and local legends.

AA recommends:
Restaurant: ◇ Watermill, Mill Hill, 2-forks, *tel.* (0736) 755019 (½m from junc A30/A3074 along unclass rd towards Lelant Downs)
Self Catering: ◇ St Ives Holiday Village, *tel.* (0872) 40400
Campsite: ◇ Sunny Meadow Caravan Park, 2-pennants, *tel.* (0736) 752243

Liskeard

Map Ref: 92SX2564

Today Liskeard is a busy market town of great charm, serving a wide agricultural community, but it was once one of Cornwall's stannary towns (for the testing of tin), and its prosperity was enhanced by the rich copper ore from the nearby Caradon mines and the granite from Cheesewring quarry. Standing at the head of a river valley, Liskeard was linked to the port of Looe by a canal early last century. This was superseded in 1859 by the railway line which now carries visitors down to the coast. Buildings of note include Cornwall's largest parish church, several Georgian houses, a Victorian Italianate guildhall, an 1833 coaching inn and Stuart House where King Charles stayed in 1644. The waters of the Pipe Well are said to have therapeutic powers.

To the west of Liskeard is one of Cornwall's foremost tourist attractions, Dobwalls Theme Park. This includes the Forest Railroad and 'Mr Thorburn's Edwardian Countryside', where the wildlife paintings of Archibald Thorburn are displayed in period settings.

AA recommends:
Hotels: Country Castle, Station Rd, 2-star Country House Hotel, *tel.* (0579) 42694
Lord Eliot, Castle St, 2-star, *tel.* (0579) 42717
◇ Webbs, The Parade, 2-star, *tel.* (0579) 43675
Self Catering: ◇ Deer Park Forest Cabins, *tel.* (031-334) 2576
Guesthouses: Elnor, 1 Russell St, *tel.* (0579) 42472
◇ Tencreek (farmhouse), *tel.* (0579) 43379
Garage: ◇ New Central, Plymouth Rd, *tel.* (0579) 45098 (day) & 62071 (night)

Castle keep, Launceston

Above: Looe fishermen set off at dawn past Banjo Pier
Left: craftsman carving serpentine marble, Lizard

display of the town's long history and a nearby former fish cellar now contains a museum of Cornish folk items.

East along the coast is Murrayton Monkey Sanctuary, where a protected breeding colony of Amazonian Woolly monkeys enjoys life in a delightful setting among trees and spacious enclosures.

St Keyne, a few miles up the deep, wooded valley from Looe, is the home of the Paul Corin Musical Collection of fairground organs and player pianos.

AA recommends:
Hotels: Hannafore Point, Marine Dr, Hannafore, 3-star, *tel.* (05036) 3273
Commonwood, St Martins Rd, 2-star, *tel.* (05036) 2929
Fieldhead, Portuan Rd, Hannafore, 2-star, *tel.* (05036) 2689
Portbyhan, West Looe Quay, 1-star, *tel.* (05036) 2071
Restaurant: ◇ Trelaske Country Hotel, Polperro Rd, Trelaske, 2-forks, *tel.* (05036) 2159 (2m w on A387)
Self Catering: ◇ Lemain Garden Apartments, Portuan Rd, West Looe, *tel.* (05036) 2073
◇ Stonerock Holiday Flats, Portuan Rd, *tel.* (05036) 2928
Guesthouses: Kantara, 7 Trelawney Ter, *tel.* (05036) 2093
Ogunquit, Portuan Rd, Hannafore, *tel.* (05036) 3105
Panorama Hotel, Hannafore Rd, Hannafore, *tel.* (05036) 2123
St Aubyns, Marine Dr, Hannafore, *tel.* (05036) 4351
Campsites: 'Treble B' Holiday Centre, Polperro Rd, 5-pennants, *tel.* (05036) 2425
Polborder House, 3-pennants, *tel.* (05034) 265
◇ Tregoad Caravan & Camping Park, St Martin, 3-pennants, *tel.* (05036) 2718
Garage: Barbican Mtr Co, The Barbican, East Looe, *tel.* (05036) 2498 (day) & (0503) 72277 (night)

Looe's picturesque quay, much beloved of holidaymakers

Lizard

Map Ref: 91SW7012

The jagged rocks of Lizard Point are the most southerly point on the British mainland, and it was from the mesembryanthemum-clad cliffs above that the approaching Spanish Armada was first sighted in 1588. A lighthouse, lit by coal fires, was built here in 1620, but the present building dates from 1751 and was provided by Sir John Killigrew, a former pirate from Falmouth. Some suggest that he wished to save vessels in the hope that they might founder on rocks nearer his home, where he owned the wrecking rights. On the high, windswept tip of the high peninsula, the village of Lizard is the only British mainland community lying south of the 50th parallel. Almost the entire Lizard Peninsula is composed of soft, colourful serpentine stone, ideal for carving in local workshops. The surrounding heathland is a botanist's paradise and supports many rare plants, including the unique Cornish Heath.

East of the village are the pretty hamlet of Landewednack and the Church of St Winwalloe, built of alternate serpentine and granite blocks. Below in Church Cove an old fish cellar has been converted into a private dwelling.

Kynance Cove to the west is a picturesque spot with tilted pinnacles of serpentine rising from a clean, white beach, deep caves and plenty of rock pools.

AA recommends:
Hotels: Housel Bay, Housel Cove, 2-star, *tel.* (0326) 290417
◇ Lizard, 2-star, *tel.* (0326) 290456
Self Catering: ◇ Penmenner House Hotel (flats), *tel.* (0326) 290370
Guesthouses: Mounts Bay Hotel, Penmenner Rd, *tel.* (0326) 290305
Parc Brawse House, *tel.* (0326) 290466
Penmenner House Hotel, Penmenner Rd, *tel.* (0326) 290370

Looe

Map Ref: 92SX2553

East and West Looe face each other across the estuary of two rivers and are joined by a broad seven-arched bridge. It was formerly a pilchard fishing community, and the arrival of the railway in 1859 also brought the first wave of summer visitors to Looe. The labyrinth of narrow lanes and flower-hung courtyards in the old quarter of East Looe has changed little during the past century, but the remainder of the town is now largely given over to tourism in summer. The bustling quayside is still lined with fishing boats and shark-fishing expeditions can be taken or more leisurely boat trips round St George's Island. Land-based anglers can cast a line from the circular end of the Banjo Pier, or view exotic species of fish in the town's aquarium. The 16th-century Guildhall houses a museum

Restormel Castle

Lostwithiel

Map Ref: 92SX1059

One of the most attractive and interesting small market towns in Cornwall, Lostwithiel was its capital for a short period in the 13th century, before passing that honour to Launceston. Surrounded by thickly wooded hills and rich meadowland, the town grew to prominence as the lowest bridging point on the River Fowey. It prospered from the profits of tin and wool, becoming the seat of the Duchy Parliament, Stannary Court and Hall of Exchequer. The present river bridge replaced an old wooden structure in the 15th century.

Today Lostwithiel is a peaceful place to browse round antique and craft shops, enjoying the well-preserved Georgian houses, narrow 'ope-ways' and old shopfronts before relaxing in the riverside gardens. A dark, cobbled passageway leads beneath an arch in the buttressed walls of the 13th-century Old Duchy Palace. Dating from the same period is the unusual octagonal Breton-style spire of St Bartholomew's Church. Inside is a charming Elizabethan slate carving depicting a lady and her family of eight children. The town's guildhall, built in 1740, houses a small local history museum. North of the town a road between flat meadows and Duchy of Cornwall woodlands leads to Restormel Castle, perched on a strategic hilltop site. Rebuilt in the Middle Ages by Edmund, Earl of Cornwall, this Norman castle has a circular keep divided into small rooms and its stout walls afford magnificent valley views.

A short drive from Lostwithiel down the eastern bank of the River Fowey leads you through high-banked lanes to the Church of St Winnow, picturesquely sited on the river's edge. Frequently used for film and television locations, this gem of a church contains some colourful 15th-century glass.

AA recommends:
Hotel: Restormel Lodge Hotel, Hillside Gdns, 2-star, *tel.* (0208) 872223
Campsite: ◇ Downend Campsite, 1-pennant, *tel.* (0208) 872363
Garage: ◇ Four Way Auto Services, North St, *tel.* (0208) 872503

Luxulyan

Map Ref: 92SX0558

The densely-forested Luxulyan Valley winding north from St Blazey is a favourite springtime beauty spot with local people, the river cascading over mossy boulders between banks of daffodils and

Spring bulbs in full bloom in the gardens at Trengwainton

bluebells. A mighty viaduct, built by local mine and quarry-owner Joseph Treffry in 1842, carried a mineral line and aqueduct across the valley to the port of Par. Higher up the valley, the tidy village of Luxulyan contains some interesting cottages which are built from locally-quarried granite, as are the fine 15th-century church and turreted tower. At the lower end of the village is St Cyor's Holy Well, now dried up, beneath a stone canopy.

A narrow lane leads north to Lowertown and across the flat, wooded expanse of Breney Common to the high vantage point of Helman Tor.

The Duchy of Cornwall

Contrary to popular belief, the Duchy of Cornwall does not refer to the entire county, but only to the estates owned by the Duke of Cornwall, mainly farms, woodlands and a few castles. The title also refers to the many Duchy estates and properties outside Cornwall, in Devon, Somerset, the Isles of Scilly – even the Oval cricket ground in London.

The Duchy was created by Edward III as an estate for the eldest son of the monarch. In 1337 Edward the Black Prince, rode to Launceston castle to be proclaimed the first Duke of Cornwall and to meet his tenants. Many subsequent monarchs failed to produce male heirs, and during periods when the title fell dormant, some ducal estates were sold by the Crown or given away in exchange for services rendered.

HRH Prince Charles became Duke of Cornwall at the age of four, on his mother's accession to the throne. In 1973 he too travelled to Launceston to be proclaimed the 24th Duke and to meet his tenants.

He also received his feudal dues, an extraordinary collection of items which included a pair of white gloves, a brace of greyhounds, a pound each of pepper and the herb cummin, a bow de 'arburne, a pair of gilt spurs, 100 specially struck silver shillings, a carriage of wood to be delivered daily and a salmon spear. A pair of puffins was originally part of this payment, but in these conservation-conscious times, they have been transmuted into a token cash payment.

The Prince receives nothing from the Civil List, his only income being derived from the Duchy. As chairman of the Prince's Council, he is ultimately responsible for the management of some 128,000 acres of land comprising almost 200 farms, leased to tenant farmers, and 2,400 acres of woodlands, all of which play an important role in Cornwall's economy. The Duke takes a personal interest in the estate's management, making frequent visits to

The Duke of Cornwall meets the crowds during a visit to the Duchy with the Duchess

its woodlands, farms, sawmills and nurseries, even occasionally lending a hand with the milking of cows, planting of crops and building of walls.

Madron

Map Ref: 90SW4531

The mother church of Penzance, dedicated to St Maddern, can be found on the moors behind the town, surrounded by a pleasant cluster of old cottages, Victorian villas and pretty gardens. A broad wagon roof spans the church, where you can see some old carved bench-ends and the Trafalgar Banner, commemorating the first news of the victory and death of Nelson in 1805. A mile north of the village a path winds through a thicket of gnarled lichen-encrusted trees to an ancient roofless baptistry with its small, stone altar. Nearby is Madron Wishing Well whose waters are said to possess healing powers. Votive offerings of scraps of rags are still found hanging from the branches of surrounding trees.

The National Trust gardens of Trengwainton, south of Madron, are rich in semi-tropical plants. An attractive stream bubbles through wooded lawns backed by banks of bright rhododendrons.

The moorland to the north of Madron is rich in prehistoric relics. Alongside the road crossing the peninsula to Morvah stands Lanyon Quoit, an exposed Neolithic chamber-tomb consisting of a mighty capstone supported by three upright stones. To the north-west a lane leads from a roadside schoolhouse at Bosullow Common to the Mên-an-Tol or 'holed stone' which stands between two upright stones. Local children were said to be cured of rickets by being passed through the stone against the sun. In a field further along the track stands Maen Scryfa or 'inscribed stone', said to mark the grave of a 6th-century chieftain.

On a hilltop to the south-west of the schoolhouse are Chun Castle and Quoit, the ruins of an Iron Age hill-fort and a Neolithic tomb.

Smugglers and Wreckers

The nefarious pursuit of smuggling, once described as a 'national failing', was nowhere more common than in Cornwall. Remote from the rest of England and easily accessible from the Continent, it was here that the practice reached its height during the 18th century. The many narrow inlets, deep coves, long creeks and cave-riddled cliffs made the concealment of contraband easy, and smuggling became a winning game played with the Preventive forces. Wine, spirits, tobacco and bullion were the principal items brought ashore by the 'free-traders'. All levels of society were involved in this stealthy evasion of the revenue laws. Fishermen carried the goods from France and villagers helped get it ashore and distribute it inland. Magistrates and landowners turned a blind eye (possibly through personal involvement), customs officers took bribes, and it was not unknown for Revenue cutters to carry and land the very contraband they were empowered to seize.

Most notable of the Cornish smugglers were John and Harry Carter who operated in Mount's Bay, five miles up the coast from Marazion. As a boy John Carter called himself 'The King of Prussia' after his hero Frederick the Great. The name stuck, and one of the deep inlets from which he operated became known as Prussia Cove. Devout Methodists (swearing was forbidden in their company), the brothers owned a 160-ton cutter with 19 guns which they used for smuggling runs to Brittany. When they arrived home one day to find that the Excise had raided their sheds and confiscated their latest cargo, the brothers led their men to Penzance and broke into the Customs House, removing their own goods, but leaving everything else untouched. The Carters mounted a battery of small cannon on the clifftop near their base, and on one occasion, when the Revenue cutter *Faery* chased a smuggling boat into the cove, the brothers opened fire, and kept up the cannonade until the cutter withdrew. The inns, cottages, manor houses and, occasionally, churches of outlying fishing communities had secret caches in their walls or under their floors for concealing contraband. Excise officers who arrived in Polperro to seize a cellarful of brandy, found themselves threatened by a large cannon. The cellar was carefully watched until reinforcements arrived. When it was opened, the cellar was empty – the brandy had mysteriously been spirited away.

Wrecking, the practice of looting wrecked ships, was also a regular and often necessary way of life in Cornwall, for wages were low and poverty rife. In its mildest form it amounted to little more than beachcombing, gleaning from the shore what the sea had thrown up from a wreck. Less often it consisted of the organised plundering of the vessel itself, sometimes with scant regard for the well-being of any crew still aboard. Tales of wreckers coldbloodedly drowning sailors while they fought for cargo were not uncommon, but stories of wreckers deliberately luring ships onto the rocky coast at night by means of false lights contain little, if any, truth.

The attitude of most Cornish wreckers was best expressed by Parson Troutbeck of Scilly: 'We pray, O Lord, not that wrecks should occur, but that if they do, Thou wilt drive them into the Scilly Isles, for the benefit of the poor inhabitants.'

'Smugglers surprised' and (inset) smugglers' refuge

Fishing

With over 250 miles of coastline, it is hardly surprising that fishing has been practised in Cornwall since Neolithic times. The heyday of the industry was between the mid-18th and mid-19th centuries, when every harbour, cove and inlet had its own fishing fleet. They served the local need for cheap food and provided France, Italy and Spain with a necessary requirement for fast days. Pilchards were the basis of the industry. They arrived in huge shoals close to the shore and were trapped by seine nets strung between three or four boats. A 'huer' posted on a nearby cliff would direct operations by signalling with a trumpet or white hoops. His semaphore-like signals and cry of 'Hevva!' gave the exact position of the shoal, allowing the boats to manoeuvre the net accurately, ready for shooting. A sturdy, white huer's house still exists on a headland at Newquay.

Pilchard catches were enormous, and it is recorded that in 1834, at St Ives, 10,000 hogshead of pilchard (30 million fish) were landed in just one hour. Drifting was also used to trap the shoals, but this method gained a bad reputation as it damaged the gills of the fish. In those early years of the 19th century, over 2,000 men were employed on

Cornish fishing boats, and 6,000 men, women and children on land. Most harbours had at least one fish-cellar or 'palace', a large undercover courtyard where the fish were salted, packed into barrels and pressed before being shipped overseas. The fish oil by-product was used as lamp fuel and rotten fish were spread on the fields as fertiliser. The smell created by this process was legendary, and many early forerunners of today's tourists were sent scurrying back across the Tamar by the intolerable stench. For many years the village of Polperro was jokingly known as Polstink.

The reason for the disappearance of the pilchard shoals in the mid-19th century is unknown, though most will agree that overfishing was certainly a contributory cause. Whatever the reason, the pilchard all but vanished and the fishing fleets dwindled. Two world wars also broke the continuity of the fishing tradition in many families and boats were left to rot as a new generation found less hazardous ways of earning a living.

Today's Cornish fishermen have to compete with trawlers and drifters from the east coast and Scotland as well as the mighty French and Russian vessels whose purse-seine nets scour the sea-bed of coastal waters. Mackerel are the chief catch, together with skate, herring, sole and whiting, and many local fishermen also supplement their living by fishing for crab, lobster and crayfish. Using radar, echo-sounders and other modern devices they glean what they can from the sea, but the Cornish fishing industry today is only a shadow of its former self. Newlyn can still boast a sizeable fishing fleet, and smaller numbers sail from Mevagissey, Falmouth, Newquay, Padstow and Looe.

Mackerel are the main catch for today's Cornish fishermen

Marazion

Map Ref: 90SW5130

Facing St Michael's Mount, to which it is linked by a cobbled causeway at low tide, Marazion is an attractive town of Georgian and Victorian houses and old inns built to serve pilgrims at their journey's end. Although Jews are said to have smelted tin nearby in the Middle Ages, the town's strange name derives from 'Marghas Vyghan', Cornish for 'Little Market', just as Market Jew Street in Penzance stems from 'Marghas Yow' or 'Thursday Market'.

Behind the fine shingle beach to the west is a marshy lagoon, a bird sanctuary often visited by spoonbills, bitterns and other waterfowl. The tiny hamlet of St Hilary, a couple of miles east of Marazion, is reached by narrow lanes of wild flowers. The spired church contains unusual decorations and sculptures dating from the 1920s.

AA recommends:
Hotels: Mount Haven, Turnpike Rd, 2-star, *tel.* (0736) 710249
◇ Cutty Sark, The Square, 1-star, *tel.* (0736) 710334
Self Catering: ◇ Clipper, Coach House, Schooner & Gun Room Flats, *tel.* (0736) 731878

Mawgan

Map Ref: 91SW7125

This string of pretty cottages, inn, shop and church lies in a wooded valley south of the Helford River. To the north are deep, winding creeks and to the south, the flat, exposed heathland of the Lizard plateau. Trelowarren, for 500 years the home of the Vyvyan family, lies in parkland nearby. This Tudor house has a neo-Gothic chapel and the stables to the rear contain a restaurant and craft centre.

Across the downs to the south, 11 vast dish-aerials of British Telecom's Goonhilly Earth Station rise from the flat landscape, picking up messages, television signals and telephone calls from satellites 22,000 miles out in space. By way of contrast, the site is surrounded by many circular burial mounds built by Bronze Age men.

Mawnan Smith

Map Ref: 91SW7827

Exotic and semi-tropical plants flourish in the mild coastal area surrounding this quiet village with its thatched inn and cottages. The 13th-century church stands amidst trees on the cliff-edge overlooking the mouth of the Helford River. To the north of the village are the gardens of Penjerrick where lawns

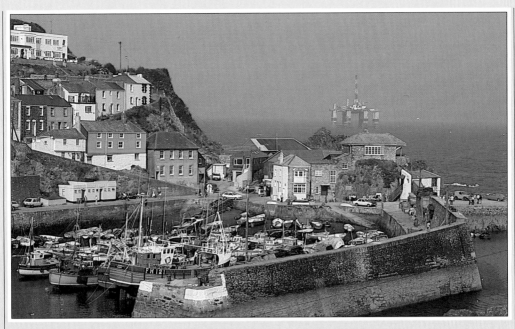

and fine shrubs surround a house belonging to the Fox family. To the south, the National Trust gardens of Glendurgan follow a valley leading steeply to the river's edge and the quaint village of Durgan. The garden boasts a maze and many fine specimen shrubs and trees. Along the riverbank to the west is Helford Passage with its waterside Ferry Boat Inn and passenger ferry across to Helford on the opposite bank. Tortuous lanes lead west from Mawnan Smith to Porth Navas, a creekside hamlet popular with the yachting fraternity and famed for its oysters, grown in beds owned by the Duchy of Cornwall Oyster Farm.

AA recommends:
Hotels: Budock Vean, 3-star, *tel.* (0326) 250288
Meudon, 3-star Country House Hotel, *tel.* (0326) 250541
Trelawne, 3-star, *tel.* (0326) 250226
Restaurant: ◇ Dionysus, 1-fork, *tel.* (0326) 250714
Garage: ◇ Goldmartin (Alanco Mtr Svcs), *tel.* (0326) 250394

Mevagissey

Map Ref: 92SX0144

Rows of colour-washed cob cottages descend the steep sides of a valley to a picturesque natural harbour bobbing with boats. Although Mevagissey is still primarily a fishing port, tourists have tended to replace pilchards as a source of income in recent years. Early this century over 100 luggers crammed into the inner harbour which was lined with fishing-stores and net-lofts. Pilchards were salted in deep quayside pits before being pressed into barrels by the fishwives. Pack-mules carried baskets of fish through the streets, though some were so narrow that the baskets had to be carried on poles by men, one behind the other. As well as providing tasty food, pilchards also provided oil

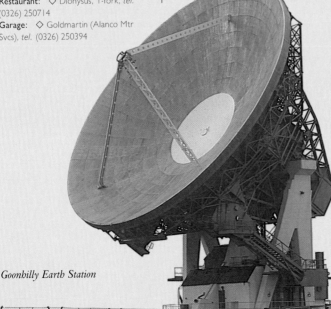

Goonhilly Earth Station

Mevagissey's inner harbour

which was used in lamps for light and warmth, hence the local fishermens' rhyme: 'Food, heat and light, All in one night.'

Despite the proliferation of gift-shops and cafés, the old port has retained much of its character and its leaning buildings and quaint courtyards are hung with flowers in summertime. A few 'old-timers' still sit and put the world to rights on a wooden quayside bench known as 'Parliament'. An old boat-building shed at the harbour's edge now contains a folk museum and there is an extensive model railway exhibition in the town.

Round the headland to the north is the small clay port of Pentewan, now a popular place for caravan holidays. South lies Gorran Haven, its cluster of cottages, sandy beach and small quay surrounded by high, protective cliffs.

AA recommends:
Hotels: Spa, Polkirt Hill, 2-star, *tel.* (0726) 842244
Tremarne, Polkirt Hill, 2-star, *tel.* (0726) 842213
Trevalsa Court, Polstreath, 2-star, *tel.* (0726) 842468
Sharksfin, The Quay, 1-star, *tel.* (0726) 843241
Self Catering: ◇ Coach House, Goose & Donner Cottage, Vicarage Hill, *tel.* (0726) 842427
Guesthouses: Headlands Hotel, Polkirt Hill, *tel.* (0726) 843453
Mevagissey House, Vicarage Hill, *tel.* (0726) 842427
◇ Valley Park Private Hotel, Tregoney Hill, *tel.* (0726) 842347
Treleaven (farmhouse), *tel.* (0726) 842413
Ship (Inn), Fore St, *tel.* (0726) 843324
Garage: ◇ Ava Mtrs, Valley Rd, *tel.* (0726) 843339

The Cheesewring, a natural rock formation at the edge of a quarry

Minions

Map Ref: 95SX2671

A scattered hamlet of low slate-hung houses lashed by wind and rain, Minions stands on the south-east fringe of Bodmin Moor. It boasts the highest pub in Cornwall, a popular place with the quarry-workers and miners who lived here up to this century. Blue-grey granite from nearby Cheesewring quarry and rich copper, tin and lead-ore from the Caradon mines were transported by rail from here to Looe. On the rim of the quarry stands the Cheesewring itself, a strange natural formation of flattish rocks. Below the quarry is a small rocky dwelling where lived Daniel Gumb, an eccentric quarry-worker who taught himself geometry and astronomy. Set in the springy turf west of Minions are The Hurlers, three Bronze Age stone circles said to be men turned to stone for playing the Cornish sport of hurling on a Sunday. A gold cup of the same period found nearby is now displayed in the British Museum.

AA recommends:
Self Catering: ◇ Cheesewring Farm (flat), *tel.* (0579) 62200

Morwenstow

Map Ref: 95SS2015

The hamlet of Morwenstow at Cornwall's northernmost tip is best known for its eccentric vicar-poet, Robert Stephen Hawker. He came to this thinly populated parish in 1834 and spent 40 years serving 'a mixed multitude of smugglers, wreckers and dissenters'.

He was much concerned with the fate of mariners wrecked on this treacherous coast and often scrambled down the high cliffs to carry back the bodies of drowned seamen for a Christian burial. He strode around the parish in long sea-boots, a fisherman's jersey and a purple coat and spent much time writing poetry in a cliff-edge hut made of driftwood. Best remembered for reviving the custom of the Harvest Festival and for his poem, *The Song of the Western Men*, which has become the Cornish national anthem, he is also renowned for dressing up as a mermaid and for excommunicating one of his cats for catching a mouse on Sunday.

The doorway of the part-Norman church is carved with the heads of men and beasts, and the unusual chimneys of the adjacent rectory are based on two Oxford colleges, three church towers and Hawker's mother's gravestone.

Mousehole

Map Ref: 90SW4626

A patchwork of fields leads down to the village of Mousehole, one of Cornwall's most ancient ports. Its tiers of pretty cottages, narrow alleyways and flowery courtyards attract many summer visitors, but the character of this fishing village remains unspoilt. There are several explanations for its odd name, pronounced 'Mouzell' by the local people. It may stem from the Cornish words for 'maiden's stream' or 'gull basin', or it may simply refer to a small cave in nearby cliffs. In 1595 the village was raided by Spanish privateers and razed to the ground. The only building to survive was the manor house, later to become the Keigwin Arms Inn and now a private dwelling. The village became a centre for pilchard fishing and up to 100 years ago over 400 boats packed into the snug refuge of its harbour walls.

Another tragedy struck the village in December 1981 when the eight Mousehole men who crewed the Penlee lifeboat 'Solomon Browne' perished while attempting to rescue the crew of the 'Union Star' which had run aground in terrible weather a few miles to the south.

Tom Bawcock's Eve, celebrated in the village's one pub, 'The Ship', every 23 December, recalls the time a local fisherman saved the local people from famine by sailing out in a storm and returning with a large catch of seven sorts of fish. A special dish, 'Starry-gazy pie', with fish-heads poking up through the

B U D E
HOLSWORTHY
Map

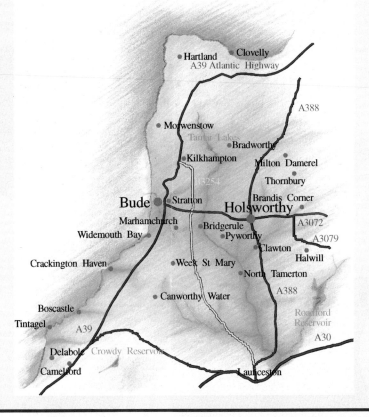

Hartland • • Clovelly
A39 Atlantic Highway

A388

• Morwenstow
Tamar Lakes
• Bradworthy
• Kilkhampton
Milton Damerel •
Thornbury •
Bude • • Stratton   Brandis Corner •
                Holsworthy
• Marhamchurch   A3072
Widemouth Bay •   • Bridgerule   A3079
                     • Pyworthy
                        • Clawton   • Halwill
Crackington Haven   • Week St Mary
                                    • North Tamerton
Boscastle •   • Canworthy Water   A388
Tintagel •   Roadford
      A39   Reservoir
• Delabole   Crowdy Reservoir   A30
Camelford •   Launceston •

BUDE

The Bude Tourist Information Centre is now part of the much larger Bude Visitor Centre situated in the Crescent Car Park, which now also incorporates displays and information material from the North Cornwall Heritage Coast & Countryside service.

The Centre is open daily throughout the season and provides a local accommodation finding service and a "book a bed ahead" service. A comprehensive range of literature is also available to the visitor seeking information of all kind.

PHONE (0288) 354240

HOLSWORTHY

Holsworthy Information Centre may be found in the Manor Car Park in the centre of the town, just behind the library. It is open throughout the season, and provides a local accommodation finding service. A range of information about the surrounding area is also carried, and the staff would be pleased to help with any of your queries.

PHONE (0409) 254185

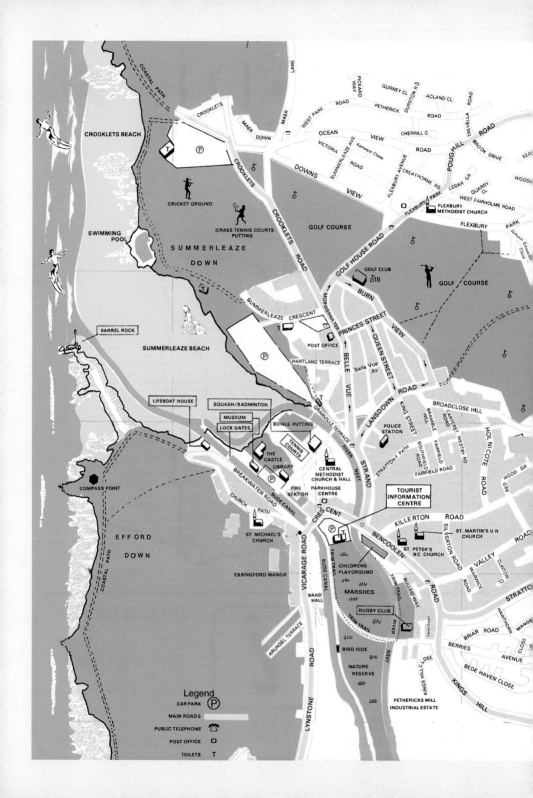

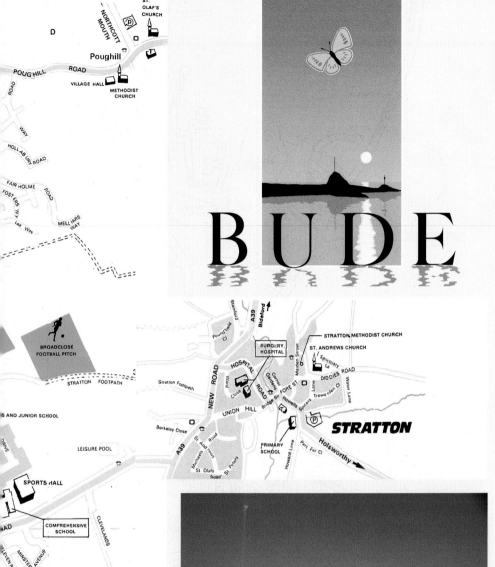

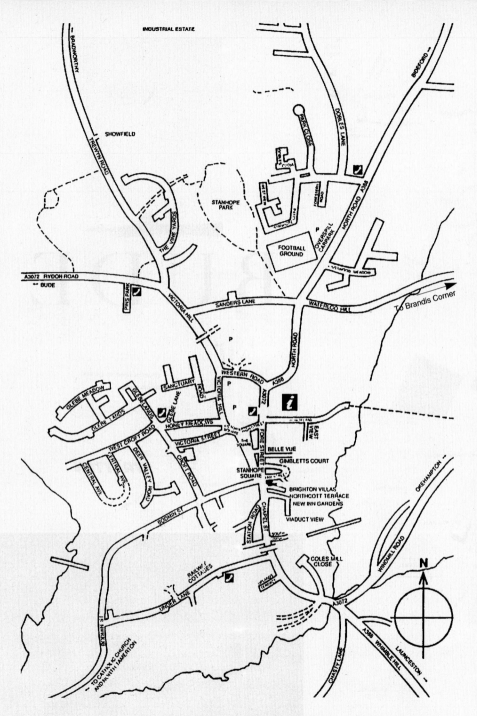

HOLSWORTHY

Main picture: the harbour at Mousehole. Inset: memorial to the crew of the Penlee lifeboat, 1981

pastry, is still baked and eaten in his honour.

Injured and oiled birds are cared for at Mousehole Bird Sanctuary. At Paul, one mile inland, the prominent church tower acts as a day-mark to shipping. In the churchyard is a memorial to Dolly Pentreath, the fishwife who died in 1777 and is said to have been the last person to converse only in Cornish. There has been a healthy revival of the language in recent years.

AA recommends:
Hotels: Carn Du, Raginnis Hill, 2-star, *tel.* (0736) 731233
Lobster Pot, 2-star, *tel.* (0736) 731251
Self Catering: ◇ Flats 1, 2 & 3 Old Coastguard Apartment, *tel.* (0736) 731222
Guesthouse: Tavis Vor, *tel.* (0736) 731306

Mullion harbour, a safe refuge from rough seas off the Lizard

Mullion

Map Ref: 91SW6719

This compactly grouped village of sturdy cottages has at its centre a broad-towered church inside which are some remarkable carved bench-ends depicting surprisingly bawdy scenes. A road descends 200ft from the edge of the Lizard plateau to Mullion harbour or Porth Mellin, owned by the National Trust. The solid granite piers of the harbour bear the full brunt of south-westerly gales whipping off the Atlantic. Exhilarating footpath walks lead north to Polurrian beach or south over cliffs of scented thyme and sea-thrift to Kynance Cove.

AA recommends:
Hotels: Polurrian, 3-star, *tel.* (0326) 240421
Mullion Cove, 2-star, *tel.* (0326) 240328
Self Catering: ◇ Trenance Farm Cottages, *tel.* (0326) 240639
◇ Pedn-y-ke Holiday Bungalows, *tel.* (0326) 240421
Guesthouses: ◇ Belle Vue, *tel.* (0326) 240483
Henscath House, Mullion Cove, *tel.* (0326) 240537
Trenowyth House Private Hotel, Mullion Cove, *tel.* (0326) 240486
◇ Old Inn, Church Town, *tel.* (0326) 240240
Campsites: Franchis, Cury Cross Lanes, 3-pennants, *tel.* (0326) 240301
Mullion Holiday Park, Ruan Minor, 3-pennants, *tel.* (0326) 240428
◇ Criggan Mill Caravans, Mullion Cove, 2-pennants, *tel.* (0326) 240496
Teneriffe Farm Caravan Site, 1-pennant, *tel.* (0326) 240293
Garage: Mullion *tel.* (0326) 240332

The Mylors

Map Ref: 91SW8235

The small village and wharf of Mylor Bridge lies at the head of a long creek off Carrick Roads. To the east is Mylor Churchtown where the waterside church and separate bell-tower are idyllically set amidst trees. The churchyard contains an impressive granite Celtic cross and the tombstone of Joseph Crapp, a local shipwright, who died in 1770. It reads:

Alass frend Joseph
His end was all most Sudden
As thou a mandate came
Express from Heaven –
His foot, it slip and he did fall
Help help he cries, and that was all.

Oyster-dredging working-boats can often be seen in Restronguet Creek to the north of Mylor Bridge. A 13th-century thatched inn, The Pandora, stands at the creekside and a ferry can be taken across to Feock.

Newlyn

Map Ref: 90SW4628

A favourite haunt of artists since Edwardian times, Newlyn is Cornwall's largest fishing port, a haven for deep-sea trawlers and small inshore craft. The long arms of its 100-year-old harbour walls enclose a tiny 15th-century pier behind which a hillside of fishermen's cottages rises above a high road known as 'Mount Misery'. Here the wives of the fishermen waited and watched for the return of the fleet. At the harbour's edge are several salty pubs, some converted fish-cellars and net-making lofts and a Deep Sea Fishermen's Mission. Catches bought at the early morning fish market are either canned in the town or sent by rail from neighbouring Penzance to Billingsgate.

It was the clear light and bustling life of the port that attracted the artist Stanhope Forbes, founder of the Newlyn School of Artists. Its best-known members were Frank Bramley, Norman Garstin, Lamorna Birch, Alfred Munnings and Laura Knight, and examples of their work, together with paintings and sculpture by the present-day generation of Newlyn artists, can be seen in Newlyn Art Gallery and at Penlee House in Penzance.

Above: Newlyn, early morning fish market – a good catch
Left: the busy port has long been a favourite with artists

The Art Colonies

The mild climate, the exceptionally clear light and Mediterranean atmosphere which first attracted artists to west Cornwall over a century ago, still draw them today, and the area west of Hayle probably contains the greatest concentration of painters, sculptors and craftsmen anywhere in Britain outside London.

In the 19th century, as today, the artistic life of Cornwall centred around the fishing villages of St Ives and Newlyn, 10 miles apart on opposite sides of the Penwith peninsula. The Irish painter Stanhope Forbes arrived in Newlyn for a few days in 1884, and stayed on. He met several other painters whom he had known in Brittany and, together with Walter Langley, Frank Bramley, Norman Garstin and Elizabeth Armstrong (later to become his wife), Forbes formed the Newlyn School of Painting. The rocky coastline, sheltered valleys, high moorland and granite outcrops provided ideal subject-matter for their paintings, but their most famous works portrayed the day-to-day life of the fishing village itself.

That same period also found many largely foreign artists settling in St Ives. Anders Zorn, Louis Grier, Julius Olsson, Algernon Talmage, Adrian Stokes, Borlase Smart and Arnesby Brown all set up studios, and formed the St Ives Arts Club in 1888.

The early years of this century found a revival of spirit in Newlyn with the arrival of Laura Knight and Dod Procter. Together with S J Lamorna Birch they produced many fine landscape paintings of the coast south of Newlyn.

The 1920s found the leading artists Ben Nicholson and Christopher Wood settling in St Ives where they 'discovered' Alfred Wallis, a retired fisherman whose primitive paintings on scraps of wood were to prove very influential. Nicholson's first wife, the sculptor, Barbara Hepworth, began to work in the town and the world-famous potter Bernard Leach set up the Leach Pottery at Higher Stennack. By the 1960s a new generation of artists had joined the St Ives colony, including Roger Hilton, Peter Lanyon, Bryan Wynter, Terry Frost and Patrick Heron. As St Ives has developed as a tourist town so many artists have moved to nearby villages, but examples of work by the leading artists can be seen in the Penwith Society of Arts gallery in Back Road West, and the St Ives Society of Artists gallery in the old Mariners' Church in Norway Square. The Wills Lane Gallery and the Salt House Gallery also contain recent work by the latest generation of St Ives artists. Many sculptures by Dame Barbara Hepworth, together with her workshop and tools, can be seen at the Barbara Hepworth Museum in Back Street.

A permanent exhibition of paintings by the Newlyn School can be seen at Penlee House in Penzance, while the Newlyn Art Gallery, which gave many original members of the Newlyn School a showcase for their work, still contains a few examples of their work as well as work by the many fine painters, potters and sculptors still working in the town.

Painting by Elizabeth Armstrong, of the Newlyn School of Artists

World class surfing at Newquay

gardens and in the grounds a barn contains an unusual Museum of Lawnmowers.

Beside the A3058 road to Summercourt is one of Cornwall's most unusual tourist attractions, DairyLand, where 160 cows are milked to music in a 'merry-go-round' parlour. The Country Life Museum on the same site contains many interesting old farm tools and implements. South of Newquay, near St Newlyn East, the Lappa Valley Railway carries you behind a miniature engine along a two-mile stretch of an old GWR line.

AA recommends:
Hotels: ◇ Glendorgal, Lusty Glaze Rd, 3-star, *tel.* (0637) 874937
Hotel Riviera, Lusty Glaze Rd, 3-star, *tel.* (0637) 874251
Porth Veor Manor House, Porthway, 2-star *tel.* (0637) 873274
Whipsiderry, Trevelgue Rd, Porth, 2-star, *tel.* (0637) 874777
Self Catering: ◇ The Barn, *tel.* (0637) 874695
◇ Treverrick House, at Gunmowsshop, *tel.* (087251) 226
Guesthouses: Copper Beech Hotel, 70 Edgcumbe Ave, *tel.* (0637) 873376
Porth Enodoc, 4 Esplanade Rd, Pentire, *tel.* (0637) 872372
Priory Lodge Hotel, Mount Wise, *tel.* (0637) 874111
◇ Rumours Hotel, 89 Henver Rd, *tel.* (0637) 872170
Garages: Globe, East Rd, Quintrell Downs, *tel.* (0637) 872410
Treloggan Mtr Svcs, Plot 1, Treloggan Ind Est, *tel.* (0637) 874884 (day) & 876774 (night)

Newquay

Map Ref: 91SW8161

Victorian holidaymakers were attracted to Newquay's bracing beaches, and large hotels soon sprang up in the town and on the grassy headlands. Now Cornwall's largest and most popular holiday resort, with all the attendant facilities, Newquay overlooks several fine sandy beaches sheltered by spectacular high cliffs and headlands. Surfers can enjoy the high, green Atlantic rollers of Fistral beach; young couples the lively nightlife; and families the wide range of entertainment from crazy golf, swimming pools and sailing to season shows at the Cosy Nook Theatre. There is an excellent golf course, a boating lake and a large zoo in Trenance Park. High on a headland overlooking the old harbour stands a whitewashed stone Huer's Hut, a reminder of the importance of Newquay's former pilchard fishing industry. From here the huer kept a watch for shoals of fish far out to sea, alerting the fleet with cries of 'Hevva! Hevva!' and guiding them to the right spot by signalling with bats known as 'bushes'.

In a peaceful, wooded valley a few miles south-east from bustling Newquay is the gabled Elizabethan manor house of Trerice, owned by the National Trust. Rebuilt in 1571 by Sir John Arundell, it contains fine moulded plaster ceilings, broad fireplaces, walnut and oak furniture and several colourful tapestries. The hall, overlooked by a musician's gallery, is lit by a vast window containing 576 panes of glass. The house is surrounded by well-tended

A wooden horse round, one of many unusual items to be seen at the Country Life Museum and DairyLand

62

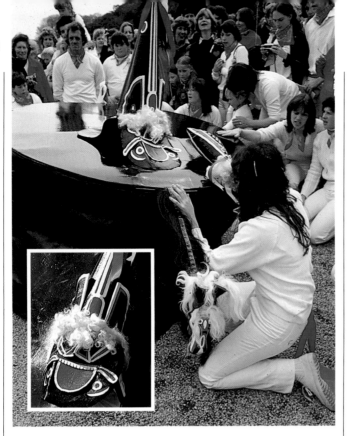

Padstow's 'Obby 'Oss takes to the streets on May Day
Inset: the 'Obby 'Oss mask

Campsite: Dennis Cove Leisure Park, Dennis Cove, 2-pennant, *tel.* (0841) 532349
Garage: Padstow (J C Tregoning & Son), Trecerus Ind Est, *tel.* (0841) 532521 (day) & 520033 (night)

Par

Map Ref: 92SX0753

The industrialist Joseph Treffry built the port of Par on reclaimed land. Today the giant firm of English China Clays uses it as its chief outlet and the beach and bay are white with clay-dust.

South-west of the town, at Biscovey, are the Mid-Cornwall Galleries and Craft Centre. Before the building of the port, the sea reached as far inland as the village of Tywardreath, or 'House on the strand', a charming group of buildings immortalised in a Daphne du Maurier novel of that name. At Polmear, east of Par, stands a delightful row of old almshouses. From here a road leads south to the tiny sandy cove of Polkerris with its small pier and Elizabethan 'Pilchard Palace'. A clifftop walk south leads to the red-and-white striped beacon on Gribbin Head.

AA recommends:
Campsite: Mount Holiday Park, The Mount, 3-pennants, *tel.* (072681) 2616
Garage: St Andrews Road Garage, St Andrews Rd, *tel.* (072681) 2318 (day) & 2189 (night)

Penryn

Map Ref: 91SW7834

Penryn flourished as a mediaeval port largely because of Glasney

Padstow

Map Ref: 92SW9175

Its sheltered position in the Camel estuary makes Padstow a welcome north-coast haven for shipping. It became an important trading and ship-building port, but the formation of the Doom Bar sandbank across the mouth of the estuary prevented large vessels using the harbour. Nevertheless, before World War II it was an important fishing port, with two fish trains leaving for Billingsgate daily from the specially built fish quay. It declined after the war, but is now seeing a revival, with many fishing boats by the quay once more.

The attractive mediaeval town has remained largely unspoilt, its warren of narrow streets and alleys lined with slate-hung and pastel-coloured houses. Abbey House on the South Quay dates from the 15th century while the Court House of Sir Walter Raleigh stands on the North Quay. Many emigrants left for America last century from the harbour. St Petroc, Cornwall's chief saint, landed at Padstow from Ireland in the 6th century, and the church dedicated to him has a fine Elizabethan pulpit and some amusing bench-ends, one of which shows the devil disguised as a fox preaching to a congregation of geese. Prideaux Place stands at the top of the town, but is not open to the public. Nearby are the Tropical Bird and Butterfly Gardens where colourful birds fly loose in an indoor jungle setting.

Padstow's Hobby Horse, or 'Obby 'Oss, takes to the flower- and flag-decked streets on 1 May, accompanied by a drum and accordian band. With swirling black skirt and grinning mask, the 'Oss cavorts through the crowds, and the slow song and rhythmic thud of the drums gives this colourful event a distinctly pagan feel.

AA recommends:
Hotels: Metropole, Station Rd, 3-star, *tel.* (0841) 532486
Old Custom House Inn, South Quay, 2-star, *tel.* (0841) 532359
Restaurant: Seafood, 2-forks 1-rosette, *tel.* (0841) 532485
Self Catering: ◇ Martinette & St Martins, Trevone, *tel.* (0752) 563594
◇ Flats 1, 2 & 3, Raintree House, Windmill, *tel.* (0841) 520358
Guesthouses: Alexandra, 30 Dennis Rd, *tel.* (0841) 532503
Dower House Private Hotel, Fentonluna Ln, *tel.* (0841) 532317
Tregea Hotel, High St, *tel.* (0841) 532455
◇ Woodlands Hotel, Treator, *tel.* (0841) 532426

Polkerris Bay, which has an Elizabethan Pilchard Palace

College, a collegiate church and centre of learning founded in the 13th century. It was closed at the Dissolution of the Monasteries, and all that remains is a small fragment of church pillar.

The old character of the distinctive town has recently been painstakingly restored. Its Georgian houses, cobbled square, slate-hung buildings and cosy courtyards stand astride a spur of land between two deep valleys leading down to old wharves and a harbour. Up-river from Falmouth, Penryn was granted its Charter in 1236 and flourished as a port in Tudor times. Stone quarried in the nearby parish of Mabe was exported from here last century, but as Falmouth's importance as a port increased, so Penryn's role declined.

Near the village of Mabe Burnthouse, west of Penryn, are Argal and College reservoirs where, with the proper licence, anglers may fish for brown and rainbow trout. The much larger Stithians reservoir, further west, also offers sailing and windsurfing facilities.

AA recommends:
Garage: ◇ Edgcumbe Service Station, Edgcumbe, Rame, *tel.* (0209) 860289

Penzance

Map Ref: 90SW4730

A lively, spacious town of great character, Penzance is worthy of lengthy exploration. The long arms of the piers were constructed in the 17th century to protect the town from pirates, but not before it had been sacked and partly destroyed, like neighbouring Newlyn and Mousehole, by the Spanish in 1595. It became the chief coinage town for the west of England and its market attracted buyers and sellers from a wide area.

The arrival of the railway in 1859 provided an efficient means of dispatching locally caught fish, flowers and vegetables direct to London. Its sheltered position at the western end of Mount's Bay and its

mild climate also made Penzance a fashionable watering place. Large hotels sprang up facing Cornwall's only 'promenade' and handsome Georgian, Victorian and Regency buildings, terraces and squares can still be found on the south side of the town. The wide main thoroughfare, Market Jew Street, rises in a gentle curve, a high stone-stepped pavement to one side. At its head a statue to Penzance's most famous son, Sir Humphry Davy, miners' lamp in hand, stands in front of the Ionic pillars and dome of the Market Hall. Causewayhead, now traffic-free, leads up to a small market, and in Alverton Street can be found a museum containing displays of rare minerals, rock specimens and fossils.

Running down to the harbour from the Market Hall is Chapel Street, the town's most fascinating thoroughfare, lined with 18th- and 19th-century houses and shopfronts. The elaborate façade of the Georgian Egyptian House, now partly a National Trust shop, faces the Union Hotel, whose Georgian façade hides an Elizabethan interior. Scorch marks on the stonework inside the doorway could be the result of the Spanish attack 400 years ago. Nelson's victory and death were first announced from a minstrel's gallery in the hotel's Assembly Room. At the rear of the building stands the shell of one of the oldest theatres in Britain, which opened in 1787. Further along Chapel Street are the ancient Turk's Head Inn and the Admiral Benbow Inn, with a model smuggler astride its roof acting as a reminder of how much the early wealth of the town was gained. Opposite is the Museum of Nautical Art which contains items recovered from wrecks around the coast of Cornwall and the Isles of Scilly. Elizabeth Branwell, mother of the Brontë sisters, lived in Chapel Street, close to the Church of St Mary, overlooking the harbour.

Semi-tropical shrubs and flowers surround a Victorian bandstand in

Model smuggler on the roof of the Admiral Benbow Inn

Morrab Gardens, while rare trees and shrubs can be seen in Penlee Memorial Gardens, together with a local history museum and paintings by the Newlyn School of Painters in Penlee House.

Regular boat and helicopter links with the Isles of Scilly are maintained throughout the year.

AA recommends:
Hotels: Higher Faugan, Newlyn, 3-star Country House Hotel, *tel.* (0736) 62076
Mount Prospect, Britons Hill, 3-star, *tel.* (0736) 63117
Estoril, 46 Morrab Rd, 1-star, *tel.* (0736) 62468
Tarbert, 11-12 Clarence St, 1-star, *tel.* (0736) 63758
Self Catering: ◇ Carne House, Newlyn (flats), *tel.* (062882) 5989
◇ Egyptian House, Chapel St (flats), *tel.* (062882) 5925
Guesthouses: Camilla Hotel, Regent Ter, *tel.* (0736) 63771
Dunedin, Alexandra Rd, *tel.* (0736) 62652
Penmorvah Hotel, Alexandra Rd, *tel.* (0736) 63711
◇ Pentrea Hotel, Alexandra Rd, *tel.* (0736) 69576
Campsite: Bone Valley Caravan Park, Heamoore, 2-pennants, *tel.* (0736) 60313
Garages: Jenning Street (R C Pender & Sons) Jenning St, *tel.* (0736) 65366 (day) & 60632 (night)
◇ Sheffield Garage, Sheffield, *tel.* (0736) 731350 (day) & 64139 (night)
Trelawny, Morrab Rd, *tel.* (0736) 62717

Boats at anchor in the sheltered harbour of Penzance

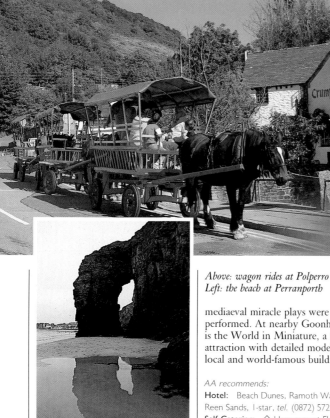

Above: wagon rides at Polperro
Left: the beach at Perranporth

Perranporth

Map Ref: 91SW7554

This popular family resort lies at the southern end of a three-mile beach of golden sand. Perranporth was originally a mining community but the remains of mine buildings have long ago been swallowed by the encroaching sand. The author Winston Graham wrote the first of his *Poldark* books here, using a combination of real and fictitious people and places to weave a story of 18th- and 19th-century mining families. To experience the atmosphere of these popular novels, walk south along the cliffs to Trevellas Coombe and St Agnes.

The odd name of the parish, Perranzabuloe, means 'Piran in the sands' and it was in the centre of the dunes north of Perranporth that the patron saint of tinners, St Piran, founded a chapel in the 6th century. An oratory-chapel was later built on the site, but this was engulfed by the sand. In 1835 the 'Lost Church' was rediscovered and encased in a protective shell. However, the site was almost permanently flooded and in 1980 the local council re-covered the oratory with sand, marking the spot with a memorial stone. A tall cross stands some distance away.

East of Perranporth, near the village of Rose, is Piran Round, an Iron Age fort transformed into a circular 'playing place', where mediaeval miracle plays were performed. At nearby Goonhavern is the World in Miniature, a tourist attraction with detailed models of local and world-famous buildings.

AA recommends:
Hotel: Beach Dunes, Ramoth Way, Reen Sands, 1-star, *tel.* (0872) 572263
Self Catering: ◇ Heronscourt Flats, The Gounce, Beach Rd, *tel.* (0872) 572168 Leycroft, Perrancombe, *tel.* (0872) 573044
Guesthouses: Cellar Cove Hotel, Droskyn Way, *tel.* (0872) 572110 Fairview Hotel, Tywarnhayle Rd, *tel.* (0872) 572278 Lamorna Private Hotel, Tywarnhayle Rd, *tel.* (0872) 573398 Villa Margarita Private Hotel, Bolingey, *tel.* (0872) 572063
Campsites: Perran Sands Holiday Centre, 5-pennants, *tel.* (0872) 573551 Perranporth Camping & Touring Site, Budnick Rd. 4-pennants, *tel.* (0872) 572174

Polperro

Map Ref: 92SX2051

The most timeless, picturesque and photogenic of all Cornish fishing villages, Polperro nestles in a green valley snaking inland from a small harbour guarded by jagged rocks. Colour-washed cottages rise in tiers above a jumble of unique and intriguing buildings, wound about with narrow alleys. Tales of local smuggling activities concerning rum and tobacco are legion, and it was not by chance that the first Preventive Service station was built nearby. But until the last century, fishing was the chief occupation of the villagers, the smell of pilchards becoming so strong that neighbouring people referred to Polperro as 'Polstink'. Colourful fishing boats still crowd the harbour and the village has retained the atmosphere of a fishing community, with its own fishermen's choir. Among the many old inns, cottages, studios and gift shops, look for the House-on-Props by the Roman Bridge, and the house of Dr Jonathan Couch, village doctor, naturalist and grandfather of Sir Arthur Quiller-Couch.

Parking is restricted to the top of the valley, near the historic Crumplehorn Mill, but at the height of the season the streets become clogged with visitors. Try to visit the village out of season to savour its unique character.

AA recommends:
Hotel: Claremont, 1-star, *tel.* (0503) 72241
Restaurant: ◇ Kitchen at Polperro, Fish na Bridge, 1-fork, *tel.* (0503) 72780
Self Catering: ◇ Beville Cottage, The Coombes, *tel.* (0503) 72485 ◇ Crumplehorn Cottages 1 & 2, *tel.* (0503) 72274 ◇ Hael-a-Gwynt, Little Laney, *tel.* (0503) 72485 ◇ Seabreeze Cottage, 88 Carey Park, *tel.* (0503) 72274 ◇ Sunny Harbour Cottage, The Coombes, *tel.* (0503) 72274
Guesthouses: Landaviddy Manor, Landaviddy Ln, *tel.* (0503) 72210 Lanhael House, *tel.* (0503) 72428 ◇ Penryn House Hotel, The Coombes, *tel.* (0503) 72157
Campsite: Killigarth Manor Holiday Estate, 3-pennants, *tel.* (0503) 72216
Garage: ◇ Central (Granthurst), The Coombes, *tel.* (0503) 72341

Polperro, one of Cornwall's most charming fishing villages

Polzeath

Map Ref: 94SW9378

The much-loved former poet laureate, Sir John Betjeman, spent many of his childhood holidays on this eastern tip of the Camel estuary, and its villages and churches form the subject-matter of many of his poems. From the heights of Rumps Point and Pentire Point to the tamarisk-bordered lanes around Trebetherick, the air is bracing and wild flowers are plentiful. High surf breaks on the beach at Polzeath and the cliff caves and rock pools to the south are a children's paradise. The high grassy mound of Brea Hill, south of Trebetherick, looks out over the Doom Bar, a submerged sandbank on which many ships have come to grief. Sheltering behind the hill, on the edge of a golf course, is the tiny Church of St Enodoc, with Betjeman's grave. The church has several times almost been overwhelmed by the sand, and on one occasion, the vicar and congregation had to enter through a hole in the roof. A ferry runs from the nearby village of Rock across the estuary to Padstow.

AA recommends:
Hotel: ◇ Pentine Rocks, 2-star, *tel.* (020886) 2213
Self Catering: ◇ Polzeath Holiday Cottage & Apartments, *tel.* (020886) 2371 ◇ Westward (flats), *tel.* (020886) 3235
Guesthouse: White Lodge, Old Polzeath, *tel.* (020886) 2370

Porthcurno

Map Ref: 90SW3822

A broad beach of white sand dips into a sapphire sea in this small cove, sheltered by jagged arms of orange lichen-covered granite. Set on the cliffside overlooking the beach is the Minack Open-Air Theatre, a Greek-style amphitheatre where professional theatre companies perform during the summer months. Begun in 1923, it

Porthcurno's Minack open-air theatre, perched on the cliff

was created by Miss Rowena Cade and offers audiences a spectacular natural backdrop of sea, sand and cliff scenery.

Along a coastal footpath to the east is Treryn Dinas, an Iron Age cliff fort on a headland of pinnacled rock. The 66-ton Logan Rock can be rocked with one hand if you find the correct point of pressure, and in 1824 it was sent crashing off its perch by a young naval lieutenant. The Admiralty made him replace it at his own expense. Delightful Penberth Cove, with its old windlass and thatched cottages, lies over grassy cliffs to the north.

AA recommends:
Guesthouse: Corniche, Trebehor *tel.* (0736) 87685

Porthleven

Map Ref: 90SW6225

Still a working port with a small fishing fleet and boat-building yard, Porthleven was developed early last century for the export of tin-ore. Its long curved harbour is in three sections, the inner one capable of being sealed off from fierce south-westerly gales. A terrace of trim Victorian villas lines the east side of the harbour, facing an old waterside inn and lime-kilns, now converted into art galleries. A straggle of old cottages runs east along the crumbling clifftop above a long, steeply shelving beach. Further along the coast is the shingle barrier of Loe Bar, behind which lies Loe Pool, Cornwall's largest natural lake.

AA recommends:
Hotel: ◇ Torre Vean Manor, 1-star, *tel.* (0326) 562412
Self Catering: ◇ Harbourside Holiday Flats (1-4), *tel.* (0736) 62834

Boats of crab and lobster fishermen at rest in Port Isaac

Port Isaac

Map Ref: 94SW9980

A fishing harbour since the Middle Ages, this unspoilt huddle of slate cottages and fish-cellars is protected by high headlands. The small shingle beach faces an old inn, and narrow alleyways known as 'drangs' wind between the houses. The narrowest is known as 'Squeeze-Belly Alley'. Over the headland to the east is Portgaverne, a stony cove which, like its neighbour, was formerly used for the export of Delabole slate.

West of Port Isaac, and reached by a lane which loops inland, is Portquin, a tiny hamlet at the head of a sheltered inlet, now owned by the National Trust. Overlooking the inlet from a green clifftop is Doyden Castle, a folly built in 1839. The church at St Kew, a few miles inland, stands in an idyllic streamside setting and has some of the finest mediaeval glass in Cornwall.

AA recommends:
Hotels: Archer Farm Hotel, Trewetha, 2-star, *tel.* (0208) 880522
Castle Rock, 2-star, *tel.* (0208) 880300
◇ Slipway, The Harbour Front, 2-star, *tel.* (0208) 880264
Self Catering: ◇ CC Ref 314 E (Character Cottages), *tel.* (03955) 77001
◇ Trevathan Farm, St Endellion, *tel.* (0208) 880248
Guesthouses: Bay Hotel, 1 The Terrace, *tel.* (0208) 880380
◇ Fairholme, 30 Trewetha Lane, *tel.* (0208) 880397
St Andrews Hotel, The Terrace, *tel.* (0208) 880240
◇ Trethoway Hotel, 98 Fore St, *tel.* (0208) 880214

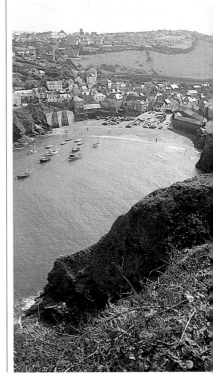

Porthtowan

Map Ref: 91SW6947

A long, peaceful valley, scarred with the waste of abandoned copper mines, winds down to a broad flat beach washed by high, powerful surf. Popular with the surfing set, this stretch of coast can be dangerous for inexperienced swimmers, and volunteer members of the Surf Life Saving Club put coloured flags on the beach to denote sea conditions. Red flags mean 'No swimming at all'. The road climbing steeply to the south, towards Redruth, passes Reg Morse's Farm Museum, a unique collection of farm machinery, tools and evocative domestic objects.

AA recommends:
Guesthouses: Beach Hotel, *tel.* (0209) 890228
◇ Torvean (farmhouse) Coast Rd, *tel.* (0209) 890536
Campsites: Rose Hill Park, Rose Hill, 3-pennants, *tel.* (0209) 890802
Porthtowan Tourist Park, Hilltop Cottage, Mile Hill, 3-pennants, *tel.* (0209) 890256

Portreath

Map Ref: 90SW6545

Now a popular family beach and small resort, well protected by surrounding high cliffs, Portreath was developed by Francis Basset to serve local mines. The Basset family who lived at nearby Tehidy estate, owned many of the tin and copper mines in the Redruth area. A long harbour was built for shipping ore and importing Welsh coal to fuel the mine engines, and one of Britain's earliest railway lines ran to the edge of the valley, the ore being lowered to the harbour by means of an ingenious incline railway. To one side of the harbour-mouth stands a white building known as the 'pepper-pot', from where ships were guided into the narrow harbour entrance. In the centre of the bay is Gull Rock, and the grassy headland to the west, from which a neat slice has been carved by the waves, is locally known as the 'Wedding Cake'.

AA recommends:
Guesthouse: Portreath Arms, The Square (inn), *tel.* (0209) 842534

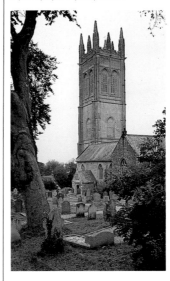

The church tower at Probus, the tallest in Cornwall

Remains of the incline railway (above), used to lower ore to the harbour at Portreath (top)

Probus

Map Ref: 91SW8947

The tallest church tower in Cornwall, 123 feet of magnificently carved moorstone, dominates Probus, once an important wool town. The broad main street leading up to the church boasts some large Georgian houses and old granite cottages with railed steps.
A mile east is Trewithen, the 17th-century home of the Hawkins family. Its attractive gardens of rare shrubs and colourful flowers are open in afternoons during the summer. Nearby, and also on the A390, is the County Demonstration Garden where you can compare different varieties of plants, fruit, vegetables and flowers grown under different conditions.

Redruth

Map Ref: 91SW6941

Once the capital of Cornish mining, Redruth is an old market town of great character, its architecture ranging in style from Georgian and Gothic to Victorian Italianate and Art Deco. Sprawling on either side of a deep valley, the town contains many interesting nooks and crannies. Its name stems from the Cornish words for the 'red river' which now runs under the foot of the steep main street. In narrow Cross Street is the former home of the Scottish inventor William Murdoch, the first house to be lit by gas, in 1792.

From the giant spans of the granite railway viaduct at the lower part of the town, a walk up tree-lined Trewirgie Road leads to Redruth's old churchtown. Alongside some well-restored cottages stands the Georgian Church of St Euny, which has a 15th-century tower. The lych-gate covers an extra-long coffin-rest for use following major mining accidents.

Towering above is the bracken-covered hill of Carn Brea, topped by a memorial to local mine-owner Francis Basset and a dramatically-sited castle. The northern slopes were once thickly wooded and the castle was used in Elizabethan and later times as a hunting lodge. It has been tastefully converted into a restaurant. Neolithic stone ramparts, partly rebuilt in the Iron Age, encircle the twin summits of Carn Brea, which can be reached by road from Carnkie, and hut circles can be seen.

AA recommends:
Hotels: Penventon, 3-star, *tel.* (0209) 214141
Aviary Court, Marys Well, Illogan, 2-star *tel.* (0209) 842256 (2m nw unclass)
Crossroads Motel Scorrier, 2-star, *tel.* (0209) 820551 (2m e of A30)
Self Catering: ◇ Rayle Farm Holiday Cottages, Bridge, Illogan, *tel.* (0209)) 842245
Campsites: Cambrose Farm Campsite, Portreath Rd, 3-pennants, *tel.* (0209)) 890747
Tehidy Caravan Park, Harris Mill, Illogan, 3-pennants, *tel.* (0209) 216489 (2m nw off B3300 on n side of A30)
Garage: Volks Eng, Wesley St, *tel.* (0209) 217161 (day) & 213842 (night)

St Agnes

Map Ref: 91SW7250

This former tin-mining village stands at the head of a steep valley winding down to Trevaunance Cove. The chimneys of ivy-clad engine-houses mark the sites of surrounding mines, bearing such names as Wheal Kitty, Blue Hills and Wheal Friendly. In the centre of the village, a stepped terrace of miners' cottages, known as 'Stippy-Stappy' descends a hill alongside the charming spired church. Lanes lined with old cob cottages and pretty gardens wind off the main street, and this bustling village also boasts a handsome Methodist church, several craft workshops and some welcoming pubs. Readers of Winston Graham's *Poldark* books may recognise St Agnes as the model for the village of St Ann in

Carn Brea Castle, Redruth

the books. There is a good small museum of local history, open in the season.

Just outside the village is St Agnes Leisure Park with plentiful attractions set in colourful, landscaped gardens. The Cornish artist John Opie was born in 1761 in a thatched cottage, 'Harmony Cot', east of St Agnes. Examples of his work can be seen in the County Museum in Truro.

Trevaunance Cove, at the mouth of the long coombe snaking down from the village, has a popular sand and shingle beach. Tin-ore was shipped from a small 18th-century quay, but this was swept away by a storm in 1934.

A footpath along the high cliffs to the west leads to St Agnes Head, with its dramatic view south along the rugged coastline. A walk to the summit of St Agnes Beacon will be rewarded with views as far as the

tors of Bodmin Moor. Further south is the charming green valley and cove of Chapel Porth, owned by the National Trust. On the cliff-edge to the north are the mine buildings of Wheal Coates and the Towanroath engine-house poised half-way down the cliffside.

AA recommends:
Hotels: Rose in Vale Country House, Rose in Vale, Mithian, 2-star Country House Hotel, *tel.* (087255) 2202
Rosemundy House, 2-star, *tel.* (087255) 2101
◇ Lamorna House, Chapel Porth Rd, Goonvrea, 1-star, *tel.* (087255) 2670
Sunholme, Goonvrea Rd, 1-star, *tel.* (087255) 2318
Guesthouses: Penkerris, Penwinnick Rd, *tel.* (087255) 2262
Porthvean Hotel, Churchtown, *tel.* (087255) 2581
Garage: Peterville & Dales, *tel.* (087255) 2296 (day) & 2877 (night)

Wheal Coates tin mine, St Agnes

St Austell

Map Ref: 92SX0152

This busy town became the capital of the china-clay country last century. Today its narrow streets and alleyways merge with modern shopping precincts and undercover markets. All the streets radiate from the delicately-carved 15th-century tower of Holy Trinity Church. Its original waggon roof is worth inspection, as is the magnificently timbered roof of the large Market Hall opposite. There are numerous interesting old inns, the most notable being the White Hart Hotel.

Those unique white pyramids of china-clay sand-spoil which dominate the landscape north of the town are sometimes known as the 'Cornish Alps'. It was William Cookworthy who first discovered large deposits of china-clay or kaolin in Cornwall in 1755. Originally used for making porcelain, it is now used for coating paper and in the manufacture of house-paint, some medicines and numerous other items. The massive industry that developed made Britain the world's leading exporter of china-clay, most being shipped from Fowey, Par and Charlestown. The giant firm of English China Clays are presently landscaping and planting grass on many of the white spoil-heaps to make them less prominent.

China-clay tips near Nanpean, a prominent feature of the landscape

Almost every one of the grey granite communities of the clay area, together with many other Cornish villages, boasts its own silver band, and each year they exhibit their prowess at a festival in the aptly-named village of Bugle.

A display of china-clay industry artefacts, equipment, clothes and locomotives can be seen at the Wheal Martyn Museum, a 19th-century clay-works situated in a deep, wooded valley two miles north of St Austell on the Bodmin road.

AA recommends:

Hotels: Carlyon Bay, Sea Rd, Carlyon Bay, 4-star, *tel.* (072681) 2304
Cliff Head, Sea Rd, Carlyon Bay, 3-star, *tel.* (072681) 2345
Porth Avallen, Sea Rd, Carlyon Bay, 3-star, *tel.* (072681) 2802
Boscundle Manor, Tregrehan, 2-star Country House Hotel, *tel.* (072681) 3557

Clifden, 36-39 Aylmer Sq, 2-star, *tel.* (0726) 73691
◇ Pier House, Harbour Front, Charlestown, 2-star, *tel.* (0726) 75272
◇ White Hart, Church St, 2-star, *tel.* (0726) 72100
Self Catering: ◇ Bosinver Farm & Holiday Centre, *tel.* (0726) 72128
◇ St Margarets Holiday Park, Polgooth, *tel.* (0726) 74283
Guesthouses: Alexandra Hotel, 52-54 Alexandra Rd, *tel.* (0726) 74242
Cornerways, Penwinnick Rd, *tel.* (0726) 61579
Selwood House Hotel, 60 Alexandra Rd, *tel.* (0726) 65707
◇ Wimereux, 1 Trevanion Rd, *tel.* (0726) 72187
Campsite: ◇ Trewhiddle Holiday Estate, 3-pennants, *tel.* (0726) 67011
Garage: Beech Mtrs, Beech Ln, *tel.* (0726) 74743
Carlyon Bay, Carlyon Bay, *tel.* (072681) 4014 (day) & 69089 (night)
Cornish Ford, Slades Rd, *tel.* (0726) 72333

Saints

Cornwall, it is said, boasts more saints than were ever enthroned in heaven. Certainly, when St Augustine arrived in Kent in AD597 to convert the heathen English, the faith was already burning bright in Cornwall.

For a hundred years Celtic missionaries had been arriving on its shores from Wales and Ireland, converting small groups of people to Christianity. They were encouraged by their own monasteries to make these pilgrimages overseas to convert and teach the heathen populace, founding a 'cell' or church before moving on to continue their work. Most established their cells near sites where the people had been accustomed to worshipping — springs, wells, rivers or standing stones. Many lived as contemplative hermits, adhering to a strict ascetic code. Many were never 'sainted' in an ecclesiastical sense, but their names live on in the dedications of over 200 old Cornish churches and even more villages and towns.

The first wave of saints arrived in the 5th century, and the effect of these simple, ragged, wonder-working proselytisers on small communities must have been quite startling. Legends of their lives and powers abounded. St Brychan, it is said, arrived from Wales with three wives, 12 sons and 12 daughters, including Endellion, Issey, Kew, Mabyn, Minver and Teath, all of whom became saints. St Keyne is supposed to have arrived on a millstone, St Budoc in a barrel and several Breton saints floating on their stone altars. St Fingar (Gwinear) arrived from Ireland with his brothers St Breaca (Breage), St

St Enodoc Church, Trebetherick

Euny (Lelant) and St Erc (Erth). Their sister Ia (Ives) arrived separately, floating on a cabbage leaf. St Piran, patron saint of tinners, is said to have had a taste for the bottle, while saints Keverne and Just gained a reputation for being aggressive rivals. A strange mixture of the old and new religions forms a part of many legends concerning battles between the saints and the old Cornish giants. The saints usually won these boulder-throwing contests, thanks to heavenly intervention.

Bizarre legends apart, the success of the missionary work carried out by these Irish, Welsh and Breton saints was genuine enough and local kings and chieftains readily gave large areas of land for the building of monasteries and colleges. The most influential saint was undoubtedly St Petroc, who travelled from Wales to found monasteries in Padstow and Bodmin, also visiting Devon, Somerset and Brittany. Another Welsh saint, Sampson, Christianised a stone pillar being worshipped by heathens by carving a cross on its side. Many such Celtic crosses, carved by or dedicated to the early saints, can be seen in Cornish churchyards. The memory of these good men and women also lives on in the annual Feast Days held in most villages and towns in Cornwall today.

St Buryan

Map Ref: 90SW4025

At the centre of this agricultural parish of squat, moorland farms, remote hamlets and tortuous lanes, rises the lofty tower of St Buryan Church, a day-mark for ships rounding the high Land's End peninsula. In the dark interior of the church is a wide rood-screen carved with hunting scenes, strange beasts and vine leaves. The surrounding houses built of granite provided the setting for the film *Straw Dogs*, made in the 1970s. Bronze Age and Iron Age relics

A stone circle near St Buryan

abound in nearby fields and a circle of 19 stones, Boscawen-Un, may be inspected with the permission of the farmer.

AA recommends:

Guesthouses: High Trevorian Hotel, *tel.* (0736) 810348
Boskenna Home (farmhouse), *tel.* (0736) 810250
◇ Burnewhall (farmhouse), *tel.* (0736) 810200
Campsites: Lower Treave Caravan Park, Crow-an-Wra, 3-pennants, *tel.* (0736) 810559
Tower. Farm Caravan & Camping Park, 3-pennants, *tel.* (0736) 810286
Treverven Camping & Touring Site, Treverven Farm, 3-pennants, *tel.* (0736) 810221

Near St Cleer may be seen a Neolithic chamber tomb, Trethevy Quoit (main picture) and (inset) the Doniert Stone, dedicated to the 9th-century King Doniert

St Cleer

Map Ref: 92SX2468

This compact group of moorstone cottages surrounding a stout-walled 15th-century church, lies on the south-west fringe of Bodmin Moor, close to a former quarrying and mining area. Down the road past the village inn is St Cleer's Well, beneath a small 16th-century roadside chapel. In a field north-east of the village stands Trethevy Quoit, an impressive Neolithic chamber tomb with a massive capstone.

Alongside a road north-west of the village is the Doniert Stone, a block of granite carved with intricate designs and dedicated to a 9th-century Cornish king who drowned nearby. Turn north at Redgate to reach an ancient packhorse bridge, from where a footpath leads along the wooded banks of the River Fowey to Golitha Falls, a series of small cascades.

A short drive north of St Cleer is Siblyback Lake, a reservoir where visitors can sail, windsurf or fish for brown or rainbow trout with a day permit. A Visitors' Centre contains a café and geological display.

St Columb Major

Map Ref: 91SW9163

At the head of the Vale of Lanherne, the little market town of St Columb Major was considered as the site for Cornwall's cathedral, but lost the battle to more centrally-placed Truro. The proud tower of the Church of St Columba looks down on a narrow, meandering main street of slate-hung buildings and interesting side-lanes. The church has a broad barrel roof vaulting its spacious interior, and there is a fine peal of bells. A former landlord of the Red Lion Inn was James Polkinghorne, a champion in the art of Cornish wrestling. The name of another inn, the Silver Ball, refers to the small silver-coated wooden ball for which two teams battle fiercely every Shrove Tuesday and second

Gwennap Pit near St Day. After sheltering here in a storm, John Wesley found this to be an ideal venue for his meetings

Saturday following. The object of these hurling matches is to carry the ball to one of two goals which are two miles apart.

The Iron Age hill-fort of Castle-an-Dinas, surrounded by three ramparts and ditches, can be found on a high hill-top west of the town.

AA recommends:
Restaurants: ◇ Old Rectory Hotel & Country Club, Bridge Hill, 2-forks, *tel.* (0637) 880656
Campsites: ◇ Tregatillian Caravan Park, Tregatillian, 3-pennants, *tel.* (0637)) 880482
Trekenning Manor Tourist Park, Trekenning, 3-pennants, *tel.* (0637) 880462
Garage: ◇ Enterprise, *tel.* (0637) 880488 (day) & 880489 (night)

St Day

Map Ref: 91SW7342

Surrounded by the brick-topped chimneys of abandoned engine-houses, St Day preceded Redruth as the mining capital of Cornwall. Its terraces of miners' cottages and mine-captains' villas were once familiar to John Wesley, who visited the town on numerous occasions. At nearby Busveal a deep hollow, Gwennap Pit, became a regular venue on his tours of Cornwall and now Methodists from all over the world gather here each year, on Whit Monday for a service.

AA recommends:
Campsite: ◇ Tresaddern Caravan Park, 3-pennants, *tel.* (0209) 820459

John Wesley

John Wesley

Poverty, violence and a contempt for the law were common amongst the hard-drinking, wild-living members of Cornwall's 18th-century mining and fishing communities. The Church offered little personal contact, seeming instead to be the province of the mine-owners and landed gentry.

When the preacher John Wesley made the first of over 30 visits to Cornwall, in 1743, he was met with suspicion and opposition. On several occasions his life was put in danger when he was pelted with stones and attacked by hounds. After several visits, however, his courage was acknowledged and his simple, personal message was gradually accepted. Travelling on horseback, he visited towns and villages from Launceston to St Just, Polperro to St Ives, preaching first at small meetings in houses and cottages, and later at large open-air gatherings. The fiery preaching and passionate singing caused many conversions to Methodism and numerous places of worship were built throughout the county. These small 'bethels', chapels and churches were simple in design, often resembling the familiar mine buildings that surrounded the towns. Some of the journeys on horseback undertaken by Wesley in all weathers were gruelling, and special accommodation was provided for him at Trewint, near Altarnun, at St Just-in-Penwith and at Crantock. On one visit he preached six sermons and rode over 50 miles in three days.

Many of Wesley's best-attended meetings were held at Gwennap Pit, a hollow in the ground near St Day, converted by miners into an amphitheatre capable of holding several thousand people. Methodists still congregate here in large numbers for the annual Whit Monday service and to visit the adjacent memorial chapel. At the nearby mining village of Carharrack a small Museum of Cornish Methodism has been created in the church, which still contains its original box-pews and gaslights.

Since Wesley's death in 1791, the Methodists have split into several sects: Wesleyan; Bible Christians (or Bryonites); Primitive Methodists; United Methodist Free Church and Methodist New Connection. So powerful is the legacy left by John Wesley that many towns and villages contain chapels or churches to two, or even three of these sects.

St Dennis

Map Ref: 91SW9558

On the high northern edge of the china-clay country, the village of St Dennis looks out over the flat expanse of Goss Moor, birthplace of the fledgling Fal. On the windswept hill above a group of clay-miners' cottages stands the Church of St Dionysius, built within an Iron Age fort. From here the view south over the white spoil-heaps of the clay country is impressive. Near the village of Roche, a few miles to the north-east, is Roche Rock, a sudden granite outcrop on which stands a ruined 15th-century chapel and hermitage where lived St Gonand, a leper.

St Ewe

Map Ref: 92SW9746

This pocket-sized village on the side of the River Luney valley, west of Mevagissey, contains some charming cottages, a set of village stocks and a 14th-century church surrounded by trees. Its spire is octagonal in shape and carvings of faces peering through foliage surround the doorway.

Below: the ruined chapel and hermitage on top of Roche Rock
Right: Polmassick vineyard near St Ewe is open to the public

In the wooded valley below is the hamlet of Polmassick where you may taste wine made from locally-grown grapes and inspect delightful miniature ponies at Polmassick Vineyard.

AA recommends:
Campsite: Pengrugla Caravan & Camp Site, 3-pennants, *tel.* (0726) 842714

St Ives: view across the harbour to the old fishing town

St Germans

Map Ref: 93SX3557

Built on a high spur at the confluence of two rivers, this showpiece village of great charm contains numerous attractive buildings with well-tended gardens. A row of balconied almshouses, built in 1538, has been carefully restored. An Augustinian priory was established here in 1162, and its magnificent priory church was the chief church in Cornwall until the completion of Truro Cathedral in 1910. Rising on either side of its deep, carved doorway are two towers, dating from the 13th and 15th centuries. The spacious interior contains many memorials to the Eliot family, whose home, Port Eliot, stands alongside the church, looking out over wooded parkland. A steep lane descends to the once-busy Victorian wharves at St Germans Quay.

St Ives

Map Ref: 90SW5140

The colourful Mediterranean atmosphere of St Ives attracts hordes of visitors every year. Of the surrounding beaches and coves, the flat expanse of Porthmeor beach is favoured by surfers, while the more sheltered Porthminster beach is popular with families and young children.

The old fishing village grew up on a narrow isthmus of land joining the mainland to a low green mound known as The Island. It became Cornwall's busiest pilchard fishing port, also exporting tin and copper from nearby mines. The sturdy main pier was built in 1767 by John Smeaton, and up to early this century hundreds of luggers crammed into the harbour.

The quaint maze of streets behind the wharf is divided into 'Downalong', the abode of the fishing community, and 'Upalong', where the mining families lived. The piercing shrieks of gulls echo in cobbled alleyways and flowery courtyards, and steep streets of whitewashed cottages bear such names as Rope Walk, Mount Zion, Virgin Street and Fish Street. The finest cottages, many with outside staircases, can be found in a lane called The Digey at the foot of which is the old artist's and fisherman's inn, The Sloop. John Wesley's frequent visits to the town as well as the firm grip of Methodism are recalled in the names of Salubrious Street and Teetotal Street. At the foot of the town, by West Pier, rises the golden tower of the parish church, dedicated to St Ia, a 6th-century female missionary who is said to have arrived here from Ireland floating on a leaf! The church contains a fine barrel roof and a tender sculpture of Our Lady and Child by Barbara Hepworth.

St Ives became the haunt of artists following a visit by the painter Turner in the 1880s. Sickert and Whistler worked here, attracted by the clear light, and many others followed in their wake. As the fishing industry declined, so net-lofts and fish-cellars were converted into studios. Ben Nicholson and Peter Lanyon headed a new wave this century, together with Barbara Hepworth. Examples of her work can be seen in a delightful garden setting at the Barbara Hepworth Museum in Back Street. The potter Bernard Leach started the Leach Pottery at Higher Stennack; and many artists of varying standards still work in or near the town, and examples of their work can be seen in the numerous galleries.

A narrow lane of old houses known as The Warren meanders behind the rocky headland of Pedn Olva to Porthminster and the railway station. The train ride from here to St Erth is one of the finest short scenic routes in Britain.

Just east of St Ives is the quieter, less hectic resort of Carbis Bay, a steep hillside of hotels and villas overlooking a wide sandy beach. The slender stone steeple on a high hill to the south is the Knill Monument, erected by an 18th-century customs officer and mayor of St Ives, John Knill, who is reputed to have taken an active part in local smuggling. He built it as a mausoleum for himself, but he died in London, where he is buried. However, he left instructions that every five years on 25 July, ten girls and two local widows should follow a fiddler up the hill to the monument where they should dance around its base before joining the assembled crowd in singing the 'Old Hundredth' psalm. A bequest allows a small payment for all concerned and this strange ceremony will next be performed in 1991, 1996, etc.

AA recommends:
Hotels: Porthminster, The Terrace, 3-star, *tel.* (0736) 795221
Tregenna Castle, Tregenna Park, St Ives Rd, 3-star, *tel.* (0736) 795254
Garrack, Higher Ayr, 3-star, *tel.* (0736) 796199
Cornwallis, Headland Rd, Carbis Bay, 2-star, *tel.* (0736) 795294
Self Catering: ◇ Casa Bella Holiday Apartments, Hain Walk, *tel.* (0736) 795427
◇ Trevalgan Farm Holiday Homes, *tel.* (0736) 796433
Guesthouses: Dean Court Hotel. Trelyon Ave, *tel.* (0736) 796023
Shun Lee Private Hotel, Trelyon Ave, *tel.* (0736) 796284
Sunrise, 22 The Warren, *tel.* (0736) 795407
Tregorran Hotel, Headland Rd, Carbis Bay, *tel.* (0736) 795889
Campsites: Ayr Holiday Park, 3-pennants, *tel.* (0736) 795855
Chy an Gweal Holiday Park, 3-pennants, *tel.* (0736) 796257
Polmanter Farm Campsite, Halsetown, 3-pennants, *tel.* (0736) 795640
◇ Higher Penderleith Site, Towednack, 1-pennant, *tel.* (0736) 796576

St Just

Map Ref: 90SW3731

The most westerly town in mainland England, St Just bustled with activity last century when nearby tin and copper mines were in full production. Its streets of gabled, grey-granite houses and old inns still have a busy working atmosphere, despite the closure of the last local tin-mine, Geevor, at nearby Pendeen. Two imposing Methodist churches, one with a Doric façade, and a sturdy 15th-century church dominate the low-roofed town. At its centre is an ancient Plain-an-Gwarry or 'Playing Place', a grass-covered amphitheatre where mediaeval miracle plays were once performed.

A lane winds west to the windy tip of Cape Cornwall, a high knoll looking out over two islands known as The Brisons, where many ships have come to grief.

From the hamlet of Botallack, a mile or so north of St Just, a track leads to the clifftop from where you can look down on the recently-restored Crown engine-houses of Botallack mine, perched on the rocky cliffside only feet from the crashing waves. The shaft of this old mine sloped down under the sea and on stormy nights miners could hear the sound of boulders shifting on the sea-bed above them. The mine Count House has been converted into a fine restaurant.

Round the headland are the ruins of Levant mine where 31 men perished in 1919 when the 'man-engine', a wooden beam used to lower and raise the miners, collapsed. The museum at Geevor Mine gives a graphic picture of life underground for the hard-rock miners. Visitors are also welcome to inspect Pendeen lighthouse at the tip of Pendeen Watch. The view from here along the coast to Cape Cornwall is superb, especially on a stormy day when the air is full of sea-spray.

The Iron Age village of Carn Euny lies in the centre of the Land's End peninsula, but is most easily reached from St Just, on the road to Sancreed. It comprises a village of four courtyard houses and a number of round houses, dating from the first century BC. There is also a magnificent 66ft-long fogou, an underground passage leading to a subterranean chamber.

AA recommends:
Self Catering: ◇ The Cottage, Tremythek, Higher Bosavern, *tel.* (0305) 67545
Guesthouses: Boscean Country Hotel, *tel.* (0736) 788748
Boswedden House, Cape Cornwall, *tel.* (0736) 788733
Kenython, *tel.* (0736) 788607
Campsites: Bosavern House Caravan Park, 2-pennants, *tel.* (0736) 788301
Kelynack Caravan Park, 2-pennants, *tel.* (0736) 787633
Trevaylor Caravan Park, Truthwall, 2-pennants, *tel.* (0736) 787016

St Just In Roseland

Map Ref: 91SW8435

The Roseland Peninsula is rather like Cornwall in reverse, with woodlands and sheltered creeks to the north-west and rocky cliffs to the south-east. Running down its centre is the winding Percuil River. The peninsula is renowned for its beauty, but nowhere is it more luxuriant than at St Just In Roseland, where a small 13th- and 15th-century church stands on the water's edge at the head of a wooded tidal creek. Behind rises a steep hillside churchyard of semi-tropical trees and shrubs, a blaze of colour in early summer. Across the

The cliff-side mines at Botallack, near St Just

peninsula is the fishing village of Porthscatho, where lobster-pots are piled on the quayside and boats cluster on the slipway.

From the National Trust hamlet of Tregassick to the south, you can walk along the creekside, past oyster-beds, to Percuil. Near the southern tip of the peninsula, a wooded lane leads down to St Anthony and a small church standing alongside Place House, former home of the Spry family.

AA recommends:
Guesthouses: Rose-Da-Mar Hotel, *tel.* (0326) 270450
Commerrans (farmhouse), *tel.* (087258) 270
Campsite: Trethem Mill Caravan Site, 3-pennants, *tel.* (087258) 504

The waterside church of St Just In Roseland

St Keverne

Map Ref: 91SW7921

Although built a mile or so inland from the coast, the tower and octagonal steeple of St Keverne Church act as a day-mark to sailors as they approach the dreaded Manacle rocks. In the churchyard are the tombstones of over 400 men who have perished along this stretch of coast. Radiating from a small square, the village is often swept by fierce gale-force winds which whip across the high Lizard plateau. It was a St Keverne blacksmith, Joseph An Gof (Michael Joseph) who, together with Thomas Flamank of Bodmin, led a rebellious but ill-fated march to London in 1497 against taxation. Both were hanged at Tyburn.

To the north and east of St Keverne are the villages of Porthoustock and Porthallow, pronounced 'P'rewstock' and 'P'raller'. Originally fishing communities, they are now devoted to roadstone quarrying.

AA recommends:
Self Catering: ◇ St James Court Holiday Cottages and Tregowris Farmhouses, *tel.* (0326) 280459
Garage: Zoar, *tel.* (0326) 280235

St Mawes

Map Ref: 91SW8433

A sunny hillside of white houses and villas rises from the harbour of St Mawes, now a popular yachting haven. Its steep lanes contain many charming old cottages overhung with flowers and a small holy well. At the mouth of the Percuil River to the west stands St Mawes Castle, built by Henry VIII in 1542 to protect the ports of Truro and Falmouth. It was built to the same

One of the biggest round castles in England, at St Mawes

'clover-leaf' design as the much larger Pendennis Castle across the mouth of Carrick Roads. Its dungeons, barrack rooms and cannon-lined walls are open to the public.

AA recommends:
Hotels: Idle Rocks, 3-star, *tel.* (0326) 270771
◇ Green Lantern, Marine Pde, 2-star, *tel.* (0326) 270502
Rising Sun, 2-star, *tel.* (0326) 270233
St Mawes, The Seafront, 2-star, *tel.* (0326) 270266

St Mawgan

Map Ref: 91SW8765

Surrounded by woodland in the deep, sheltered Vale of Lanherne, this picturesque village consists of charming cottages, the old Falcon Inn, a turret-towered church and a pair of bridges spanning a slow-moving stream. The 13th-century manor house of the Arundell family has been the convent of a closed order of nuns since 1794. A remarkably carved lantern-cross dating from 1420 stands in the churchyard, near to a boat-shaped wooden memorial recording the fate of nine men and a boy who froze in their lifeboat after a shipwreck in 1846.

At the foot of the Vale is the sheltered sandy cove of Mawgan Porth, and a mile to the north are Bedruthan Steps, owned by the National Trust – high outcrops of rock on a flat sandy beach, said to be the stepping-stones of the Cornish giant Bedruthan.

AA recommends:
Hotels: Dalswinton Country House, 2-star, *tel.* (0637) 860385
◇ Pen-y-Morfa Country, 1-star, *tel.* (0637) 860363

Bedruthan Steps, gigantic granite rocks, strangely shaped by the Atlantic waves

St Merryn

Map Ref: 94SW8874

Cottages cluster around the Church of St Marina in this tiny village of grey slate. To the west Trevose Head juts out into the Atlantic, a lighthouse at its tip. Padstow lifeboat is based on its sheltered eastern side in Mother Ivey's Bay. This popular family beach is divided from another safe beach at Harlyn Bay by Cataclews Point, where much of the blue-grey greenstone used to make church fonts and window tracery was quarried.
On the western side of Trevose Head, below a superbly-sited golf course, are the beaches of Booby's Bay and Constantine Bay, where powerful surf makes swimming less safe.

St Michael's Mount

Map Ref: 90SW5129

In its time, the high pinnacle of St Michael's Mount, rising like a fairytale castle from the sea, has been a church, a priory, a fortress and a private house. Tradition also holds it to be the abode of Cormoran, the Cornish giant slain by brave Jack. It has been a place of pilgrimage since the Middle Ages, and today about half a million people a year either walk across the cobbled causeway at low tide or use one of the small ferries that ply between the Mount and Marazion on the mainland.
The small port at the foot of the Mount is thought to be the site of Ictis, from where tin was shipped to the Mediterranean in the Iron Age. The archangel St Michael appeared to a group of fishermen on the rocky south side of the Mount and the monks of Mont St Michel, its

larger cousin in Normandy, built a priory on its summit. Annexed by Henry IV during the war with France, the Mount was transformed into a fortified garrison. Later owned by a series of noble families, it was acquired by Sir John St Aubyn in 1660, and his descendant, Lord St Levan, still lives here. A magnificent east wing was added to the mediaeval castle in the 1870s. There are splendid plaster reliefs of hunting scenes in the Chevy Chase room and Chippendale furniture in the elegant Blue Drawing Room. Lord St Levan gave the Mount to the National Trust in 1954 and it is open to the public on certain days throughout the year; should it be closed, the harbourside village of Victorian houses is charming.

St Neot

Map Ref: 92SX1867

Formerly a centre for wool and locally-mined tin and slate, this quiet village is tucked away in a deep wooded hollow on the edge of Bodmin Moor. Water which began life in the mysterious Dozmary Pool rushes under a stone bridge beside a friendly old inn. The church, which contains some of the most magnificent mediaeval stained glass in England, is dedicated to St Neot. Standing only 4ft tall, he lived upstream from the church by a pool which miraculously always contained two fish. He was only allowed to eat one at a time, and when his servant accidentally caught and cooked both fish, the good Neot threw one back into the pool where it returned to life.
A couple of miles to the west, steep moorland lanes lead up to the remote hamlet of Warleggan. Here lived the eccentric Rev Frederick Densham, who became parish priest

At low tide St Michael's Mount can be reached on foot

in 1931. Disliked by his parishioners, he surrounded the rectory with a high wall and withdrew from the world. A young musician who braved Densham's guard-dogs to take up the post of organist, fled in the night from a window when he found himself securely locked in his room. Lacking a Sunday congregation, the priest preached to a group of cards propped in the pews, each one bearing a name. One entry in his service book reads: 'No fog, no wind, no rain, no congregation.' He died alone in the rectory in 1953.
North of St Neot lies Colliford Lake Reservoir, the largest in the South West. Permits can be purchased for brown trout fishing.

There is a wealth of colour in St Neot's mediaeval stained glass

Above: rail and road bridges span the Tamar at Saltash
Right: The county Coat of Arms on the Tamar Bridge, Saltash

Saltash

Map Ref: 93SX4258

The original link between Saltash and Plymouth was provided by a small ferry which crossed the Tamar from the Passage Inn. Isambard Kingdom Brunel's magnificent iron single-track railway bridge was opened by Prince Albert in 1859 and a road link was provided by the three-lane suspension bridge in 1961.

The steep streets of the old town contain many fine buildings, and in Culver Street is Mary Newman's Cottage, where the first wife of Sir Francis Drake was born. In the town centre is a 17th-century pillared guildhall, now used for markets, and the parish church with an unusual 17th-century clock in its slate tower.

On the hillside facing south-west is the old churchtown of Saltash where some old cottages and an inn stand by St Stephen's church,

whose tower and granite arcades date from the 15th century.

Across a wooded creek are the battlemented walls of Trematon Castle, not open to the public. Built by Robert of Mortain, half brother of William the Conqueror, it passed to the Black Prince in 1337.

The leafy lanes and creeks north of Saltash are worth exploring. This is a fruit-growing region and the cherry orchards make a delightful sight in early summer.

AA recommends:
Hotel: Holland Inn, 1-star, *tel.* (0752) 844044
Garage: Westward Recovery Relay, Unit 21F, Brunel Rd, Saltash Ind Est, *tel.* (0752) 847480 (night)

Sennen

Map Ref: 90SW3525

Sennen, standing on the clifftop, has several 'First and Last' shops, for this is the westernmost village on mainland England. Down in Sennen Cove is the fishing village. An old wooden roundhouse, now an art gallery, used to contain a windlass for drawing boats out of the water during storms. The lifeboat station is only a mile from the reefs of Land's End and its volunteer crew has to be ready and willing to set sail in all weathers. Whitesand Bay is popular with surfers.

North-east of Sennen, alongside the St Ives road, is Land's End Airport, from where short flights can be taken along the coast.

AA recommends:
Hotels: ◇ Tregiffian, 2-star, *tel.* (073687) 408
Self Catering: ◇ Tregiffian Cottages, *tel.* (073687) 408
Guesthouses: Old Manor, *tel.* (0736) 871280
◇ Sunny Bank Hotel, Sea View Hill, *tel.* (073687) 278
Garage: First & Last Filling Station Z Nicholas & Sons, Mayon Gar, *tel.* (0736) 871203

Tintagel

Map Ref: 94SX0588

Tennyson's poem *The Idylls of the King* drew throngs of Victorian tourists to see the birthplace and castle of the legendary King Arthur. In fact, whether he existed or led the Celts against the Saxons from these parts, remains pure speculation. Certainly, the precipitous headland, joined to the cliffs by a narrow neck of land, is easily defendable, and there was a castle here in the Iron Age. The scant remains of what was formerly thought to be a Celtic monastery, dating from the fifth to the eighth centuries AD, are now interpreted as being a trading settlement or chieftain's stronghold. Perhaps those hazy Arthurian connections have some substance. However, the more prominent remains that we see are the ruins of a castle built in 1145. In the 14th century it passed to the Black Prince, who used it as a prison. Nevertheless the romance of those Arthurian legends hangs heavily in the air.

The small town of Tintagel is almost entirely devoted to the 'Arthur industry', but worth seeing are the 14th-century Old Post Office, a National Trust property with an undulating slate roof, and King Arthur's Hall, which contains an exhibition of the Arthurian legends.

Apart from the town is the low-towered cliff-top Church of St Merteriana, with its carved Saxon doorway and five-legged Norman

St Nectan's Kieve, near Tintagel

font. Along the coast north-east of the town, a stream gushes down a woody glen from St Nectan's Kieve, home of a Celtic hermit, past an old mill to meet the sea in Rocky Valley. Carved on the rock-wall near the mill is a small maze, possibly dating from the Bronze Age.

AA recommends:

Hotels: Atlantic View, Treknow, 2-star, *tel.* (0840) 770221
Bossiney House, 2-star, *tel.* (0840) 770240
Self Catering: ◇ CC Ref 345 E (Character Cottages), *tel.* (03955) 77001
◇ Halgabron Holiday Cottages, Halgabron, *tel.* (0840) 770667
Guesthouses: Belvoir House, Tregatta, *tel.* (0840) 770265
Penallick Hotel, Treknow, *tel.* (0840) 770296
Trebrea Lodge, Trenale, *tel.* (0840) 770410
Trevervan Hotel, Trewarmett, *tel.* (0840) 770486
Trewarmett Lodge, *tel.* (0840) 770460
Willapark Manor Hotel, Bossiney, *tel.* (0840) 770782
Campsites: Headland Caravan & Camping Site, 2-pennant, *tel.* (0840) 770239
Garage: Tonkins, Bossiney Rd, *tel.* (0840) 770259

Sunset at Tintagel. The ruins (inset) are perched dramatically above the shingle beach

Language and Traditions

Remote and unaffected by the Roman Conquest, Cornwall was a Celtic country whose strongest links were overseas. Its people were first cousins to the Welsh and Bretons and second cousins to the Scots, Irish and Manx. Until the 18th century it had a language of its own, similar to those of the other Celtic nations. Iron Age tribes introduced the Brythonic branch of the language to Cornwall, and its similarities with the other Celtic languages can be found:

English	river	island	sweet
Cornish	avon	enys	melys
Welsh	avon	ynys	milis
Breton	avon	enez	melys
Irish	abbahn	inis	milis
Scottish Gaelic	abhainn	innis	milis
Manx	awin	innys	millish

A local rhyme states:
By Tre, Pol and Pen,
Ye shall know Cornishmen'

and a quick glance at any map or telephone directory will show an abundance of names beginning with the prefixes Tre (a homestead or hamlet), Pol (a pool or pond) and Pen (chief, a headland or hill). Many poems and plays written during the golden age of the Cornish language in the 14th and 15th centuries have survived, but the imposition of Anglicanism and strengthening links with England caused a steady decline in the language. Only in the far west was it kept alive until the death in 1777 of Dolly Pentreath, a fisherwoman from Mousehole who was reputed to be the last monoglot Cornish-speaker.

Recently there has been a resurgence of interest in the ancient tongue and it is now taught at evening classes and in some local schools.

Cornish-speaking evenings are held in pubs and many church services contain elements in the old language.

A ceremony held entirely in Cornish is the annual Gorsedd of the Bards of Kernow (Cornwall), held on the first Saturday in September at some historic site. Similar in style to the Welsh and Breton Gorsedds, this colourful event is part prize-giving to the writers of poems and songs in Cornish, and part rejoicing in Celtic tradition.

Many other Cornish customs and traditions have their roots in the dim Celtic past. The ancient custom of hurling, when opposing sides race through the streets trying to catch and carry a silver ball to one of two goals, is kept alive in St Ives and St Columb Major, while the sport of Cornish wrestling is still a popular summer event in Cornwall and Brittany. Padstow's 'Obby 'Oss is led by a 'teazer' through the streets of Padstow on May Day, and the ancient 'Hal-an-Tow' mumming play precedes the Flora Day dances at Helston on 8th May. Midsummer bonfires blaze from Cornish beacons on the eve of the Feast of St John, and the custom of 'Crying the Neck', when the last sheaf of corn is scythed, has been revived by the Old Cornwall Society.

Dolly Pentreath

Torpoint

Map Ref: 93SX4355

Until the opening of the road bridge at Saltash in 1961, the car-ferry linking Torpoint with Devonport and Plymouth was one of the leading 'gateways' to Cornwall. Ship-building and repairing were the industries here, and this small working town retains strong links with the naval dockyard across the water. The Torpoint ferry still regularly crosses the Hamoaze, taking workers across to Devonport and bringing Plymothians across for a breath of Cornish fresh air.

The National Trust property of Antony House, north of the town, is surrounded by thickly-wooded gardens and lawns sloping down to the riverside. The Carew family have lived on this estate since the 15th century, and the present house, built in 1721, is in the Classical style with a central block of Pentewan stone joined by colonnades to red-brick wings. The house contains exquisite tapestries, a large library and dining room and some fine pieces of 18th-century furniture. In the village church of Antony, a couple of miles to the west, is a splendid full-length brass of Lady Margery Arundell dating from 1420. Lanes winding south-east, past the old boat-building town of Millbrook, lead to the twin coastal villages of Kingsand and Cawsand, where pastel-coloured cottages sprawl around a small quay.

Close by are the attractive 900-acre gardens of Mount Edgcumbe. Dating back to Elizabethan times, they contain a deer park, a temple folly, Italian gardens, an orangery and masses of colourful shrubs. Mount Edgcumbe House, open various days in summer, is a recent copy of a 16th-century building, destroyed during the Blitz.

AA recommends:
Self Catering: ◇ Whitsand Bay Holiday Park, Chalets 1-7, Millbrook, *tel.* (0752) 822597

Tree ferns in the gardens of Trelissick House (inset)

Come-to-Good Quaker meeting-house

Tregony

Map Ref: 91SW9244

Large ships once sailed up the River Fal to this port to collect hides and unload limestone and coal. Market produce from the Roseland Peninsula was sold here and until 1832 it sent two MPs to Westminster. As the river became clogged with silt, so Tregony's importance declined, and it is now a quiet village where the pace of life is slow. In the steep main street are a row of balconied almshouses and a Gothic clock-tower. The small Church of St Cuby contains a Norman font.

Trelissick

Map Ref: 91SW8339

The National Trust gardens of Trelissick overlook a bend in the beautiful River Fal. Extensive park and woodlands surround a large garden of flowering shrubs, best seen in the spring and early summer. The elegant 19th-century house with its Grecian façade is not open to the public, but there are a National Trust shop and a restaurant in the stables.

The King Harry Ferry provides a close-up view of the massive oil-tankers 'lying-up' in the deep, sheltered waters. The creekside hamlets of Cowlands and Coombe a little up-river are surrounded by fruit trees, and a visit at 'plum-time' can be rewarding.

Beside the road from Trelissick to Carnon Downs stands the thatched Quaker meeting-house of Come-to-Good. Built in 1710, this charming whitewashed building has small latticed windows and a thatched stable. Its name stems from the Cornish words for 'House in the wooded coombe'.

Truro Cathedral, built between 1880 and 1910. Above: the vaulted nave. Inset: the west front

Tresillian

Map Ref: 91SW8646

This former port and lowest bridging point on the River Tresillian had its moment of fame in 1646 when negotiations between Parliamentary and Royalist forces on the bridge led to the signing of a 'cease-fire' in the Civil War. The Parliamentary army had their headquarters at the Wheel Inn, which has a spoked wheel made of straw on its thatched roof. On the opposite bank is a charming lodge entrance to the Tregothnan estate and mansion, home of Lord Falmouth. Tregothnan is not open to the public, but lanes leading south wind through dark woods and rolling estate farmland to St Michael Penkevil. Victorian estate-workers' cottages cluster round a village green at the imposing gates to the Falmouth family seat.

Truro

Map Ref: 91SW8244

Cornwall's cathedral city and centre of business and administration, Truro will also become the county's capital with the opening of the new Crown Court building. (At present it is Bodmin.)

Truro grew as an inland seaport in the Middle Ages. Well protected from direct attack by sea, it became a prosperous market and stannary town, ore from local mines being shipped from its wharves. Mine waste and silt slowly clogged the higher reaches of the Truro River,

and by the late 17th century, the town was in decline. Truro's revival and virtual rebuilding came during the 18th century when the high price paid for tin and copper caused an expansion in the mining industry. Wealthy merchants and banks moved to the town, and several important local families built town houses. Elegant Georgian terraces and Queen Anne houses attracted fashionable society, and the arrival of the railway in 1859 put Truro firmly on the map. It gained its city status in 1877 and the completion of the cathedral in 1910 made it the focus of social and business life.

Today Truro is a busy, spacious shopping city with much new development in the city centre. The main quay was filled in some years ago to provide a shoppers' car-park and very little shipping now navigates the narrow approach to Truro's wharves. The three-spired cathedral, one of the few to be completed in Britain this century and the first to be constructed for 800 years, is built of granite and Bath stone in Gothic and Early English styles. It was built on the site of the existing 16th-century Parish Church of St Mary, which the architect John L Pearson

incorporated into the cathedral's south wall. The interior of the richly-carved building is spacious and light, with slender columns rising to a vaulted roof. Amongst the cathedral's treasures are a magnificent Bath stone reredos and a delicate terracotta relief in the choir aisle. The Georgian Assembly Rooms and Theatre in Pydar Street were at the centre of Truro's social life in the 1800s.

On the south side of Boscaven Street is the imposing City Hall, behind which is situated the indoor Pannier Market. The wide street rising steeply to the south of the city is Lemon Street, lined with elegant Georgian houses and considered a marvel of its age in the 18th century.

Running off Victoria Square is Walsingham Place, a delightful small crescent of Georgian houses. Truro is also a city of narrow alleyways or 'opes' with names like Squeezegutts Alley and Burton's Ope. Tippet's Backlet runs from High Cross through to River Street, where stands the Royal Institution of Cornwall and County Museum, with a superb collection of minerals, paintings by Cornish artists and displays of prehistoric and later finds.

Roads wind south-east from the city along the wooded banks of the Truro River to Malpas, from where it is possible to sail to Falmouth, or through wooded farmland to the riverside hamlet of St Clement where pretty thatched cottages stand alongside an old church.

AA recommends:

Hotels: Brookdale, Tregolls Rd, 3-star, *tel.* (0872) 73513

Carlton, Falmouth Rd, 2-star, *tel.* (0872) 72450

Royal, Lemon St, 2-star, *tel.* (0872) 70345

Restaurant: ◊ Withies Country, Penmount Farm, Newquay Rd, 1-fork, *tel.* (0872) 70007

Self Catering: ◊ CC Ref 351 EL (Character Cottages), *tel.* (03955) 77001

Guesthouses: ◊ Colthrop, Tregolls Rd, *tel.* (0872) 72920

◊ Farley Hotel, Falmouth Rd, *tel.* (0872) 70712

◊ Manor Cottage, Tresillian, *tel.* (087252) 212

Marcorrie Hotel, 20 Falmouth Rd, *tel.* (0872) 77374

Campsites: Leverton Place, Greenbottom, Chacewater, 4-pennants, *tel.* (0872) 560462

Liskey Touring Park, Greenbottom, 3-pennants, *tel.* (0872) 560274 (3m w off A390)

Summer Valley, Allet, Shortlanesend, 3-pennant, *tel.* (0872) 77874 (3m nw off B3284)

Carnon Downs Caravan & Camping Park, Carnon Downs, 2-pennants, *tel.* (0872) 862283 (3m off A39)

Garages: Hicks & Son, Lemon Quay, *tel.* (0872) 74321

Kenwyn Hill, Kenwyn Hill, *tel.* (0872) 72609

Shortlanesend Garage, Shortlanesend, *tel.* (0872) 72359

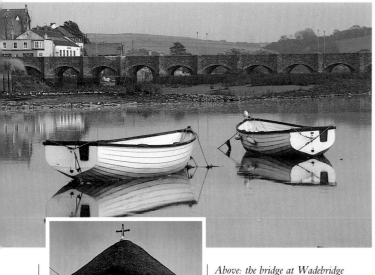

Above: the bridge at Wadebridge
Left: round house at Veryan

Veryan

Map Ref: 91SW9139

A tranquil village in a lush wooded hollow, Veryan is best known for its circular 19th-century round houses, each topped with a conical thatched roof and a cross. Their shape stems from an old tradition that the devil likes to hide and lie in wait in corners. Luxuriant trees and shrubs surround the church above a small water garden.

A deep lane runs south-west from the village down to sandy Pendower Beach, a safe bathing place. East of Veryan, the fishing village of Portloe straggles down a long narrow inlet in the cliffs to an old inn and slipway.

The road winding north-east from Veryan descends the high cliffs to the sandy cove of Portholland before looping inland to Tubb's Mill and returning to the coast at Porthluney Cove. Look inland from the flat sandy beach to see the battlements, towers and turrets of Caerhays Castle against a dark background of high trees. Designed by John Nash for the Trevanion

family, it was completed in 1808, its high cost absorbing most of the family's money. Its fine gardens contain many rare species of camellia, rhododendron, magnolia and azalea, but they are not open to the public except on certain days in spring, when proceeds go to charity.

AA recommends:
Hotels: Nare, 3-star, *tel.* (0872) 501279
Elerkey house, 2-star, *tel.* (0872) 501261
Restaurant: Treverbyn House, Pendower Rd, 1-fork, *tel.* (0872) 501201
Self Catering: ◇ Elerkey Cottage, *tel.* (0647) 21287
Campsite: Tretheake Manor Tourist Site, 3-pennants, *tel.* (0872) 501658

Wadebridge

Map Ref: 94SW9972

The 14-arch bridge of this ancient port, the lowest on the River Camel, is also the longest in Cornwall and originally had 17 spans. It is known as 'The Bridge on Wool', traditionally thought to mean that its 15th-century foundations were laid on wool-packs for stability. However, it seems more likely to refer to the money raised to pay for the bridge, which came mainly from wealthy sheep-farmers who wanted an easier passage across the river. The importance of the town grew when Wadebridge was linked to Bodmin by one of Britain's earliest railways

in 1834, the line later being extended as far as Padstow. It was closed in 1967, but the five-mile riverside stretch to Padstow now makes a pleasant scenic walk. Today Wadebridge is a busy shopping centre serving a wide agricultural area. Upstream and on the opposite bank is Egloshayle, a landing place even older than Wadebridge. A hillside of cottages with well-tended gardens climbs from an old inn and the riverside Church of St Conan.

AA recommends:
Hotel: Molesworth Arms, Molesworth St, 2-star, *tel.* (020881) 2055
Campsite: Little Bodieve Holiday Park, 3-pennants, *tel.* (020881) 2323
Garages: R. Eyres, *tel.* (020881) 2758

Zennor

Map Ref: 90SW4538

The unspoilt stretch of north coast between St Ives and St Just is Celtic Cornwall at its finest, with rugged, boulder-strewn moorland topped by granite tors, sloping down to bracken-covered cliffs and the sea, glinting beyond the stark ruins of old mine buildings. Low farmhouses huddle close together in the brooding landscape of this wild and windswept coast, and many of the irregular field-patterns date back to the Iron Age.

The tiny village of Zennor shelters in a hollow just north of the road, the tip of its weathered church tower only just visible as you drive along the switchback of a road. Inside the Church of St Senara, dating from the 12th century, is a bench-end carved in the form of a mermaid, the subject of a local legend. One Matthew Trewhella, the squire's son and a tenor in the church choir, became bewitched by a beautiful young woman who appeared in the church each week. On her third visit she lured him away, down to the cove, and he was never seen again. But on stormy nights, it was said his voice could be heard singing beneath the waves. Alongside the church stands the Tinner's Arms, an inn of great character. D H Lawrence drank here when he lived in a nearby cottage during the First World War, writing *Women in Love*. Both he and his German-born wife were driven out of the village, suspected of being German spies.

Alongside a bubbling stream is the charming Wayside Folk Museum, a cottage containing a traditional Cornish kitchen and an outdoor exhibition of domestic and mining implements. A rocky track from the church leads down the lush valley to Pendour Cove and Zennor Head, owned by the National Trust.

Traditional kitchen at the Wayside Folk Museum, Zennor

Directory

Sailing and mackerel fishing trips on offer at Looe

ANGLING
Day tickets for river fishing are available from local shops. Day tickets for coarse and game fishing at a number of reservoirs owned by the South West Water Authority are also available from self-service units. For further details contact: South West Water, Peninsula House, Rydon Lane, Exeter. *Tel.* (0392) 219666. For Sea-fishing, *see* 'Boat Trips'.

ARCHAEOLOGY
Cornwall contains a rich diversity of ancient sites to visit and explore. What follows is a list of just a handful of the most easily accessible and interesting sites.
Lanyon Quoit: Two-and-a-half miles north of Madron on the Penzance to Morvah road. A Neolithic chamber tomb of the fourth millennium BC.
Carn Euny: Signposted from the A30 at Lower Drift, west of Newlyn. An Iron Age and Romano-British courtyard-house village with an Iron Age fogou. Literature available.
Chysauster: Signposted from the B3311 at Badger's Cross on the Penzance/Gulval to St Ives road. A large Iron Age Romano-British courtyard-house village. Literature available.
Tintagel: Footpath from Tintagel. 12th-/13th-century castle built by the Earls of Cornwall, overlying a 6th-/7th-century royal stronghold.
Dupath Well: Footpath east of

Callington. An attractive building covering a mediaeval holy well.
Launceston Castle: A 12th-century castle of the Earls of Cornwall, dominating the formerly walled town of Dunheved (Launceston).
Restormel Castle: Road north of Lostwithiel. The 13th-century shell-keep of a Duchy castle, twice visited by the Black Prince in the 14th century.
St Mawes Castle: Road west of village. Henry VIII's castle, built with Pendennis to guard Falmouth haven.
Pendennis Castle: Road east of Falmouth. This Henry VIII castle sits within defences of all periods up to the Second World War.
Wheal Coates: Cliff path north from Chapel Porth, St Agnes, or by road/track from Goonvrea. Spectacularly-sited buildings of 19th-century mine.
Cornish Engines: Pool. Two miles east of Camborne on A3047. Working beam and winding engines.
Charlestown: South-east of St Austell. A purpose-built china-clay port of the 19th century.

ART GALLERIES
Falmouth Art Gallery: The Moor, Falmouth. Regularly changing exhibitions and one-man shows by contemporary artists. Permanent collection includes works by Tuke and Burne-Jones. (Open all year, weekdays.)
Hepworth Gallery: Back Road, St Ives. Sculpture by the late Barbara Hepworth in a garden setting. (Open March to October, Monday to Saturday.)

Newlyn Art Gallery: New Road, Newlyn. Exhibitions by leading West Country artists. Also permanent collection of works by Newlyn School of Painters. (Open all year, Monday to Saturday.)
North Cornwall Museum and Gallery: The Cleese, Camelford. Changing exhibitions by local artists. (Open April to September, Monday to Saturday.)
Penlee House Gallery: Morrab Road, Penzance. Fine collection of paintings by Newlyn School of Painters. Open all year.
Penwith Galleries: Back Road West, St Ives. Exhibitions of work by leading local artists. (Open all year, Tuesday to Saturday.)
Porthleven Galleries: Harbourside. Paintings by local artists. (Open daily, April to October.)
Thorburn Gallery: Dobwalls Theme Park, West of Liskeard. Wildlife paintings by Archibald Thorburn in a unique 'living-museum' setting. (Open Easter-early Nov, seven days a week.)

BOAT TRIPS
Falmouth: Prince of Wales Pier. Cruises round the docks, Roseland Peninsula, Helford River, River Fal to Malpas and Truro. (May to end of September, Monday to Saturday.)
From Customs House Quay. Cruises up River Fal to Smuggler's Cottage. (May to end of September, Monday to Saturday.)
Fowey: Town Quay. Cruises to Mevagissey and Polperro.
Looe: East and West Looe quays. Boat trips to St George's Island or up Looe River to Sandplace.
Lostwithiel: Town Quay. Cruises down the River Fowey.
Mevagissey: Town Quay. Trips around St Austell Bay.
Newquay: Harbour. Trips around the harbour.
Penzance: North Pier. Day trips to the Isles of Scilly on the *Scillonian*. Cruises along the coast to St Michael's Mount, Porthcurno. (Whitsun to mid-September, daily).
Polperro: Harbour. Boat trips along coast.
St Ives: Town Quay. Boat trips around St Ives Bay.
Truro: Worth's Quay. Cruises to Falmouth and St Mawes.
Sea fishing trips are available from the following harbours: Falmouth, Looe, Mevagissey and Padstow.

CRAFTS
Almost every Cornish village and town has its craft workshop. This is a list of just a few centres offering a wide range of high-quality craft work.
Leach Pottery: Stennack, St Ives. Work by Janet Leach. Exhibition of pottery by the late Bernard Leach.
Mid-Cornwall Galleries: Biscovey, Par. Craft work by craftsmen living in Cornwall.

Peter Marshall Furniture:
Porthgwidden, St Ives. Handmade
furniture in English hardwoods.
Trelowarren: Off the A3083,
south of Helston. Headquarters of
the Cornwall Craft Association.

GARDENS

Cornwall's mild climate allows
plants, shrubs and trees to flourish
in some of the most attractive and
luxuriant gardens in the country.
They range from the large gardens
of castles and country homes (many
owned by the National Trust) to
the small gardens of country
cottages. It is impossible to provide
a full catalogue of places to visit;
further details may be found in the
National Gardens Scheme's
booklets, available locally. See also
pages 28-31.
Antony House: Torpoint. Lawns,
woods and shrubs. (Open April to
October, Tuesday to Thursday and
Bank Holiday Mondays.)
Cotehele: St Dominick. Terraced
hillside garden with unusual shrubs.
(Open April to October, daily.) NT.
County Demonstration Garden:
Probus. Display giving hints on
gardening. (Open weekdays.)
Glendurgan Garden: Mawnan
Smith, 40-acre wooded valley
garden. Maze (Open March to end
October, Monday, Wednesday and
Friday.) NT.
Ken Caro Garden: Bicton,
Pensilva. Two acres of flowering
shrubs and fine trees. Water fowl
collection and aviary. (Open May
to June, Wednesday and Sunday.)
Lanhydrock: Bodmin. In grounds
of historic home. (Open April to
October, daily.) NT.
Mount Edgcumbe Gardens:
Torpoint. Ornamental shrubberies
and lawns leading down to river's
edge. (Higher gardens open May to
September, Monday and Tuesday.
Lower gardens open all year, daily.)
Pencarrow House Gardens:
Washaway, Bodmin. Formal
gardens and woodlands. (Open
Easter to 15 October, Monday to
Thursday and Sunday.)
Penjerrick Gardens: Mawnan
Smith. Spring-flowering shrubs.
(Open March to September,
Wednesday and Sunday.)
Trelissick Estate: Truro. Parkland
and woods, superb shrubs. (Open
March to October, daily.) NT.
Trengwainton Garden: Penzance.
Shrub garden and stream
overlooking Mount's Bay. (Open
March to October, Wednesday to
Saturday and Bank Holiday
Mondays.) NT.
Trewithen: Probus. 20-acre garden
of flowering shrubs and rare trees.
(Open March to September,
Monday to Saturday.)

GOLF

Bude & North Cornwall Golf Club,
Burn View, Bude. *Tel.* (0288)
2006. 18-hole seaside links.
Budock Vean Golf Club, Mawnan

Smith, Falmouth. *Tel.* (0326)
250281. 9-hole parkland.
Carlyon Bay Golf Club, Carlyon
Bay Hotel, St Austell. *Tel.* (072681)
4250. 18-hole clifftop course.
Falmouth Golf Club, Swanpool
Road. *Tel.* (0326) 311262. 18-hole
seaside parkland.
Launceston Golf Club, St Stephens.
Tel. (0566) 3442. 18-hole parkland.
Looe Bin Down Golf Club. *Tel.*
(050 34) 247. 18-hole parkland.
Mullion Golf Club. *Tel.* (0326)
240276. 18-hole seaside links.
Newquay Golf Club, Fistral,
Newquay. *Tel.* (0637) 872091.
18-hole links course.
Perranporth Golf Club. *Tel.* (087
257) 2454. 18-hole seaside links.
Praa View Golf Club, near Helston.
Tel. (073 676) 3445. 9-hole.
St Austell Golf Club. *Tel.* (0726)
2649. 18-hole parkland.
St Enodoc Golf Club, Wadebridge.
Tel. (020 886) 3216. 18-hole
seaside links.
St Mellion Golf Club, Callington
Tel. (0579) 50101. 18-hole
downland.
Tehidy Park Golf Club, Camborne.
Tel. (0209) 842208. 18-hole
parkland.
Tregenna Castle Golf Course, St
Ives. *Tel.* (0736) 795254. 18-hole
parkland.
Trevose Golf Club, Padstow. *Tel.*
(0841) 520208. 18-hole downland.
Truro Golf Club, Treliske. *Tel.*
(0872) 72640. 18-hole parkland.
West Cornwall Golf Club, Lelant.
Tel. (0726) 753401. 18-hole seaside
links.
Whitsand Bay Hotel, Crafthole.
Tel. (0506) 276. 18-hole seaside
links.

HISTORIC HOMES

Antony House: Torpoint. NT.
(Open afternoons April to October,
Tuesday to Thursday and Bank
Holiday Mondays.)
Bochym Manor: Mullion. (Open
all year, daily.)
Cotehele: Calstock. NT. (Open
April to October, gardens daily but
house closed Friday.)

*Barbara Hepworth sculpture in the
Hepworth Gallery, St Ives*

Godolphin House: Helston. (Open
May and June, Thursday; July to
September, Tuesday and Thursday.)
Lanhydrock: Bodmin. NT. (Open
April to October, daily.)
Mount Edgcumbe House:
Torpoint. (Open May to
September, Monday and Tuesday.)
Pencarrow House: Washaway,
Bodmin. (Open Easter to 15
October, Monday to Thursday and
Sunday.)
St Michael's Mount: Marazion.
NT. (Open November to May,
Monday, Wednesday and Friday;
June to October, Monday to
Friday.)
Trelowarren House and Chapel:
Helston. (Open Easter to October,
Wednesday; end July to early
September, Wednesday and
Sunday. Chapel open daily.)
Trerice: Newquay. NT. (Open
April to October, daily.)
Trewithen: Probus. (Open April to
July, Monday and Tuesday.)

MUSEUMS

As space does not allow a complete
listing of all town museums, the
following is a list of some of the
larger or more unusual museums.
Automobilia Motor Museum: St
Stephen, west of St Austell. Vintage
vehicles. (Open April-September,
Tuesday-Sunday; October-March,
Saturday and Sunday.)
Barbara Hepworth Museum: Back
Street, St Ives. Exhibition of
sculpture and tools in the artist's
workshop/studio. (Open March to
October, Monday to Saturday.)
**Bude Historical and Folk
Exhibition:** The Wharf, Bude.
Local history and folk items. (Open
Easter to October, daily.)
**Camborne School of Mines
Geological Museum:** Pool,
Camborne. Display of rock and
mineral specimens from Cornish
mines and overseas. (Open all year,
weekdays.)
Cornish Engines: Pool. Beam
engines used for pumping water
from 2,000ft. (Open April to
October daily.)
Delabole Slate Quarry Museum:
Camelford. History of slate industry
and display of mining equipment.
(Open Easter to November,
weekdays.)
Falmouth Maritime Museum:
Custom House Quay, Falmouth.
Maritime exhibits on board the tug
St Denys. (Open April to October,
daily.)
Farm Museum: Mawla Well, near
Porthtowan. Large collection of
farm and domestic items. (Open all
year, daily.)
Geevor Mine Museum: Pendeen.
Models and history of mine. (Open
April to October, daily.)
Helston Folk Museum: Helston.
Old Buttermarket transformed into
lively folk museum. (Open all year,
Monday, Tuesday, Thursday to
Saturday.)
King Arthur's Hall: Tintagel.
Craftsman-built Hall of Chivalry

The China Clay Museum

WHEAL MARTYN

A GREAT FAMILY DAY WITH CORNWALL'S CHINA CLAY INDUSTRY

HISTORIC TRAIL - NATURE TRAIL - EXHIBITIONS
AUDIO VISUAL THEATRE - CHILDREN'S ADVENTURE TRAIL
POTTERY - PICNIC AREA - COFFEE SHOP - GIFT SHOP
FREE CAR PARK

A TOTALLY DIFFERENT DAY OUT

The China Clay Museum

WHEAL MARTYN

Wheal Martyn staff, ready to welcome you.

Lee Moor No. 1 0-4-0 Pecket (1899)

Visiting family at spectacular pit view.

Fun for all on the adventure trail.

Quiet woodland walks, the nature trail.

The China Clay Museum

WHEAL MARTYN

26 ACRES OF FUN AND ADVENTURE FOR ALL THE FAMILY

Production of Cornish China Clay has been a 200 year saga, and a visit to Wheal Martyn will give you a fascinating and memorable insight into this historic industry.

The stimulating **AUDIO VISUAL** arms you with a knowledge of China Clay and Wheal Martyn itself, you can then take the **HISTORIC TRAIL**, a journey into the past, through the fascinating 19th Century Clay Works with Working Water Wheels. There are two old steam locomotives and a very rare 1916 Working Peerless Lorry.

Nature lovers will enjoy the beautiful **NATURE TRAIL** which explores a unique range of habitats, both man-made and natural with many species of birds, insects, trees and flowers, not to mention a spectacular view into a working clay pit.

Wheal Martyn Museum, Carthew, St Austell
PL26 8XG   Tel: St Austell (0726) 850362

Registered under the Charities Act 1960.
No. 1001838

Even the children are specially cared for with their own **ADVENTURE TRAIL** which for the over 10's is a challenging commando style trail full of fun and adventure.

Admittance times:
Open from 10.00 a.m. to 6.00 p.m. Daily, Easter to October 31st inclusive.

Last admission - 1 hour previous to closing time.

Guided parties by arrangement.
Special rates for parties of 12 or more.

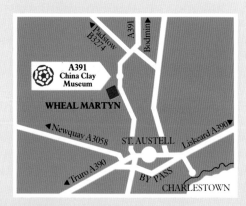

DOGS WELCOME
(ON LEADS PLEASE)

A TOTALLY DIFFERENT DAY OUT

containing Arthurian items. (Open Easter to October, weekdays.)
Lanreath Mill and Farm Museum: Lanreath. Model railway and pets corner. (Open Easter to June, daily.)
Lawrence House Museum: Launceston. Georgian house containing local history items. (Open April to September, weekdays.)
Mevagissey Folk Museum: East Quay, Mevagissey. Fascinating items of port's history. (Open Easter to September, daily.)
Military Vehicle Museum: Lamanva, south-west of Falmouth. Unique collection of vehicles. (Open all year, daily.)
Museum of Cornish Methodism: Carharrack, St Day. Items connected with Wesley's visits to Cornwall housed in old Methodist chapel. (Open Easter to September, weekdays.)
Museum of Lawnmowers: Trerice, near Newquay. Unique and unusual collection. (Open April to October, daily.)
Museum of Nautical Art: Chapel Street, Penzance. Many items recovered from sunken ships around the coast of Cornwall and the Isles of Scilly. (Open April to October, Monday to Saturday.)
Museum of Sailing Ships: Falmouth Arts Centre. Model-making at its best. (Open all year, weekdays.)
Museum of Witchcraft: Boscastle. Unusual exhibits connected with local legends and folklore. (Open Easter to October, daily.)
National Maritime Museum: Cotehele Quay. Restored Tamar barge *Shamrock*. (Open April to October, daily.)
Noah's Ark Folk Museum: Fore Street, Fowey. Local folk items. (Open all year, Monday, Tuesday, Thursday and Friday.)
North Cornwall Museum: The Clease, Camelford. Evocative display of local folk items. (Open April to September, Monday to Saturday.)
Paul Corin Musical Collection: St Keyne, Liskeard. Automatic music boxes, pianos and organs. (Open Easter week and May to September, daily.)
Regimental Museum: Victoria Barracks, Bodmin. History of the Duke of Cornwall's Light Infantry. (Open all year, weekdays.)
Royal Geological Society of Cornwall Museum: Alverton Street, Penzance. Excellent collection of minerals and fossils. (Open May to September, weekdays.)
Royal Institution of Cornwall and County Museum: River Street, Truro. Mineral collection; paintings by Cornish artists; displays of archaeological finds; fine library. (Open all year, Monday to Saturday.)
St Agnes Museum: St Agnes. Local history. (Open Easter to September, daily.)

Smuggler's Museum: Polperro. Items of local smuggling history. (Open April to October, daily.)
Wayside Folk Museum: Zennor. Collection of domestic tools, mining and quarrying instruments and traditional Cornish kitchen inside old cottage. (Open Easter to October, daily.)
Wheal Martyn Museum: Carthew, north of St Austell. History of the china-clay industry in pictures and items. (Open April to October, daily.)

TOURIST ATTRACTIONS
Unless otherwise stated, the following attractions are open from Easter to October, daily.
Charlestown Visitor Centre: East of St Austell. Shipwreck, diving and local history displays.
Cornish Leisure World and Cornwall Coliseum: Carlyon Bay, St Austell. Swimming pool; night club; naturist beach; roller-skating and large concert hall.
Cornucopia and Lelant Model Village: Lelant. Smuggling, shipwreck and mining displays; junior commando course.
Cornwall Aero Park and Flambards Village: Helston. Award-winning leisure park with historic aircraft and vehicles; large indoor reconstruction of Edwardian village; Britain in the Blitz exhibition; war gallery; bumper-boats; rides; ball-pool; delightful gardens.
Dobwalls Theme Park: near Liskeard. Forest Railroad – two railway rides behind model steam trains through authentic American Railways scenery; Mr Thorburn's Edwardian Countryside – unique 'living-museum' exhibition of wildlife paintings.
Goonhilly Earth Station: south of Helston. Guided tours of giant dish aerials of satellite communications centre. (Open Easter to end of September, daily.)
Holywell Bay Leisure Park: Newquay. Ponies; bumper-boats; go-karts; roller-skating. (Open May to September, daily.)
Land's End Experience: Land's End. Exhibitions of 'Man and the Sea', 'Land's End Heritage' and 'Air and Sea Rescue'.
Land of Legend and Polperro Model Village: Polperro. Cornish legend displays.
Lappa Valley Railway: St Newlyn East. Miniature railway; boating; engine-house; maze; woodland walk.
Poldark Mine and Ha'Penny Park: Helston. Walk safely underground in genuine old tin mine; beam engines; mining displays; childrens' leisure park; rides; beautiful gardens.
St Agnes Leisure Park: St Agnes. Colourful gardens surrounding models and rides.
World in Miniature: Goonhavern, south-west of Newquay. Models of local and world-famous buildings set in beautiful gardens.

A windsurfer's paradise . . .

WATER SPORTS
A variety of sports activities including sailing, water-skiing and windsurfing are available at the following centres:
Falmouth Windsurfing Centre: Stithians Reservoir. *Tel.* (0209) 861083.
Outdoor Adventure: Widemouth Bay. *Tel.* (028 885) 312.
Padstow Boardsailing School: Padstow. *Tel.* (0841) 532383.
Portscatho Windsurfing School: Portscatho. *Tel.* (0872) 75342.
Sailaway: St Anthony. *Tel.* (032 623) 357.

WILDLIFE AND FARMS
Bodmin Farm Park: Fletchersbridge, east of Bodmin. Working farm with animals and rides. (Open May to September, Monday to Saturday.)
Cornish Seal Sanctuary: Gweek, Helston. Injured seals cared for in large tanks; superb riverside setting. (Open all year, daily.)
DairyLand: Tresillian Barton, south-east of Newquay. 160 cows milked to music; friendly farm animals; Cornish Country Life museum; blacksmith's shop. (Open late May to early September, daily.)
Monkey Sanctuary: Murrayton, east of Looe. Protected breeding colony of Woolly Monkeys in spectacular setting. (Open early May to end September, Sunday to Friday.)
Newquay Zoo and Leisure Park: Trenance, Newquay. Wild animals in pleasant gardens. (Open April to November, daily.)
Paradise Park: Hayle. Tropical and rare birds, including Cornish Choughs, in seven-acre garden setting; rare breeds; railway. (Open all year, daily.)
Tamar Otter Park and Wild Wood: North Petherwin, Launceston. Breeding colonies of otters, owls, pheasants, peacocks, nature trail. (Open April to October, daily.)
Tropical Bird and Butterfly Gardens: Padstow. Unusual birds and butterflies flying free in tropical house; two-acre garden of subtropical plants. (Open all year, daily.)

CALENDAR OF EVENTS

February
Hurling. St Ives and St Columb
Major. On Feast Day at St Ives the
hurling match begins on the beach.
On Shrove Tuesday and the second
following Saturday at St Columb
Major, two teams battle for the
silver ball, trying to carry it to one
of two goals, two miles apart.

March
5th: St Piran's Day. Cornish flags (a
white cross on a black background)
are flown to honour the Patron
Saint of Tinners;
Spring Flower Shows at Penzance,
Falmouth and Truro;
Trevithick Day, Camborne. A
procession of dancers leads a
cavalcade of steam through the
streets in honour of the 'Father of
the Steam Locomotive', Richard
Trevithick.

May
*1st. 'Obby 'Oss and May Day
celebrations, Padstow.* The swirling
'Oss is led through the streets by an
accordian band and a 'teazer'.
*8th. Hal-an-Tow and Flora Day
celebrations, Helston.* Following an
early morning mumming-play, the
townsfolk dance through the streets
and in and out of houses behind a
silver band.

June
*Royal Cornwall Agricultural Show,
Wadebridge.* Large three-day event
featuring show-jumping, main-ring
attractions, trade stands, livestock
shows, etc.
Three Spires Festival, Truro. Two
weeks of concerts, readings, master
classes and fringe events, centred on
Truro Cathedral.
23rd. Midsummer Bonfires, lit on
beacons throughout Cornwall at
sunset.
*Whitsun weekend, Skinners Bottom
Folk Festival,* Blackwater, near
Truro. Three days of folk music,
craft stalls, children's events.

July
*Liskeard, Stithians and Launceston
Agricultural Shows:* Three large one-
day shows. Show-jumping,
livestock, etc.
Culdrose Air Day. Helicopters, jet
fighters and aerobatics at Royal
Naval Air Station, Culdrose, near
Helston.

*John Raw, international surfer, rides
'off the lip' at Newquay – see August*

August
St Mawgan International Air Day.
Air show by fighters, aerobatic
teams, etc, at RAF St Mawgan,
near Newquay.
Traction Engine Rally, near St
Agnes. Steam-powered engines and
machinery.
*Fosters Lager Surf Masters
Championship.* Fistral Beach,
Newquay, during the week leading
to Bank Holiday. The world's top
surfers in action.
Cornwall Folk Festival, Bank
Holiday weekend, Wadebridge.
Top folk acts from all over Britain.

September
Cornish Gorsedd Ceremony. The
Cornish Bards gather at an historic
site.
Summercourt Fair. The A30 comes
almost to a standstill as the village
celebrates.
'Crying the Neck' ceremony, as the
last sheaf of corn is cut.

October
Lowender Perran Celtic Festival,
Perranporth. Celtic musicians and
dancers gather to perform.

CORNWALL

Atlas

The following pages contain a legend, key map and atlas of Cornwall, three motor tours and sixteen Cornish coast and countryside walks.

Above: Tintagel Castle at sunset

Cornwall Legend

GRID REFERENCE SYSTEM

The map references used in this book are based on the Ordnance Survey National Grid, correct to within 1000 metres. They comprise two letters and four figures, and are preceded by the atlas page number.

Thus the reference for Bodmin appears 92 SX 0767

92 is the atlas page number

SX identifies the major (100km) grid square concerned (see diag)

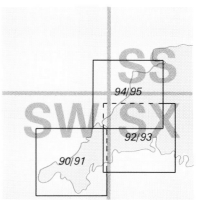

TOURIST INFORMATION

Ȧ	Camp Site	♞	Nature reserve
⌂	Caravan Site	☆	Other tourist feature
ℍ	Information Centre	⚏	Preserved railway
Ⓟ	Parking Facilities	⚘	Racecourse
☀	Viewpoint	⋎	Wildlife park
✗	Picnic site	🏛	Museum
⚑	Golf course or links	⚘	Nature or forest trail
🏰	Castle	m	Ancient monument
🏛	Cave	((	Telephones : public or motoring organisations
⛨	Country park		
❀	Garden	PC	Public Convenience
🏛	Historic house	▲	Youth Hostel

ORIENTATION

True North

At the centre of the area is 1° 33'E of Grid North

Magnetic North

At the centre of the area is about 4½° W of Grid North in 1987 decreasing by about ½° in three years

0767 locates the lower left-hand corner of the kilometre grid square in which Bodmin appears.

Take the first figure of the reference 0, this refers to the numbered grid running along the bottom of the page.
Having found this line, the second figure 7, tells you the distance to move in tenths to the right of this line. A vertical line through this point is the first half of the reference.

The third figure 6, refers to the numbered grid lines on the right hand side of the page, finally the fourth figure 7, indicates the distance to move in tenths above this line. A horizontal line drawn through this point to intersect with the first line gives the precise location of the places in question.

KEY-MAP 1:500,000 or 8 MILES to 1"

ROAD INFORMATION

—[M 5]—Ⓢ—◆—⑳—	Motorway with service area, service area (limited access) and junction with junction number
—[M 5]—Ⓛ—㉙—	Motorway junction with limited interchange
====[Mid 1987]===✦=	Motorway, service area and junction under construction with proposed opening date
—[A 30]—Ⓢ—◆—	Primary routes } Single and dual carriageway with service area
—[A 387]—◆—	Main Road
– – – – – – –	Main Road under construction
—▬—▬—▬—	Narrow Road with passing places
[B 3302]————	Other roads { B roads (majority numbered) / Unclassified (selected)
◀—‖ TOLL	Gradient (1 in 7 and steeper) and toll
𝄞 24 ⧘15	Primary routes and main roads }
𝄞 24 ⧘15	Motorways }

Primary Routes

These form a national network of recommended through routes which complement the motorway system. Selected places of major traffic importance are known as Primary Route Destinations and are shown on these maps thus TRURO . This relates to the directions on road signs which on Primary Routes have a green background. To travel on a Primary Route, follow the direction to the next Primary Destination shown on the greenbacked road signs. On these maps Primary Route road numbers and mileages are shown in green.

Motorways

A similar situation occurs with motorway routes where numbers and mileages, shown in blue on these maps correspond to the blue background of motorway road signs.

Mileages are shown on the map between large markers and between small markers in large and small type

1 mile = 1·61 kilometres

GENERAL FEATURES

———————	Railway
AA..:A RAC..:R PO..:T	Telephone call box
+–+–+–+–+–+–+–+–+	National Boundary
– – – – – – – – –	County or Region Boundary
✈ ○	Large Town Town / Village
⊕	Airport
427.	Height (metres)

WATER FEATURES

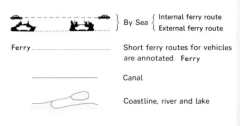

🚗– – –🚗 } By Sea	{ Internal ferry route / External ferry route
Ferry..................	Short ferry routes for vehicles are annotated Ferry
———————	Canal
~~	Coastline, river and lake

TOURS 1:250,000 or ¼" to 1 MILE
ATLAS 1:208,545 or 3¼ MILES to 1"

ROADS   Not necessarily rights of way

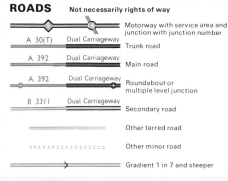

Motorway with service area and junction with junction number

A 30(T)   Dual Carriageway   Trunk road

A 392   Dual Carriageway   Main road

A 392   Dual Carriageway   Roundabout or multiple level junction

B 3311   Dual Carriageway   Secondary road

Other tarred road

Other minor road

Gradient 1 in 7 and steeper

RAILWAYS

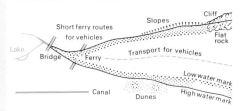

Road crossing under or over standard gauge track

Level crossing

Station

Narrow gauge track

WATER FEATURES

Cliff
Slopes
Flat rock
Lake
Bridge   Ferry   Transport for vehicles
Short ferry routes for vehicles
Low water mark
Canal   Dunes   High water mark

ANTIQUITIES

⊞   Native fortress

------   Roman road (course of)

Castle ·   Other antiquities

CANOVIVM ·   Roman antiquity

GENERAL FEATURES

Buildings

Wood

⊕   Civil aerodrome (with custom facilities)

Ⴎ   Radio or TV mast

Ⴎ   Lighthouse

ℂ ℂ   Telephones : public or motoring organisations

RELIEF

Feet	Metres	
		.274
		Heights in feet above mean sea level
3000	914	
2000	610	
1400	427	
		Contours at 200 ft intervals
1000	305	
600	183	
200	61	
		To convert feet to metres multiply by 0.3048
0	0	

WALKS 1:25,000 or 2½" to 1 MILE
ROADS AND PATHS Not necessarily rights of way

M 5   Motorway

A 30(T)   Trunk road

A 387   Main road   Narrow roads with passing places are annotated

B 3311   Secondary road

A 392   Dual carriageway

Road generally over 4m wide

Road generally under 4m wide

Other road, drive or track .... Path

RAILWAYS

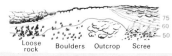

Multiple track   Level crossing
Single track   Cutting
Narrow Gauge
Road over & under   Embankment
Siding   Tunnel

GENERAL FEATURES

▲ Church with tower
● or   with spire   Electricity transmission line
+ Chapel without tower or spire   pylon pole

⊙ Gravel pit   NT National Trust always open

⬭ Sand pit   NT National Trust opening restricted

⬭ Chalk pit, clay pit or quarry   FC Forestry Commission pedestrians only (observe local signs)

⬭ Refuse or slag heap   National Park

HEIGHTS AND ROCK FEATURES

Contours are at various metres / feet vertical intervals

50 ·   Determined   ground survey
285 ·   by   air survey

Surface heights are to the nearest metre / foot above mean sea level. Heights shown close to a triangulation pillar refer to the station height at ground level and not necessarily to the summit .

Vertical Face

75
60
50

Loose rock   Boulders   Outcrop   Scree

PUBLIC RIGHTS OF WAY

Public rights of way shown in this guide may not be evident on the ground

---------   Public Paths { Footpath / Bridleway

+++++++   By-way open to all traffic

-+-+-+-   Road used as a public path

Public rights of way indicated have been derived from Definitive Maps as amended by later enactments or instruments held by Ordnance Survey between 1 February 1968 and 1st November 1985 and are shown subject to the limitations imposed by the scale of mapping Later information may be obtained from the appropriate County Council .
The representation on this map of any other road, track or path is no evidence of the existence of a right of access.

WALKS AND TOURS (All Scales)

7   Start point of walk

→   Route of walk

Line of walk

▶▶▶   Alternative route

3   Start point of tour

→   Route of tour

Featured tour

Key to Atlas pages

| Distances in miles to BODMIN | | | |
Map Ref: 92 SX 0767			
Barnstaple	64	London	236
Bournemouth	148	Oxford	218
Bristol	146	Penzance	46
Cardiff	185	Plymouth	31
Exeter	66	Southampton	180

CORNWALL

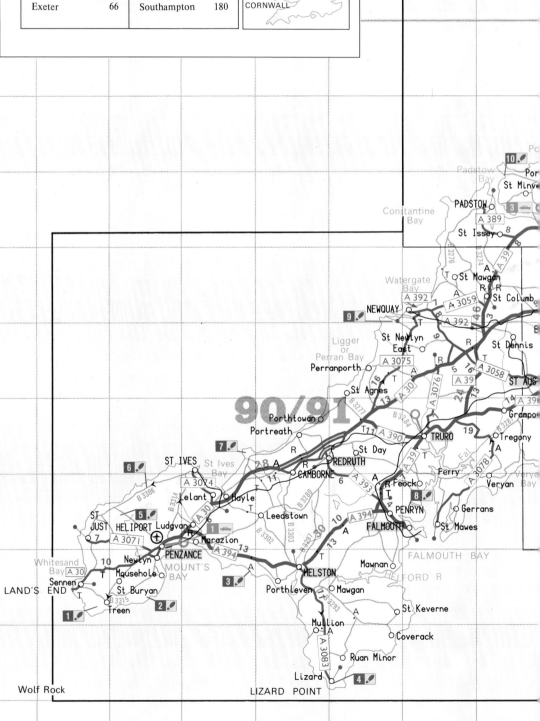

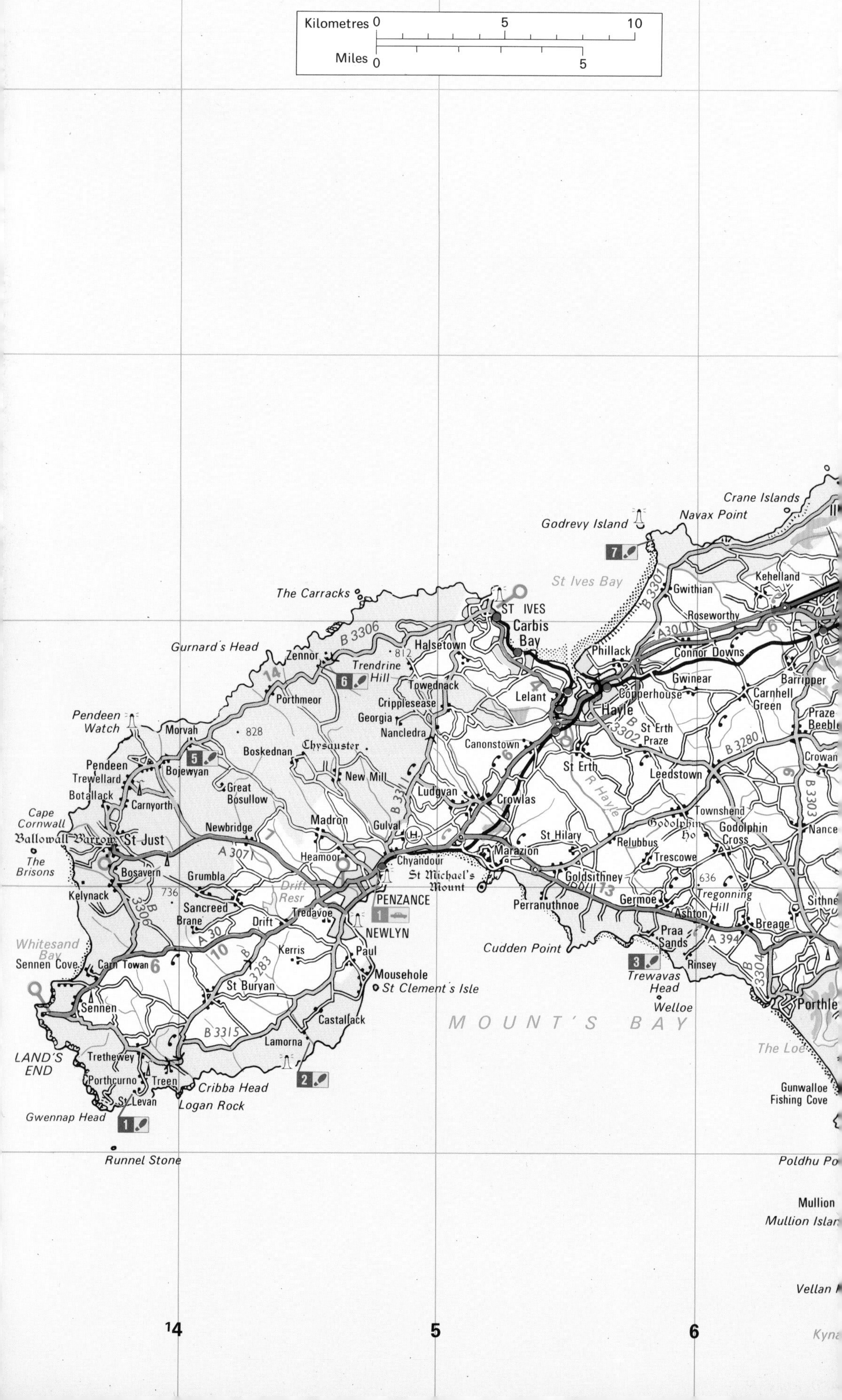

Kilometres 0   5   10

Miles 0   5

Crane Islands

Navax Point

Godrevy Island

7

St Ives Bay

Gwithian

Kehelland

The Carracks

Roseworthy

ST IVES

Carbis Bay

Phillack

Connor Downs

Gurnard's Head

B 3306

Zennor

Halsetown

812

Trendrine Hill

6

Lelant

Hayle

Gwinear

Barripper

Carnhell Green

Praze Beeble

Towednack

Copperhouse

St Erth Praze

Porthmeor

Cripplesease

Georgia

Nancledra

Canonstown

St Erth

Leedstown

Crowan

Pendeen Watch

Morvah

828

Boskednan

Chysauster

New Mill

St Hilary

Townshend

Godolphin Ho

Godolphin Cross

Nance

Pendeen

Trewellard

Bojewyan

Great Bosullow

Ludgvan

Crowlas

Relubbus

Trescowe

Botallack

Carnyorth

Madron

Gulval

Marazion

Goldsithney

636

Sithne

Cape Cornwall

Ballowall Barrow

St Just

Newbridge

Heamoor

Chyandour

St Michael's Mount

Germoe

Ashton

Tregonning Hill

Breage

The Brisons

Bosavern

Grumbla

Drift Resr

PENZANCE

1

Perranuthnoe

13

A 394

Kelynack

736

Sancreed

Brane

Drift

Tredavoe

NEWLYN

Cudden Point

Praa Sands

Rinsey

Whitesand Bay

A 30

Kerris

Paul

3

Porthle

Sennen Cove

Carn Towan

St Buryan

Mousehole

St Clement's Isle

Trewavas Head

Welloe

Sennen

B 3315

Lamorna

Castallack

MOUNT'S BAY

The Loe

LAND'S END

Trethewey

Porthcurno

Treen

Cribba Head

Logan Rock

2

Gunwalloe Fishing Cove

St Levan

Gwennap Head

1

Runnel Stone

Poldhu Po

Mullion

Mullion Islan

Vellan

14   5   6

Kyna

Cambeak

Fire Beacon Point
13

B 3263

Boscastle

Castle
Trevalga

Tintagel Head
Bossiney

Tintagel

Treknow
1009
Trewarmett

B 3266

Start Point

Treligga

Delabole

Camel

A 39

Port Isaac Bay

B 3314

Helstone

Rumps Point   **10**

Port Isaac

St Teath

Pentire Point   *Port Quin Bay*   Portquin   Portgaverne

Tregeare Rounds

727

New Polzeath

Trelights   Pendoggett

B 3267   11

Gulland Rock   *Padstow Bay*

Michaelstow

St Endellion   8   Trelill

St Breward

Polzeath
Trebetherick

Gunver Head

Trevose Head   Crugmeer   Tredrizzick   St Minver

St Kew

Row

St Breward

Quies   243   257   Rock   Chapel Amble   St Kew Highway   St Tudy

R Allen

Treyarnon   PADSTOW   Bodieve   435   Blisland

Constantine Bay   St Merryn   A 389   Trevanson   St Mabyn   B 3266

Porthcothan Bay   Shop   Little Petherick   8   St Breock   WADEBRIDGE   Egloshayle   Helland   21

Park Head   B 3276   **91**   Penrose **19**   St Issey   3   **92**

Bedruthan Steps   St Eval   Rumford   Tredinnick   Burlawn   Washaway   Cardinham

St Ervan   *St Breock Downs*

TOUR *1* 46 MILES
The Land's End Peninsula

Starting at Penzance, the drive visits the fishing villages of Newlyn and Mousehole, then veers inland and continues to Land's End. The coastal road to St Ives passes through rugged moorland interspersed with farms. Beyond St Ives Bay a detour is made to view St Michael's Mount before returning to Penzance.

The drive starts from Penzance (see page 63). A mild climate encourages the growth of exotic plants, and Regency buildings testify to its long popularity as a resort.

Follow signs to Newlyn and Mousehole (A3077) alongside the harbour. Newlyn (see page 60), a busy fishing port, became famous for its artist colony in the 19th century. Painters still live and work among the quaint old cottages and fish-cellars.

From Newlyn, continue along the A3077. After crossing a bridge, turn left on to an unclassified road to Mousehole (see page 58). With its granite houses and workmanlike harbour the village has a flavour of traditional Cornwall. Drivers must take care as the streets are narrow.

Turn left and drive to the harbour, then turn right and right again, signed Paul. This is the burial place of Dorothy Pentreath, one of the last people to speak the ancient Cornish language.

Go past the church (signed Land's End). In just over half a mile, turn left on to the B3315. After passing Sheffield, take the last turning to Lamorna Cove (see page 50). Huge granite boulders and rocky outcrops contrast with gentler countryside around. Today the cove is visited for its lovely scenery.

Re-join the B3315 and continue for 3¼ miles. At the T-junction, turn left. The road descends steeply, with a hairpin bend, then goes up to Treen. The tiny village stands near the end of a fortified headland known as Treen Castle (NT). A relative of Oliver Goldsmith overturned the 66-ton Logan rock, a rocking stone reached by a footpath from Treen, and was made to replace it at his own expense. Beautiful walks can be taken in the area.

Continue on the B3315 for ¾ mile, then turn left (unclassified) to Porthcurno (see page 65). To the west of the good beach, the Minack Theatre was built in 1931, with an auditorium cut into the rock and a stage above the sea.

Re-join the B3315 and continue westwards. After two miles, turn left on to the A30 and drive for about ½ mile to Land's End (see page 51). This is England's most westerly mainland point. On a fine day the Isles of Scilly are visible 28 miles away to the west.

Return along the A30, and reach Sennen (see page 76). Sennen Cove offers good bathing and fine scenery.

Leave Sennen on the A30. After 1¼ miles, turn left on to the B3306, signed St Just. After 3 miles turn left at the T-junction on to the A3071 and enter St Just (see page 73). The old church in the lovely village has a wall painting, an inscribed stone of the 5th century, and the shaft of a 9th-century cross.

Continue on the B3306 to Pendeen. All around are old mine workings.

Continue along the B3306 to Morvah. About 1 mile south of the village, which lies on the edge of Penwith moorland, are Chûn Castle and Chûn Quoit, an Iron Age stone fort and a Neolithic chamber tomb.

Continue on the B3306 to Zennor (see page 80). Zennor is famous for a mermaid carving in the church, and for an associated legend.

Continue on the B3306 to St Ives (see page 72). Old houses and winding alleys cluster beneath the 120ft spire of the 15th-century church.

Leave St Ives on the A3074, signed Hayle. Pass Carbis Bay on the left and continue into Lelant (see page 52) on the River Hayle.

At Lelant turn right and in ½ mile bear right at the mini-roundabout, signed Penzance, with the 'Cornucopia' on the left. At the next roundabout, take the third exit on to the A30, passing Canonstown and Crowlas. After a mile, at the next roundabout, take the second exit on to an unclassified road, signed Marazion (see page 56). St Michael's Mount (see page 75), with its splendid castle (NT) and priory, can be reached by boat from Marazion, or on foot along a causeway at low tide.

Return along the unclassified road, signed Penzance. Re-join the A30 at the roundabout at Longrock, and return to Penzance.

The mermaid of Zennor, carved on a bench-end in the church

St Michael's Mount, worth a detour at any time of day

St Ives, view across the harbour. Popular with tourists and artists alike, St Ives has now spread up the hill from the maze of old streets behind the wharf

TOUR 2 79 MILES

Woods and Bays of the South-East

Running through a region of deep wooded valleys stretching to the sea, the route also takes in one of Cornwall's finest houses, a miniature cathedral city and a sanctuary for monkeys.

The drive starts from Looe (see page 53). Now one town, until 1883 West and East Looe were separate. Looe has a double role, as a resort with good bathing and as Cornwall's main centre for shark fishing.

Follow signs to Plymouth via Torpoint along the A387. In ½ mile branch right on to the B3253. In 3¾ miles re-join the A387 and at Hessenford turn right on to the B3247, signed Seaton. From Seaton an unclassified road on the right may be taken to the Woolly Monkey Sanctuary at Murrayton (see page 83). Part of the wooded valley at Murrayton has been turned into a sanctuary where visitors can observe the animals at close quarters (OACT).

From Seaton take the steep ascent (1 in 7) to Downderry. An ascent with a hairpin bend follows. After ⅓ mile, bear right, signed Crafthole. Go straight on, signed Millbrook, then in 2 miles turn right (unclassified), signed Whitsand Bay. On the outskirts of Cawsand keep left, and in ½ mile turn left. (To visit Kingsand, turn right.) Turn left on to the B3247, signed Millbrook. Alternatively, turn right to visit Mount Edgcumbe House and Country Park. First built in the 16th century, Mount Edgcumbe House was a victim of the 1941 Plymouth Blitz and afterwards was restored. It has fine Hepplewhite furniture, and most of the large estate has been turned into a country park with scenic walks.

Continue with the B3247, signed Millbrook. At Millbrook, turn left, signed Torpoint, then bear right. The road ascends steeply (1 in 6). In 2¾ miles turn right, signed Torpoint A374. The road descends steeply (1 in 7) to Antony. From here a 1¼-mile detour to the right can be made, to Antony House (see page 82). This dignified, Queen Anne mansion (NT) has associations with the Cornish Carew family who played an active part in politics. One of the most impressive houses in Cornwall, it has panelled rooms and stands in 250 acres of parkland.

From Antony, follow the A374 Liskeard road and continue through Sheviock to Polbathic. Here turn right on to the B3249, signed St Germans. In 1 mile keep left under the railway bridge, signed Saltash, and enter St Germans (see page 72). Until 1043 this little village was Cornwall's cathedral town. The existing church was consecrated in 1261 and is one of Cornwall's best examples of Norman architecture. In the village itself are six gabled almshouses and a fine 19th-century gatehouse.

At the far end of the village branch left on an unclassified road, signed Liskeard. In 1 mile go over the crossroads and in another ¼ mile turn right on to the A374. At Trerulefoot roundabout take the second exit to join the A38. Follow for 5½ miles before branching left on to the A390 to reach Liskeard (see page 52). A pleasant market town with steep, narrow streets, Liskeard was one of Cornwall's four stannary towns. Charles I slept at Stuart House during 1644, and the water of Pipe Well in Well Lane is said to have healing properties.

From Liskeard proceed to the bypass, following signs for Bodmin A38, and after 3¼ miles reach Dobwalls. From Dobwalls, remain on the Bodmin road and descend into the Fowey Valley. After crossing the River Fowey a road on the right, signed St Neot (see page 75), leads to Carnglaze Slate Caverns. St Neot's 15th-century church has remarkable stained glass. The quarry has been in use since the 14th century and may be visited. Perhaps its most remarkable feature is a blue-green underground lake.

Continue on the A38 for another two miles, then turn left into the unclassified road, signed Looe scenic route. In one mile turn left on to the A390. After one mile turn right on to the B3359, signed Looe. In 9 miles, turn right to Lanreath. Lanreath Mill and Farm Museum has vintage tractors, engines and old farm implements, such as a turnip and cattle-cake cutter and grappling irons. The church is Norman. The 'Giant's Hedge', believed to be an ancient rampart, runs through the village.

Rejoin the B3359 and continue to Pelynt. In 1½ miles turn right, signed Polperro, then right again on to the A387. The road descends steeply (1 in 10) to Polperro (see page 64). A car park is provided on the approach to the village, which has tiny streets and alleyways leading down to the harbour in the cliffs. Artists are attracted here, and there is a smuggling museum, once the home of naturalist Jonathan Couch.

Return along the A387 to Looe.

21

The magnificent Norman doorway of
the church at St Germans

PLYMOUTH to ⛴
Roscoff................7-9 hrs
Santander.............24 hrs

View from the clifftop down to Polperro, an artist's haven, its narrow streets running
down to one of Cornwall's quaintest harbours

TOUR 3
King Arthur's Country

A drive of contrasts, including Tintagel, rich in legends, Boscastle, with its stern cliffs, the sweeping sands of Bude, and inland villages steeped in the past.

The drive starts from Wadebridge (see page 80), which has one of England's best mediaeval bridges.

Leave Wadebridge on the A39, following signs to Bude. Cross the river bridge, then at the mini-roundabout turn left. In ½ mile at the traffic signals turn left on to the B3314, signed Port Isaac. In 1½ miles Trewornan Bridge is crossed over the River Amble. In 2 miles turn left on to the unclassified road, signed Rock. 1¼ miles further, keep left for Pityme. From here a detour can be made to Rock where the small church of St Michael, at nearby Porthilly, was dug from drifting sand. It has a simple Norman font.

From Pityme the main tour continues on the Polzeath road. The road goes through Trebetherick and descends steeply (1 in 5) to Polzeath (see page 65). Its main attractions are safe bathing and excellent sands that offer some of the best surfing in Cornwall. On the golf links, the tiny church of St Enodoc was excavated from the sand in 1863. John Betjeman is buried there.

Leave Polzeath and ascend sharply (1 in 7). After 2 miles branch left on to a road signed Port Isaac. In ½ mile turn left on to the B3314 for St Endellion. Inside the church, are several quaint bell-ringer's rhymes. A number of amusing Georgian epitaphs can be seen in the churchyard.

Leave St Endellion and continue along the B3314 for 1 mile, then turn left on to the B3267 for Port Isaac (see page 65). This is an exceptionally picturesque fishing village. The streets are narrow; no turning possible.

From Port Isaac continue on an unclassified road and descend to Portgaverne. Pass through the village and ascend (1 in 10). After 2¼ miles rejoin the B3314 and continue to Delabole (see page 45). At one time most of the roofs in Cornwall came from Delabole's slate quarry.

Leave Delabole and continue on the B3314 for 1¾ miles, then turn left on to an unclassified road signed Tintagel B3263, then keep left on the B3263, and pass through Trewarmett to Tintagel (see page 76). Linked by Geoffrey of Monmouth and many later writers with King Arthur, the 12th-century castle on its wave-lashed promontory has traces of a Celtic settlement, identified as the trading part of a chieftain's stronghold. The Old Post Office (NT) is a 14th-century manor house; King Arthur's Hall was built in 1933.

From the Wharncliffe Hotel in Tintagel turn right (signed Boscastle). In about ¾ mile descend (1 in 9) then ascend steeply (1 in 6). 2 miles further on turn left (signed Bude). The road descends with a hairpin bend to Boscastle (see page 40). The attractive village is ranged round a long, broad street that climbs steeply through woodland. Close to the harbour is a witches' museum.

Leave Boscastle on the Bude road B3263, cross a river bridge, and ascend steeply (1 in 6). After 3½ miles turn left and immediately left on to an unclassified road signed Crackington Haven. In 2½ miles descend steeply (1 in 5) into the village of Crackington Haven (see page 44). There is a good surfing beach here.

Continue through Crackington Haven and ascend steeply (1 in 6). After 3 miles reach Wainhouse Corner and turn left on to the A39 (signed Bude). Continue past Treskinnick Cross and Poundstock, then ½ mile further turn left on to an unclassified road. After ¾ mile follow the wide sweep of Widemouth Bay to Bude (see page 40). Strong winds that have caused hundreds of wrecks over the centuries provide a constant supply of rollers, ideal for surfing, at Bude.

Leave Bude following signs for Bideford (A39). Shortly turn right (signed Camelford A39). After 1 mile turn right on to the A39 then turn left on the unclassified road signed Marhamchurch. At Marhamchurch turn left (signed Week St Mary), then bear right. At Week St Mary turn right (signed Canworthy Water) and at the end of the village branch right. In 3½ miles at the T-junction turn left. Just over a mile further, turn right and cross the river bridge to Canworthy Water. Continue with the Hallworthy road, and pass through Warbstow to Hallworthy. At Hallworthy turn right on to the A395 (not signed). In 2¾ miles turn left on to the A39 (signed Wadebridge), and in 5¾ miles reach Camelford (see page 42). One tradition places King Arthur's Camelot at Camelford. Slaughterbridge, which crosses the Camel River a mile north of the town, is one of the contenders for his last battleground.

Leave Camelford on the A39 and keep straight on, passing the edge of St Kew Highway to re-enter Wadebridge.

Port Isaac. The houses in the old part of this beautiful fishing village huddle together on the steep descent to the harbour

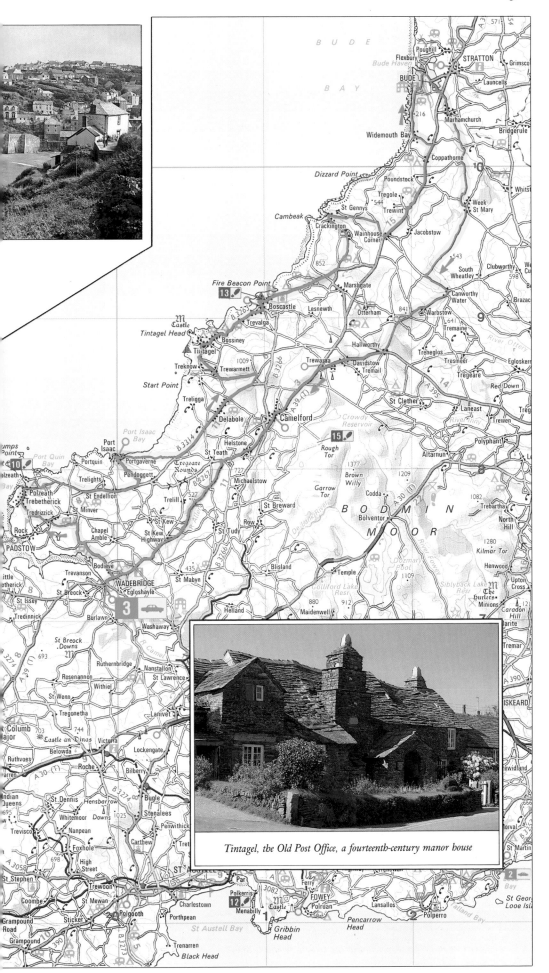

Tintagel, the Old Post Office, a fourteenth-century manor house

WALK 1
The Other
Land's End

Allow 2 hours

From the little granite church of St Levan, the walk follows an ancient field track before linking up with the coast path above the spectacular granite cliffs at Gwennap Head, the 'Fisherman's Land's End'.

Park in the field above the church (SW381222) then walk to the road end, ignoring the beach path on the left. St Levan, or Selevan to give him his ancient name, was one of a number of Celtic saints who settled in Cornwall in the 6th century. He seems to have been something of a genial eccentric, a qualification well-suited to this remarkable landscape with its green and gentle countryside linked to a rugged Atlantic coast.

The present church which is worth a visit has a remarkable font in the Norman style. In the churchyard there is a large granite rock, split in two, known as St Levan's stone.

Turn left at the road end and walk uphill past a cottage. A narrow path leads to a granite stile into a field, whose left edge is followed for 50 yards to another stile. As you cross, on the right is another stile by a Celtic cross. Follow the left side of two fields to stiles, then cross three fields to stiles, all the time aiming north-west for a single house and farm buildings. Follow the left side of another field to a stile and road that leads south

past Lower Roskestal Farm. *After about three-quarters of a mile, where the road bends sharply left, take the second obvious track on the right. It leads downhill, across a stream and up to the coastguard road. Turn right for a few yards then take the track on the right up to the coastguard lookout, at Gwennap Head.* The sea-cliffs along this stretch of coast are particularly magnificent. Grey, lichened pinnacles crown the lower walls of golden granite, above a sparkling Atlantic. A mile offshore lies the Runnel Stone Buoy, marking the outer end of a notorious reef.

Turn left in front of the look-out and follow the coast path to Porthgwarra Cove. The two painted cones on the left are navigation marks, once used by vessels for avoiding the Runnel Stone reef. At Porthgwarra there is a lovely little beach flanked by granite bluffs with caves and tunnels carved from the rock. They were used by fishermen in earlier times for storing gear and beaching their small boats.

Go past the café/shop and turn right at the signpost. Then go left and uphill past a house before turning right along the cliff top. Keep right at the next junction until reaching St Levan's holy well above the lovely Porth Chapel beach. The saint's holy well was said to cure eye troubles. It stands next to a roofless baptistry and just below is the site, now empty, of St Levan's original cell and chapel. Both are within easy reach of the beach and headland where he caught the single fish that made up his daily diet.

Go down the rocky path towards the beach then continue along the cliff-top to the next headland of Pedn-mên-an-mere. On the far edge of this headland is the open air Minack Theatre, carved out of the cliff, like a classical amphitheatre.

Follow the path to the theatre car park. (The theatre can be viewed if no play is in progress.) Follow the track from the car park to the road, then turn left and so go back to St Levan's church.

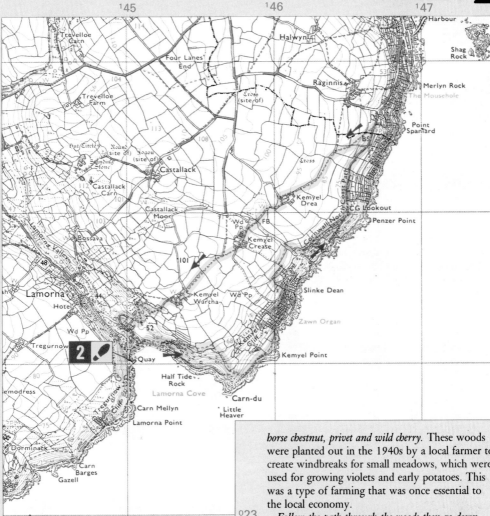

Lamorna's Sunshine Coast

Allow 3½ hours

The coast to the west of Penzance and Mousehole is less rugged than the rest of the Land's End sea-cliffs. It faces east across Mount's Bay and catches a great deal of sunlight; a softer landscape than the more open coast. The walk follows the coast from Lamorna then turns inland across a well-trodden field path that leads back to the cove. This path may be very muddy.

There is a car park at Lamorna Cove (SW450240). From the café and shop, walk in front of a row of cottages and across the stream, then continue along the coastal footpath past large heaps of quarried granite on the left. Last century, the Lamorna Quarries were worked extensively for their high quality stone, some of which was used for the building of the Thames Embankment. In 1851 a solid block of Lamorna granite was carved into a 22ft obelisk weighing 21 tons. It was sent to the Great Exhibition in Hyde Park.

Keep to the coastal path until reaching the Kemyel Woods, a fine stand of Monterey pines and cypresses, horse chestnut, privet and wild cherry. These woods were planted out in the 1940s by a local farmer to create windbreaks for small meadows, which were used for growing violets and early potatoes. This was a type of farming that was once essential to the local economy.

Follow the path through the woods then go down right to the coast before a steep uphill climb leads to the coastguard look-out at Penzer Point. Several hundred yards ahead look for a stile on the left by a wooden sign post. Cross the stile and reach another stile in the left-hand corner of the small field. Cross this and go diagonally right across a field to a stile, in the middle of the opposite wall. Cross the next field diagonally right to a stile in the top corner, then follow a line of stiles to the farm at Kemyel Drea. The path across these fields is part of a network of old rights-of-way between farm 'touns' and hamlets used intensively in the past. The removal of hedges in places has changed the nature of these paths but not their importance.

At Kemyel Drea go through the system of stiles and gates to the road. Turn left and follow the road round to the right then go sharp right at a signpost. This leads through a marshy wood to the road at Kemyel Crease. Turn left here and go through the buildings to a stile in the right-hand wall. Cross this and go diagonally right across the field to a stile then follow the line of stiles to the farm at Kemyel Wartha. At the road turn left and go through the farm, then take the left-hand path at the sign-post in front of the last house. From here the path leads down into the Lamorna Valley. It is interesting to note the way that nature has reclaimed the site of an extractive industry like quarrying. Even the abandoned quarry workings are nature reserves in their own right.

Follow the path as it winds downhill until reaching a rocky open space. Go left here until reaching the large quarry on the left, then follow the path round to the right past a ruined building. A little further on, bear round to the left and so downhill to Lamorna Cove.

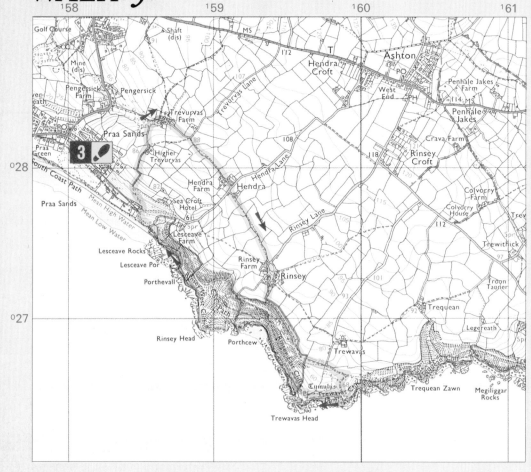

Camel on the Coast

Allow 2½ hours

A pleasant walk which takes you through fields and along the coast on the eastern shores of St Mount's Bay. The walk passes the remains of some 19th-century mine stacks and skirts the granite headlands of Rinsey and Trewavas. At the start and finish of the walk there is a beach which might well be very tempting if the weather were favourable.

There is a car park above the beach at the end of Hendra Lane (SW585276). Turn right at the car park entrance and walk a few yards uphill, then take the footpath on the left. Go left at the next junction until reaching a metalled road by some houses. This leads towards the charming little hamlet of Higher Trevurvas. Continue along the road and where it swings sharply left, cross the stile into a field on the right. Keep the hedge on your right and continue over two more stiles before reaching a lane that leads to the road at Hendra.

From these fields, out of sight and sound of the sea, the twin hills of Godolphin and Tregonning can be seen inland. On the right is Tregonning. It was in this neighbourhood that the 18th-century chemist William Cookworthy found the first Cornish deposits of china-clay (decomposed and altered granite). The site was not extensive and the main clay extraction now takes place near St Austell's 'Cornish Alps'.

Turn right at Hendra then left by a cottage. Go right across a stile then left to another stile. Cross the centre of the next field and follow the hedges over stiles until reaching the road at Rinsey, by a large barn. Turn right and go through Rinsey, leaving the National Trust car park sign to the right. Between the buildings on the right ahead there is a footpath sign pointing the way to Rinsey Cove. Follow the path to Rinsey mine stack.

This restored mine engine-house served the Wheal Prosper Mine which was first worked for copper in 1836 and runs for some distance beneath the sea. Both Rinsey and Trewavas are granite headlands on this coast of sedimentary rocks. Where the molten granite came into contact with the older, predominant slates and shales it formed liquids and gases which solidified into minerals.

Go left from the mine stack and follow the track across two stiles by a connecting wall until reaching an open field. Go along the left edge of the field then join a grass track that leads down to a granite stile in a wire fence. Turn right on to the coast path which crosses Trewavas Head. From the Head look back along the coast to the remarkable formation known as 'Camel Rock'. Millions of years ago, as the molten granite cooled, vertical and horizontal shrinkage cracks appeared and subsequent weathering along these joints has produced such characteristic shapes as the 'camel'.

Continue along the coast path on to National Trust land. Go along the coast path below the Wheal Prosper mine stack and continue uphill to the National Trust car park. Go through the car park then turn left and then right and follow the coast path avoiding all paths to right and left until the car park above the beach is reached.

Lizard, Lion and Lifeboat

Allow 3 hours

A walk from Lizard town round the famous headland of the Lizard, taking in cove and cliff-top and the Lizard lifeboat house before reaching the lovely Church Cove. Here amid trees and thatched cottages stands the delightful little church of Landewednack.

Please take care with children: the path goes close to the cliff-edge.

There is ample parking at Lizard town (SW703126). From the car park take the road that leads past the public toilets and on to Caerthillian Cove. Where the road ends by a house, follow the footpath down to the sea. The Lizard area is noted for wild flowers and for the many rare and alien species that flourish here. These include the tamarisk, a salt-resistant Mediterranean bush, on the way down to the cove, while the cliff faces at the Lizard headland are smothered with the exotic Hottentot fig.

On reaching the cove go left and follow the coast path round a series of headlands towards Lizard Point (old Lizard Head). From here there are views across

Mount's Bay to the far west of Cornwall. *Go down into Pistol Ogo Cove and cross a wooden bridge beneath tamarisks.* 'Ogo' is the Cornish word for 'cave', while the name 'Pistol', although associated with a notorious wreck of 1720 when 197 people drowned and firearms were washed ashore in crates, is more likely to come from the old Welsh word 'pystell' which means 'waterfall'.

Continue to the modern Lizard Point, taking great care on the path which although perfectly safe is sometimes close to the cliff edge. Cross the point where there are cafés and souvenir shops and continue past the Lizard Lighthouse. There has been a warning light on the Lizard since 1752, although unsuccessful attempts had been made in the previous century. Today the Lizard light is the most powerful in the country, visible for 21 miles in clear conditions. Its twin foghorns rise menacingly above the path.

Follow the path through the blackthorn groves of Housel Cove keeping right at the junction, and continue to Pen Olver Head and Bass Point coastguard lookout. There is a good view across Housel Bay to the 'Lion's Den', a vast chasm in the cliff-top formed by the collapse of a sea cave in 1847. The offshore rock pinnacle is called Bumble Rock.

Follow the path to Hot Point and to the lifeboat station at Kilcobben Cove, then on to Church Cove. Turn left here and go up to the church, past delightful thatched cottages. Landewednack Church is the most southerly church in Britain. It is centuries old and in 1678 the last sermon in the Cornish language was preached here.

Follow the road straight back to Lizard town.

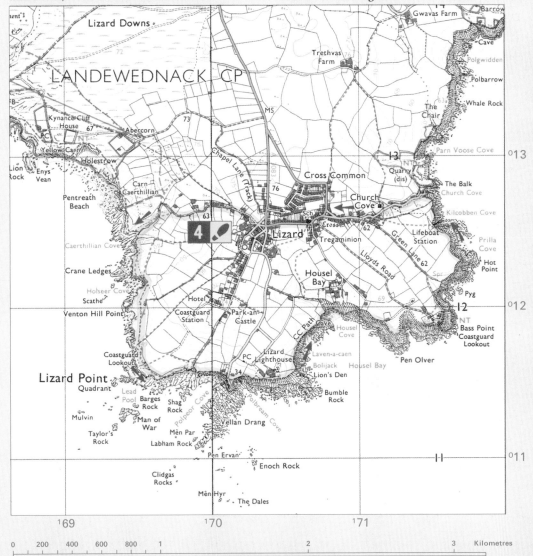

SCALE 1:25 000

Ding Dong Moors

Allow 1¾ hours

The granite hills and heath-covered moors that lie north of Penzance are rich in archaeological remains and this exhilarating walk takes in several ancient monuments.

Park opposite the Mên-An-Tol Print Studio (SW418344) and take the broad track leading inland. This track is said to be part of the ancient 'Tinners' Way' from Sennen to St Ives along which the early traders collected copper and tin from moorland smelting works.

Some distance along the track, pass the sign to the Mên-An-Tol, which we visit later on, and continue to the Mên Scryfa, an inscribed stone in the middle of a field on the left. Rejoin the track and continue to a junction of several paths. Nearby is a large 'whaleback' rock, with a cross-hole carved in it. This rock is called 'Four Parishes' and was the original meeting place of the ancient parishes of Madron, Morvah, Zennor and Gulval, names that excite interest in their own right.

Return to the junction and take the right hand of the two paths leading east uphill to the stone circle of Boskednan, known as 'Nine Maidens'. This Neolithic or Bronze Age monument of the period 2,000–1,500BC probably had an original 20 upright stones. Its present name is a traditional one that perhaps reflects early Christian superstition related to young ladies dancing on the Sabbath and being turned to stone for their sins.

Continue along the path that leads on from Nine

The Mên-An-Tol, or 'stone of the hole'

Maidens. If clear, there are views across Mount's Bay to the Lizard and St Michael's.

On reaching a pot-holed track, turn right towards Greenburrow mine shaft. This was the pumping house for the old Ding Dong mine which extends beneath the surrounding moorland.

From the mine shaft, and facing the distant rocky tor of Carn Galver, walk a few yards down the slope then take the left-hand path. Keep left at the next junction. One hundred yards before a gate in a low wall, take the right-hand junction. Continue along path until reaching a square, granite boundary stone. A few yards further on, ignoring gate on left, bear left along track, then cross a low wall and go right following an obvious path that crosses a stream before leading to the Mên-An-Tol, the 'boled stone'. Archaeologists are reticent about defining the Mên-An-Tol, since the present stones have been moved within the past 100 years. The central stone which may have been part of a burial chamber is also known as the 'crickstone' and is reputed to have curative powers if crawled through nine times against the track of the sun (an exercise more likely to encourage 'cricks' than to cure them).

Continue to rough lane and turn left to go to the car park.

Mermaid Walk

Allow 2 hours

The village of Zennor with its handsome Norman church lies between a high rocky moorland and a magnificent coast, and is the ideal starting point for a coast and inland walk through this most ancient and impressive of Cornish landscapes.

Park at the car park between the Wayside Museum and the Tinners Arms (SW454384). The story of the Mermaid of Zennor who lured a squire's son to her watery lair is the most enduring legend of the district although the reality of ancient settlement, subsistence farming and tin-mining has created a more fascinating history. The Zennor area has attracted writers including D H Lawrence who once lived near by and it still inspires many famous painters.

Follow the lane between pub and church (both worth a visit), and continue sharply left. The lane leads to the coast path at a National Trust sign and a waymarking stone. Go straight ahead for a detour to Zennor Head only a few hundred yards away. The main walk goes left and down some steep steps and slippery rocks, and across a little stream. Below here is Pendour Cove where the legendary Mermaid is said to have lured the squire's son after hearing him singing.

Follow the path across the slope then turn left and go uphill to a welcome wayside seat. The path now skirts the steep slopes that run down to Veor Cove. Follow the path down the edge of the next headland with superb views of Zennor Head across the bay. The cliffs here are a mixture of greenstone, a much older rock than granite, and killas, which is the Cornish name for the ancient sedimentary rocks that once lay beneath the sea. It is along the junctions of these older rocks with the inland granite that mineral seams occur, and the Carnelloe area, where the path now leads, was once heavily mined.

Continue round the base of the headland. Where the path branches by some rocky pillars, take the left-hand branch that leads uphill and along the back wall of an isolated cottage (this section may sometimes be overgrown). Join a track that leads inland past some old mine workings with fine views to Gurnard's Head. At the coast road, turn left in front of some houses and where the track swings sharply left, go straight ahead over a granite stile. From here, the traditional field path that once linked all the small farms and hamlets of the coast leads back to Zennor, through characteristic small Cornish fields, bordered by 'hedges' of stone and witch-like blackthorn.

Cross a second stile and go past an open gapway, keeping the hedge on your left. Then cross a stile and go straight across the next field to another stile. Continue with Zennor church tower directly ahead to yet another stile, then across the next two fields at a slight rightward angle to a final stile. From here make for the farm buildings ahead, and into a muddy lane. At the main road turn left and go down the steep hill past the museum and so back to the car park.

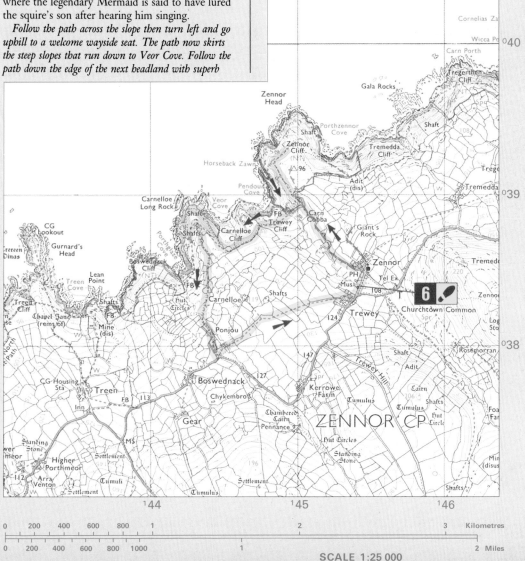

SCALE 1:25 000

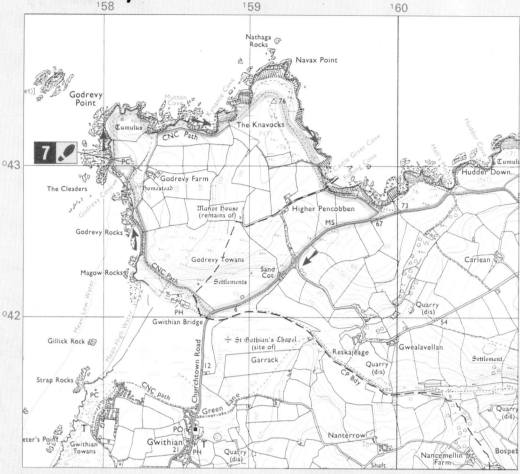

To the Lighthouse

Allow 2½ hours

A high level cliff path leads round the headlands of Godrevy and Navax Points with views to dramatic cliffs and coves. It is an area that is particularly rich in wild flowers.

Please take care with children: the path goes close to the cliff edge.

Most of the walk is on National Trust property. Park at the Trust car park (SW582431) and walk in the direction of the lighthouse, crossing a stone stile in the boundary wall. Follow the broad track directly uphill. The view to Godrevy lighthouse is particularly fine. It was built in 1859 in hope of reducing the number of wrecks that occurred on the notorious reef known as The Stones, running for a mile directly offshore. Moves to close the lighthouse in the 1930s were thwarted after protests by local fishermen and it is now automatic and unmanned. Its walled gardens, used by the early keepers, can still be seen, giving the island an intriguing but infinitely lonely atmosphere. The writer Virginia Woolf is said to have based her novel *To the Lighthouse* on Godrevy's romantic island.

Continue across the headland, following the track with care where it occasionally skirts the abrupt edge of the cliff. The cliffs here are of sedimentary rocks

The shag is a fierce defender of its cliff nest

that once lay beneath the ocean. They have been greatly altered by heat and by vast earth movements that have folded them into fantastic shapes. In the coves below the cliffs, the grey (or Atlantic) seal can often be glimpsed playing.

Continue along the path until reaching a stile into a field. Keep left and go down the side of the hedge until reaching another stile. Cross this and continue as far as the road. In summer the predominant colours along these paths and lanes are the purple of foxglove and the brilliant yellow of ragwort.

Turn right at the road and go downhill until the track (second on right) that leads right on to Godrevy headland. The sand to the west covers much of the mediaeval town of Conerton which was steadily overwhelmed by the shifting dunes from the 13th century onwards. The modern village of Gwithian a few hundred yards away has a handsome church with a fine 15th-century tower.

Continue along the road across Godrevy Towans with fine views to St Ives and so back to the car park.

A Few Miles Round Mylor

Allow 3 hours

This lovely walk reveals coastal Cornwall in a different light from that of rugged headland or sandy bay. Flanked on three sides by Mylor Creek, Restronguet Creek and the great sheltered anchorage of Carrick Roads, the wooded country around Mylor Bridge is delightful. The route passes many private houses in enviable positions but a Right of Way throughout ensures pleasure for the walker as well. There is a pleasant riverside pub midway.

There are parking facilities at Mylor Bridge (SW804363). The walk starts at Trevellan Road next to the river. Walk down the road and along the path in front of some houses. Then go left, along a narrow alleyway before crossing a road end, then turn right and into a field. Continue through a number of fields and gates, passing an old quarry and crossing a small causeway until reaching Greatwood Quay. Short sections of the path are often muddy in wet weather. After tantalising glimpses of the river through trees, the whole splendid panorama of Carrick Roads is viewed from Greatwood Quay. Across the creek on the right is Mylor Harbour, once the scene of a Naval dockyard where stores and equipment were shipped aboard. Post Office sailing ships were also serviced here during the era of the 'packet' services, up to the mid-19th century. Across the broad sweep of Carrick Roads lies the lovely Roseland Peninsula. This whole area is now a popular yachting and water-sports centre.

Continue along the track from Greatwood Quay and on reaching a narrow road turn right then left by the gates of Greatwood House. The path leads on delightfully to Restronguet Weir. Go along the beach or use the alternative permitted path at high tide, and continue to Restronguet Passage. The Passage was on the route of the old Post Road from Falmouth to Truro and there was a rowing-boat ferry here for at least 500 years. The Pandora Inn is situated at the side of the river.

From the Pandora, follow the track along the shore. There is a rash of 'Private' notices here, but they have no relevance to the public right of way which is clearly marked. One of the great pleasures of this walk in spring and summer is the delightful mix of wild flowers and cultivated garden plants. There is a luxuriance here that is rarely seen on the coast.

After about half a mile, the track curves inland, and goes across three cattle grids to Halwyn. Go left at the junction by Halwyn and follow the lane to the public road. Go left here keeping to the right at the next junction, and down Bells Hill to the car park.

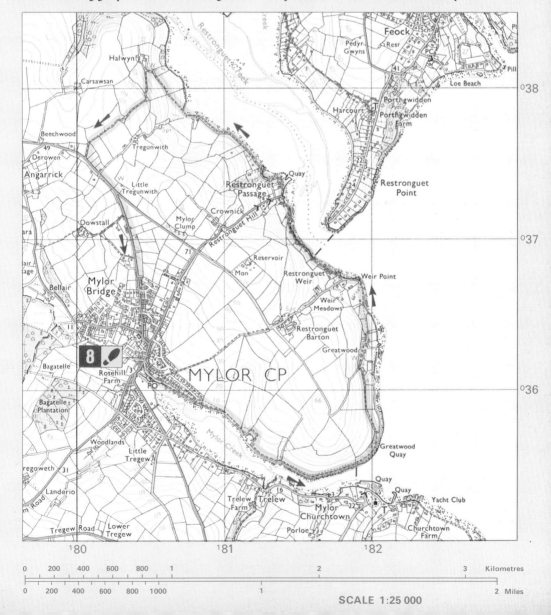

The map shows grid references 176, 177, 178 along the top and 61, 60, 59 along the left side. Notable labels include: The Chick, Kelsey Head, Settlement, Tumulus, Cave, Holywell Bay, DANGER AREA, Holywell Beach, Dunes, Penhale Point, Monk, Shaft (dis), Shafts (dis), Mine (dis), Resr, Shaft (dis), Settlement, Hoblyn's Cove, Ligger Point, Tip (dis), Mine (dis), Pentire Point West, Quarry (dis), Vugga Cove, Crantock Beach, Halwyn Farm, West Pentire, Treago Mill, Treago Farm, Quarry (dis), Pit (dis), Cubert Common, Quarry (dis), The Kelseys (National Trust), The Common, Tumulus, Lewannick, Holy Well (restored), Holywell, Trevornick, Camping Park, Pentire Point East, Lewennick Lodge, Salt Cove.

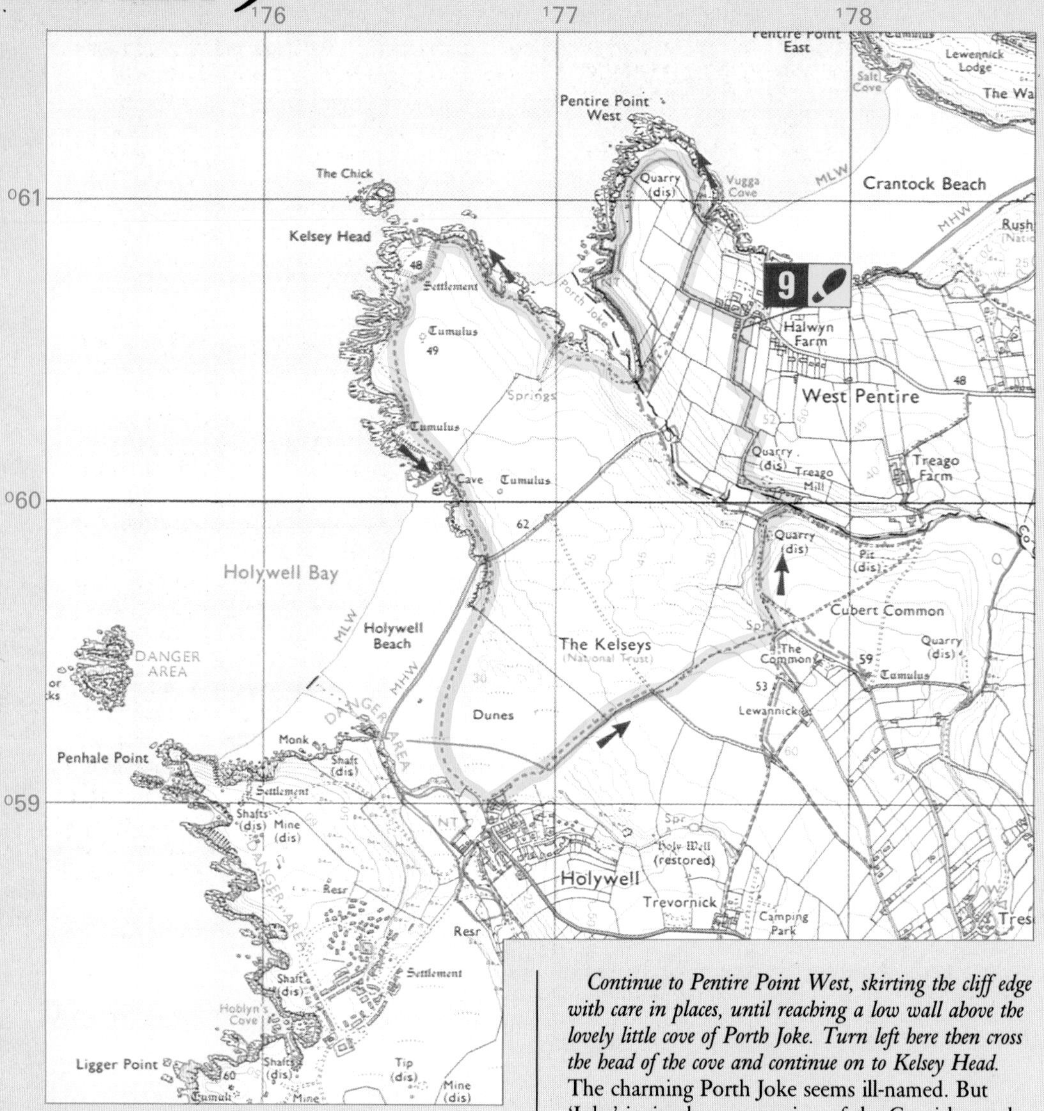

Sand Country

Allow 3 hours

The headlands of Pentire Point West and Kelsey lie to the west of the splendid Crantock Beach near Newquay where the River Gannel reaches the sea. This stretch of coast has large areas of sand lying between rocky headlands and the latter part of the walk crosses the Kelseys, an area of open grazing now in the hands of the National Trust. Please take care with children: the path goes close to the cliff edge.

There is a car park at West Pentire village (SW776606). From the car park entrance, walk straight down the road and turn left. Continue through the gate and along the track past the footpath to Porth Joke, and some yards further on, turn right at a gate and so on to the coast path above Crantock Beach. The River Gannel reaches the sea at the north end of Crantock Beach. It is now heavily silted but was once the natural port for Newquay and a landfall on the Ireland-Brittany route used from prehistoric times by travellers seeking to avoid the treacherous passage round Land's End. From here they would trek across Cornwall to re-embark on the south coast.

Continue to Pentire Point West, skirting the cliff edge with care in places, until reaching a low wall above the lovely little cove of Porth Joke. Turn left here then cross the head of the cove and continue on to Kelsey Head. The charming Porth Joke seems ill-named. But 'Joke' is simply a corruption of the Cornish word 'gwic' meaning creek. Porth means bay.

Continue round Kelsey Head, the site of an Iron Age cliff castle. Follow the cliff path to a gate at the beginning of the sand dunes at Holywell Bay, and go down a wooden boardwalk. On the other side of Holywell Beach lie Penhale Point and Ligger Point, beyond which is the great expanse of Penhale Sands. Legend claims that an ancient city lies beneath the offshore sand between Newquay and Perranporth. The sands of Holywell are certainly mobile enough and there is much reclamation in progress here. Walkers are requested to keep to the boardwalk through this part of the dunes.

On reaching the car park and shop/café at Holywell village, turn left in front of a row of houses. Keep to the sandy path that climbs up through the dunes and skirts a golf course until the broad grassy expanse of the Kelseys is reached. In summer, these dunes support a variety of flowering plants unique to such an environment including the attractive sea-holly.

The path enters the Kelseys through a wooden gate. A short distance ahead where the golf course ends behind stone walls, go right, through another gate, past a National Trust sign and turn sharp left. When the wire fence on the left bends away to the left, carry straight on until joining the track from the house up on the right known as 'The Common'. Continue to the valley bottom, ignoring a stile and gate with 'No Camping' sign. Cross a stile by a footpath sign to West Pentire, then go over the stream and turn left at the track that leads steeply uphill to the car park.

Above Doom Bar

Allow 2½ hours

Pentire Point and Rumps Point lie on the eastern side of Padstow Bay. Both headlands dominate this dramatic stretch of coastline with the great cliff faces of Pentire, best viewed from Rumps Point. Most of the area is in the care of the National Trust.

Convenient parking is available at New Polzeath (SW936795). Leave the car park by the main entrance and turn right then right again into Gulland Road. Walk to the end of the road and where it joins with the charmingly named Baby Beach Lane, join the coastal path opposite. Go round the small cove of Pentireglaze Haven on to National Trust property, and continue to Pentire Point, ignoring any paths coming in from the right. The views across Padstow Bay from this

Lifeboat rescue on Doom Bar

stretch of pathway are magnificent. On the western shore lies Stepper Point and beyond is Trevose Head with the off-lying Gulland Rock. In fine conditions, the Camel Estuary seems a calm and secure waterway but it is marred by the suitably named Doom Bar – a dangerous ridge of sand and silt that has built up between the headlands.

Yet Padstow which lies on the west bank of the Camel was a busy port in years past and is still a flourishing holiday resort and fishing harbour. On May Day the ' 'Obby 'Oss' celebrations take place.

From Pentire Point with its off-lying Newland rock, continue along the coast path until reaching the path that leads on to the Rumps Headland. Follow this path on to the head. The Rumps with their remarkable pinnacles are composed of greenstone, a hard igneous rock, whereas the rest of Pentire is pillow lava that erupted from ancient volcanoes. From the Rumps the vast main wall of Pentire is visible.

Return to the main path and continue with the wall on your right. Looking back to the Rumps it can be appreciated how the promontory made an ideal cliff castle. Three Iron Age earth ramparts with ditches were constructed across the saddle.

Where the coast path turns sharply left at the junction of two walls, go right over a stile and head for a line of tamarisk trees. At the National Trust sign turn left. On reaching Pentire Farm go straight through the yard. Opposite the farmhouse go through a gate on the right into a lane (muddy in wet weather). This becomes a path leading downhill to the coast path above Padstow Bay, where a left turn up some wooden steps leads back to New Polzeath.

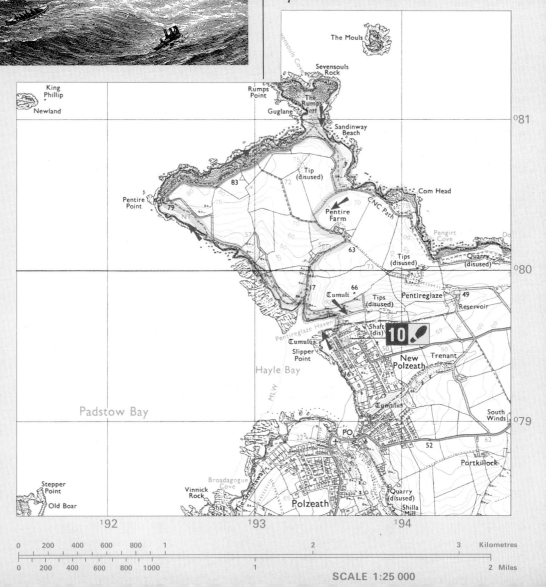

Razorbills live mostly at sea, but nest on rocky shores

Haven & Cross

Allow 3 hours

Dodman Point, or 'Deadman' as it is known locally, is the focus of this coastal walk from the old fishing village of Gorran Haven to the high headland, with its 19th-century stone cross and its remarkable Iron Age ditch and rampart fortification.

There is a substantial car park in Gorran Haven (SX011415). From the car park walk down towards the harbour and beach and turn right at Foxhole Lane before joining the coastal path at the top of some steps. Although surrounded by modern houses, Gorran Haven has at its heart a traditional complex of buildings and narrow lanes with names like Rattle Alley. It has an intriguing little 15th-century church on a site directly above the beach, probably sacred for many centuries before the present church was built. Gorran Haven has had seven quays since the 13th century. The present quay was built in 1885 and has been repaired since. The six previous quays were all washed away.

Follow the path along the cliff-top before turning right just past a stone bench. Note the memorial plaque set in the rock. (Alternatively, the path can be followed at a lower level around the headland.) At Vault Beach follow the path to the right and uphill, and go on to Dodman Point, keeping left at the obvious junction, before reaching open fields. Keep to the left edge of the fields until rejoining the path at the headland proper. The Dodman is a superb feature composed of hard sedimentary rocks that have resisted weathering. The rather stark-looking cross on the summit was erected in 1896 for spiritual glory, although it has served a more practical purpose as a guide to seafarers.

From the foot of the cross return to the junction of the paths and take the left-hand branch at signpost along the coast with views to the Lizard Point. Cross a wooden stile and by the gate a few yards further on, turn sharp right and walk up the ancient 'Bulwarks'. The Dodman was a classic Iron Age promontory fort defended by this magnificent ditch and rampart that is now in the care of the National Trust. With steep cliffs on the eastern and western flanks of the headland and panoramic views to seawards, the fort must have been hard to storm.

Follow the track, ignoring side paths until reaching Penare. Turn right past some handsome buildings in local stone and follow the road until reaching a T-junction. Go straight across and through a gate by a sign-post to Treveague. Cross some fields that are used in summer for tents and caravans and turn right at the farm buildings. Go left alongside the farmhouse, then right to a gate on the left. Go through the gate and follow the path downhill to where it leads right on to a lane between houses. A right turn at the main road leads back to the car park.

Du Maurier Country

Allow 3 hours

Gribbin Head makes up the eastern arm of St Austell Bay. It seems a gentle and passive headland without the raw, spectacular cliffs of the Land's End and Lizard areas but it is ringed by rocks against which the sea breaks heavily during storms. On its summit there is a remarkable navigational beacon, erected in 1832.

The walk starts at the secluded little cove of Polkerris and skirts the Menabilly Estate, long associated with the novelist **Daphne du Maurier**.

There is a large car park a few hundred yards before Polkerris (SX094523). Turn right on leaving the car park and walk down the lane to Polkerris. Turn left at the beach and go up the path, ignoring a flight of steps on the right. Continue uphill until reaching a quiet road. Turn right here. Polkerris was one of the busiest fishing harbours of last century. Beside the beach are the ruins of the old 'pilchard palace', one of the largest in Cornwall. Here the pilchards were 'baulked' in salted piles and pressed for their oil.

Follow the road keeping straight ahead at Tregaminion Chapel until reaching Menabilly Barton. Follow the track, keeping left at the junction as you pass through the farm, down to Polridmouth Cove. Inland lies the old Rashleigh family estate of Menabilly, associated in recent times with Daphne du Maurier. This was a classic Cornish estate in its heyday, complemented by woods, lakes, parkland and secluded cove. Note the fine herring-bone pattern in the old field wall on your left on the way down to the cove.

At the wooden stile above the cove, turn right and follow the coastal path. On reaching an open field, make directly for the tall beacon tower. Gribbin Head is National Trust property, and the view towards Fowey and the fine eastern headlands is magnificent. The 84ft-high beacon was erected by Trinity House in 1832 to help vessels navigate safely past the headland.

From the beacon follow the coast path along the western side of the headland, keeping left at all junctions. The views across St Austell Bay take in a broad mix of coast and landscape, from cliffs to sandy beaches and from the industrial complex round Par to the china-clay 'alps' above St Austell.

Where the path reaches the trees above Polkerris, go along the brow of the wood, ignoring the stiles, until you reach a coastal footpath sign. This leads down a series of inclines to the cove and so back to the car park.

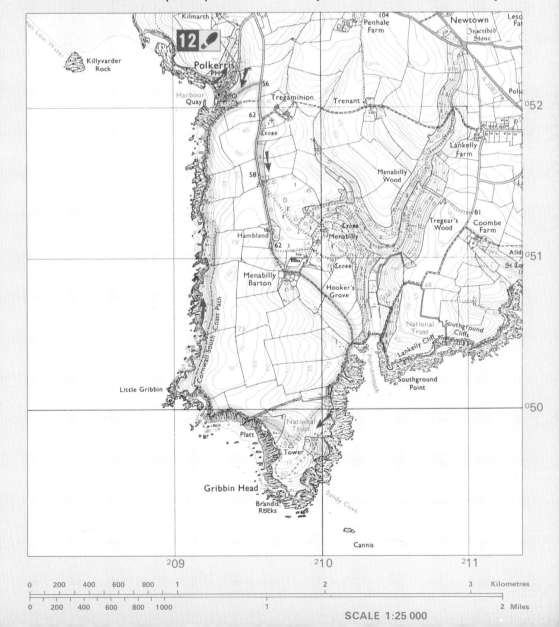

SCALE 1:25 000

WALK *13*
Boscastle Coast and Country

Boscastle – the harbour

Allow 3½ hours

Boscastle Harbour lies at the mouth of the Valency Valley, from where this walk follows the coastline to the south-west before striking inland past St Petroc's Church. From here the route goes inland until reaching a high-level right of way across the fields and a downhill stroll through the charming older part of Boscastle to the harbour once more.

From the car park at Boscastle Harbour (SX100913) walk to the bridge over the Valency River. Cross the bridge and turn right along by the harbour, then go up some steps and bear left along the cliff path. Boscastle Harbour, impressively situated in a break in the dramatic cliffs, dates from the mid-16th century. For many years it served the inland town of Launceston as a port, the two being linked by packhorse and wagon transport. Slate was also shipped out from here, the vessels being towed in and out by rowing gigs.

Willapark headland with its disused coastguard look-out is worth a detour for the magnificent views along the coast. On returning to the main path turn right. Walk with due care along the cliff top, ignoring inland paths before going down some wooden steps and over a stile. From here on the path is obvious.

Where the path drops into a shallow valley just before the 'Manor House', turn left through a gate and go straight up the lane past the farm to St Petroc's Church at Trevalga. St Petroc's is said to be a 13th-century foundation that was extensively restored in 1875. It has some charming features including a Norman font in greenstone and a hagioscope or 'squint'

between the chancel and the north transept.

From the church go to the main road. Cross over and continue up the steep lane past a chapel on the right before reaching the Old Rectory. By the rectory gate there is a path leading off to the left. It is sometimes very overgrown but does not run far before a field is reached.

From here the right-of-way is direct but not always obvious. On reaching Trehane Farm go on past the farmhouse to a field gate. From here, four fields must be crossed before the next lane is reached. Follow the right-hand hedge of the first field to a gap then cross the next field at a leftward diagonal angle until reaching a gate. Stay in the field but from the gate follow the hedge round to the right until reaching a stile. Cross this then go diagonally left across the next field to the middle of the opposite wall. Cross the wall and cross the next field to a stile near the bottom corner. This leads into a lane. Go left down the lane and at its end go right (not on to main road) then left at a cross roads and so past the Napoleon Inn. Go straight over at next cross-roads and on downhill through the delightful older part of Boscastle to the car park.

WALK 14
Hawker's Morwenstow

Allow 3 hours or more, depending on visits to various establishments along the way

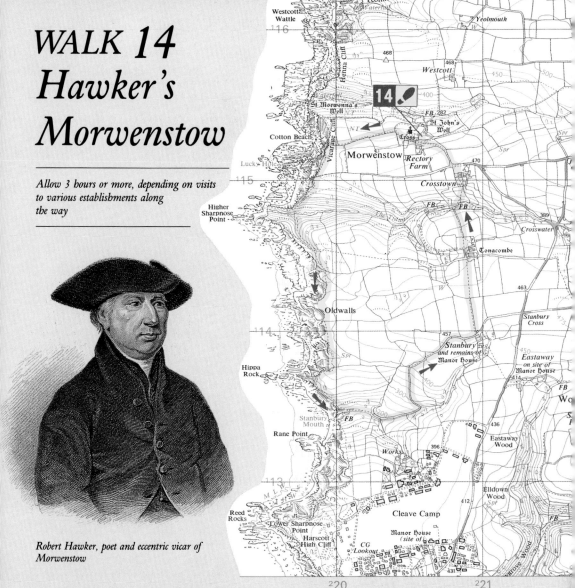

Robert Hawker, poet and eccentric vicar of Morwenstow

Here, the northern corner of Cornwall reluctantly gives way to Devon at Marsland Mouth. Even by Cornish standards it is a remote and secret place where the land runs deep and green to the very edge of the cliffs. A fitting place for the remarkable Victorian, Robert Stephen Hawker, poet, cleric and engaging eccentric.

Cars can be parked above Morwenstow Church which is certainly worth a visit. There is a magnificent Norman doorway and inside are some fine Norman arches and splendidly carved bench-ends.

From the car park (SS205153), follow the path towards the coast and go left on reaching the coastal path. It is difficult to sum up in a few words the celebrated Vicar of Morwenstow, the Rev Robert Stephen Hawker (1803–1875). Victim of legend and exaggeration he was nevertheless an extraordinary man. He has left his mark on the Morwenstow vicarage itself, whose chimneys he designed as replicas of two Oxford colleges, of three church towers associated with his family and of his mother's grave. He built for himself an even more eccentric reputation, re-created the pagan harvest festivals in Christian form and wrote among many other verses, the Cornish anthem, *The Song of the Western Men.* Some of these poems he wrote in a hut he built on the cliffs, using timbers from shipwrecked boats.

To follow in the steps of the good vicar in his seaman's boots and jersey, striding along the cliff, continue along the coast path, visiting Hawker's Hut on the way. Descend into the steep valley of Tidna Shute then climb to Higher Sharpnose Point and past the old coastguard look-out. From Higher Sharpnose there are superb views of Vicarage Cliff with its classic 'comb' of shaly rock known as 'culm', thrusting seawards, a coastal feature that repeats itself all the way to Bude and beyond. From the base of the Morwenstow cliffs, the Reverend Hawker recovered the bodies of over 40 drowned sailors throughout the years. He gave them all a Christian burial in the churchyard. Each had his own grave but there are no headstones or other marks.

Continue over a stile and stream then follow the path to the right over a second stream. Ahead can be seen the Cleave Camp Satellite Station. Continue down the steep slope to Stanbury Mouth then take the track leading pleasantly inland until it reaches a metalled road. At Stanbury Farm look for the stile in the left-hand wall just opposite the farm buildings. Cross this stile and follow the right-of-way across the field to a stile in the opposite wall, then continue across the next field and through a gate to Tonacombe. Tonacombe is a Tudor Manor House of the 15th century with splendid gateposts. It has three courtyards and a walled garden; within are contemporary wooden panellings and vast open hearths, and a minstrel's gallery.

Take the muddy track just left of the farm track or go directly along the farm track for a few yards then go left over a stile into a field. Follow the right-hand hedge until reaching the Tidna stream then go right and uphill over two stiles and so to the Bush Inn. Turn left at the road and return to Morwenstow.

0 200 400 600 800 1 2 3 Kilometres
0 200 400 600 800 1000 1 2 Miles
SCALE 1:25 000

WALK 15
The Roof
of Cornwall

The major part of this walk crosses private land, as there are no public footpaths on this part of Bodmin Moor. Before this walk can be undertaken, therefore, written permission must be obtained from the landowner. See below for details.

In complete contrast to the coast, this moorland walk leads across the high ground of Bodmin Moor and takes in the rocky summits of Rough Tor. Throughout the area there are traces of Bronze Age settlement with the remains of burial chambers, hut circles and ancient field systems that are approximately 3,000 years old.

Unlike other areas so far described, Bodmin Moor has few clearly marked paths and this walk should be tackled only in fine weather. Walkers must also be prepared for sudden weather changes. Suitable footwear and weatherproof clothing should be taken.

There is heavy grazing by cattle, sheep and ponies here. Walkers must keep dogs on leads at all times and should leave no litter.

There is a car park at the end of Rough Tor Road or Jubilee Drive as it is sometimes known (SX138819). Follow the track on to the moor and past the National Trust sign. On the right by the stream bank there is a stone memorial to a young servant girl, Charlotte Dymond, who was murdered by her lover on the

moor in 1844 and immortalised in a fine ballad by the Cornish poet Charles Causley.

Continue directly uphill to the saddle between Showery Tor and Rough Tor, keeping to the track that is marked on the map. It is faint in places but direct. On reaching the saddle bear right (south-west) along the ridge that links Little Rough Tor and Rough Tor main summit. At 1311ft, Rough Tor is a handsome moorland summit. It is in the care of the National Trust above the 950ft contour line and was given to the Trust in 1951 by Sir Richard Onslow, as a war memorial to the men of the 43rd Wessex Division. From the summit, where there was once a medieval Chapel of St Michael, the views are magnificent in clear weather. The high hill lying to the south-east is Brown Willy, the highest point in Cornwall.

Retrace your steps to the saddle. Just north of here is the summit of Showery Tor with its remarkable wind-eroded 'Cheesewring' rock, itself once part of a prehistoric ring cairn of significance. From the saddle retrace the track downhill. All along the slopes on your left are extensive remains of Bronze Age remains of settlements and field systems with hut circles, tumuli and lynchets, grass terraces formed by early ploughing methods. Although this area is bleak in the present day it is likely that the milder climate 3,000 years ago made the area more habitable.

Further west, the moor is scarred by the china-clay works at Stannon, a sharp contrast between Bronze Age agriculture and 20th century industry.

Cross the stream and reach the car park.

Detailed application for written permission must be made at least two weeks ahead to Mr Rodney Hall, Lord of Hamatethy Common, Penrose Burden, St Breward, Bodmin, Cornwall PL30 4LZ, enclosing s.a.e.

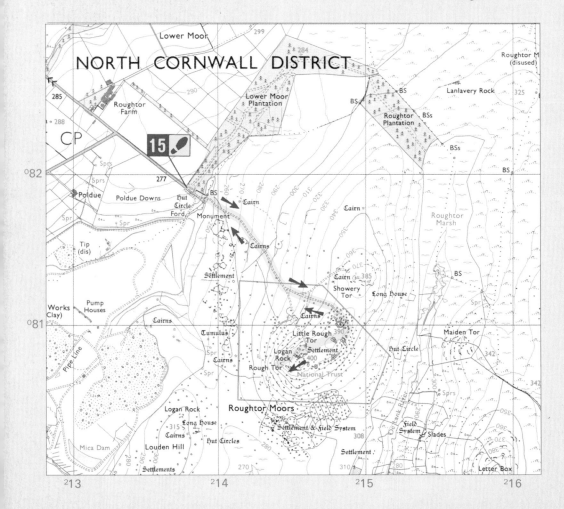

Rame Head Ramble

Allow 2½ hours

A circular walk on the Rame Peninsula, starting and finishing at Cawsand village, with views across Plymouth Sound to the Devon shore. After a pleasant stretch of woodland the second part of the route takes in Rame Head and the eastern shore of Whitsand Bay.

There is a large car park at Cawsand village (SX432503). From the car park take the road towards the village square (signposted) and turn right at Pier Lane by a small coast path sign. This leads to Penlee Point along the 'Earl's Drive', built by a 19th-century Earl of Edgcumbe. Keep to the lower track before climbing towards Penlee Point. Cawsand and Kingsand are linked villages once divided by the ancient Cornwall-Devon boundary. Both are wholeheartedly Cornish now and are worth exploring for their vernacular architecture. The Cawsand Bay fishermen were great pilchard catchers and noted smugglers. Seventeen thousand casks of spirits are said to have passed through the two villages in the single year of 1804.
From Penlee Point follow the metalled track until it turns inland. Keep straight ahead over a stile and on to Rame Head. A short diversion to Rame Head and the 14th-century Chapel of St Michael is recommended. The headland was once an Iron

Looking towards Whitsand Bay – over three miles of sand

Age fort protected by a deep ditch (still visible) across its narrow neck. Rame Head has been used ever since, as a chapel, hermitage and a light beacon for shipping.
Rejoin the path and turn left below the coastguard look-out to a wooden stile. Continue along the side of the headland with the great sweep of Whitsand Bay on your left. Cross two more stiles then go left down some stone steps and straight across a track by the gate of a house. Go down more steps and through a gate until reaching another track. Turn right here and follow the track uphill. The road above Whitsand Bay was originally a military road, part of the mid-18th-century system of batteries and forts created to protect Plymouth Sound and the Royal Docks.
On reaching the road go straight across and down the opposite lane for about 50 yards. Just before a farm go left into a field at the signpost and follow the path keeping the hedge on your right. On reaching a gap turn right and go down to a stile into a lane. Turn right then left on to the road, and so back to Cawsand car park.

Other Ordnance Survey Maps of Cornwall

How to get there with Routemaster and Routeplanner Maps

Reach Cornwall from Cardiff, Bristol, Birmingham, London, Dover, and Bournemouth using Routemaster map sheets 8 and 9.
Alternatively use the Ordnance Survey Great Britain Routeplanner which covers the whole country on one map sheet.

Exploring with Landranger and Holiday Maps

Landranger Series
1¼ inches to one mile or 1:50 000 scale

These maps cover the whole of Britain and are good for local motoring and walking.
Each contains tourist information such as parking, picnic places, viewpoints and rights of way.
Sheets covering Cornwall are:

190 Bude and Clovelly
200 Newquay and Bodmin
201 Plymouth and Launceston
203 Lands End, The Lizard
204 Truro and Falmouth

Holiday Map and Guide
Holiday Map and Guide to the West Country
3¼ miles to one inch

This particular map is geared to the needs of the holiday maker and shows items of interest for all the family.
On the back of the map there is a detailed guide of ideas on what to do and see.

Acknowledgements

The Automobile Association wishes to thank the following photographers,
organisations and libraries for their assistance in the compilation of this book.
Many of the photographs reproduced are the copyright of the AA Photolibrary.

M Adelman 97 St Ives; *BBC Hulton Picture Library* 22 The Death of Arthur; *Ray Bishop* 36 St Petroc;
Camera Press 54 Prince Charles; *John Conway/Wavelength* 60, 84 Surfers, Newquay;
Cornish Life Magazine 15 Flamank Plaque, 21 St Pirans Oratory, 36 Holy Well Luxulyan;
County Museum & Art Gallery, Truro 8 Gold Collar, 10/11 Botallack Mine, 17 Pendennis Castle, 19 Jan Tregeagle,
60 Lamorna Mill, 77 Dolly Pentreath; *Cornwall Archaeological Unit* 7 St Dennis, 8 Zennor, 9 Restormel Castle,
75 St Michaels Mount; *Cornwall Garden Society* 28 Tregothnan, 30 Trewithen, 31 Trebah;
Bob Johnson 32 Walker near Zennor, 33 Sunset Cape Cornwall, 34/5 Lizard Point, 35 Mên Scryfa;
Andrew Lawson Front Cover Boscastle, 1 St Agnes, 3 Looe, 5 Mevagissey, 6 The Hurlers, 7 Mên an Tol,
9 St Cleer's Well, 11 Engine House, 11 miner's helmet, 12 Trevithick statue, 13 Tamar Bridge, 14 Antony House,
15 Mount Edgcumbe, 17 St Mawes Castle, 19 Dozmary Pool, 21 St Neot's window, 22 Arthur's tomb, 37 The Hurlers,
38 Altarnun, bench end, 40 Boscastle, St Juliot Church, 40 wall painting, 41 Bude, Cadgwith,
43 Charlestown Harbour, Camborne, 44 Crackington Haven, Cotehele Morden Mill, 45 Pendennis Castle,
46 Feock Cross, Flushing fish, Mackerel, 47 Fowey, pasties, 48 Gunwalloe, 49 Helford, Ponsance Cove, 51 Lands End,
52/3 Looe, 55 Jamaica Inn, 56 Mackerel, Unloading Mackerel, 57 Mevagissey, Goonhilly, 58 Cheesewring,
58/9 Mousehole, Memorial, Mullion, 60 Fish Market Newlyn, Old Harbour, 62 Polkerris Bay, 63 Smuggler,
63 Penzance, 64 Perranporth, Polperro, 65 Porthcurno, Port Isaac, 66 Portreath, Inclined railway, Probus,
67 Carn Brae, St Agnes, 68 China-clay tips, St Enodoc Church, 69 Trethevy Quoit, 69 St Bunyan stone circle, 70 St Day,
71 Polmassick vineyard, St Dennis Roche rock, 72 St Ives, 73 St Just in Penwith, St Just in Roseland,
74 St Mawes castle, Bedruthan steps, 75 St Neot, 76 Saltash, Tamar bridge, 77 St Nectan's Kieve, Tintagel,
78 Quaker meeting house, Trelissick House, 80 Wadebridge, Zennor Museum, 81 Looe, 82 Sculpture, 83 Surfer,
85 Sunset, 96 Zennor mermaid, St Michael's Mount, 99 St Germans church, Polperro, 100/101 Port Isaac,
106 Mên an Tol, 114 Boscastle; *The Mansell Collection* 16/17 St Michael's Mount, 19 Giant Killer,
20 Mermaid, Little People, 39 D H Lawrence, 55 Smugglers, 111 Lifeboat rescue;
Mary Evans Picture Library Back Cover St Michael's Mount, 18 The Giant Bolster, 115 Robert Hawker;
S & O Mathews 16 John Robartes, 39 Bodmin Moor, 52 Launceston Castle, 53 Lizard marble, 54 Restormel,
79 Truro Cathedral, 80 Veryan; *National Trust Cornwall Regional Office* 14 Sir Richard Carew,
29 Cotehele Valley garden, 31 Glendurgan; *Nature Photographers Ltd* 23 Rock Pool, 23 Shore crab,
24 Burnet Rose, 25 Dog Whelk, 27 Marsh Orchid (A Cleave) 24 Fulmar, Water Spider, 25 Puffin (P Sterry),
26 Yellow Flag (C Grey Wilson), 27 Otter (W Paton) 27 Grey Seal (D Smith); *Doc Rowe* 50 Flora Day Dance Helston,
62 Padstow 'Obby Oss; *Graham Sutton* 26 Green Hairstreak; *H Williams* 11 Camborne, 32/33 Kynance Cove,
42/3 East Pool whim, 42 Upper chamber engine, 45 Falmouth Harbour, 48 Gweek, 51 Lanhydrock House,
54/55 Trengwainton, 61 DairyLand Museum; *Wyn Voysey* 64 Polperro, 101 Tintagel Post Office,
117 Whitsand Bay.

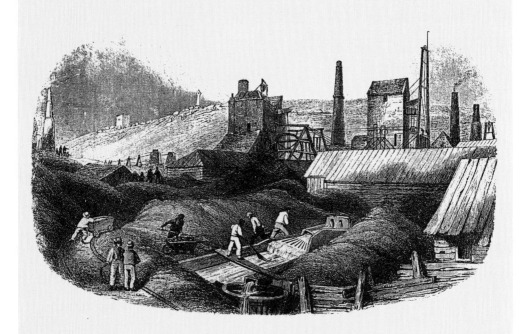

Other titles available in this series are:

Channel Islands   Lake District   Peak District
Cotswolds   New Forest   Scottish Highlands
Ireland   Northumbria   Yorkshire Dales
North York Moors